The Trial of Martin Luther King

THE TRIAL OF MARTIN LUTHER KING

ALAN F. WESTIN / BARRY MAHONEY

THOMAS Y. CROWELL COMPANY
NEW YORK / ESTABLISHED *1834*

The publisher wishes to thank the following for granting permission to use photographs from their files:

United Press International: 107 (top and bottom), 108, 109 (top), 111 (bottom), 114 (bottom), 115, 116 (bottom); Wide World Photos: 109 (bottom), 110, 112 (top and bottom), 113, 114 (top), 116 (top); *Birmingham Post-Herald:* 111 (top); Ed Bagwell (for NVI): 117 *The New York Times*/George Tames: 118, 119 (top and bottom); Wyatt Tee Walker: 120

Copyright © 1974 by Thomas Y. Crowell Company, Inc.

Designed by Ingrid Beckman
Manufactured in the United States of America

ISBN 0-690-83565-5

Library of Congress Cataloging in Publication Data

Westin, Alan F
    The trial of Martin Luther King.

    Bibliography: p.
    1. King, Martin Luther.   2. Negroes—Civil rights.
I. Mahoney, Barry, joint author.   II. Title.
KF224.K56W48   342'.73'0850269   74-9945
ISBN 0-690-83565-5

1 2 3 4 5 6 7 8 9 10

Preface

BOOKS HAVE both origins and intentions. This one grew out of an experimental course on the role of the Supreme Court in the American political system that Alan Westin taught at Columbia College in the fall of 1969, with the assistance of three younger colleagues who were then graduate students in the Department of Public Law and Government at Columbia University—Barry Mahoney, Christopher Pyle, and Stephen Chaberski. When the planning for the course was begun in the early months of 1969, we decided to develop special reading materials that would show the legal and political realities of the American constitutional system, along the lines of Westin's *The Anatomy of a Constitutional Law Case* (Macmillan, 1958), a documentary reconstruction of the famous *Steel Seizure* case of 1952 that is widely used in college courses on the Supreme Court and American Government. Westin and Mahoney agreed to work on this project while Pyle and Chaberski developed other materials for the course.

Our problem was to find a case decided by the U.S. Supreme Court that was even more pertinent for the late 1960s and 1970s than the *Steel Seizure* decision. *Walker v. Birmingham,* decided by the Supreme Court in 1967, seemed to have all the right elements: racial conflict in the South; Martin Luther King, Jr., and the civil rights movement of the 1960s; protest demonstrations; the use of court injunctions; and the role of law and the courts in dealing with pressures for social change. We prepared a set of documentary materials for *Walker* that drew on the memoirs of the participants;

media coverage of the Birmingham demonstrations of 1963; the trial transcript, briefs, and appeal papers, and the oral arguments in the courts; and many other such primary sources. These materials were used for our teaching in 1969, and for another experimental course in 1971 (on "American Politics and Social Change"). The reaction of students was enthusiastic, and the materials taught well.

At this point we had a finished manuscript in the style of the *Anatomy* volume. When this was read by our editors at Thomas Y. Crowell, they agreed with us that it dealt with such major issues of American law and politics that a fuller, narrative treatment of the case would have considerable appeal to a broader audience. They recommended shifting our treatment from the marshaling of edited, primary materials connected by our explanatory essays to a full-scale trade book, in the manner of Anthony Lewis' superb study of the Supreme Court's right-to-counsel decision, *Gideon's Trumpet* (Random House, 1964).

To do this required a great deal more research. We had to seek out people involved in the *Walker* case who were still available for personal interviews—King's colleagues in the Southern Christian Leadership Conference; lawyers who worked with Dr. King; white and black leaders and officials in Birmingham; key figures in the U.S. Department of Justice during the Kennedy and Johnson Administrations; and many others. It also meant consulting press clippings and other materials at the Martin Luther King, Jr. Center for Social Change in Atlanta, the Southern Regional Council, the National Archives, the Library of Congress, and elsewhere.

With this expansion of the project, we spent until the winter of 1974 researching, writing, and verifying our in-depth reconstruction of the *Walker* case and its aftermath, and wrestling with the enormously difficult problem of balancing the free speech rights of protest groups with respect for court orders, the issue on which the *Walker* case turned.

This account of the origins of *The Trial of Martin Luther King* recalls to mind the many intellectual and personal debts that we have incurred, and which we are happy to acknowledge in this Preface.

For personal interviews, some of them several times, mostly in person but a few in lengthy telephone conversations, we are grateful to present or former Southern Christian Leadership Conference aides and officers Bernard Lee, Andrew Young, James Orange, Wyatt Tee Walker, and Stoney Cooks; former Justice Department officials Nicholas deB. Katzenbach, Ramsey Clark, Louis Claiborne, Louis Oberdorfer, Joseph F. Dolan, Burke Marshall, and John Doar; Fred Shuttlesworth, David Vann, Charles Morgan, Jr., and George Peach Taylor, each of whom was in Birmingham in 1963; Harry Wachtel and Chauncey Eskridge, legal advisers to Dr. King; NAACP Legal Defense Fund lawyers Jack Greenberg, James Nabrit III, Norman Amaker, and Charles S. Ralston; King's friend and political consultant, Bayard Rustin; William A. Jenkins, judge of the Alabama Tenth Judicial Circuit, Birmingham, in 1963; Memphis lawyer Lucius Burch; Chicago lawyers Lee J. Vickman and Richard Watts; Washington *Post* reporter John MacKenzie; Professor Charles Hamilton of Columbia University, who was in Birmingham in 1963; former U.S. Supreme Court law clerks Benno Schmidt, Jr., Richard Stewart, and Edward Bruce; and persons currently active in Birmingham who were interviewed about that city's present racial scene: John Drew, George Quiggle, Walter Jackson, Jack Drake, Barney Weeks, Frank Parker, William Pugh, Richard Arrington, and Massey Gentry.

While the lawyers for the city of Birmingham who handled the *Walker* case from 1963 to 1967, J. M. Breckinridge and Earl McBee, declined to be interviewed, saying that they preferred to allow the record and their briefs to stand by themselves, they were kind enough to send us materials on the City Attorney's Office and biographical data on their careers.

To the following institutions, we are indebted for the use of manuscript and newspaper collections and general library resources: the Martin Luther King, Jr. Center for Social Change, Atlanta, Georgia; the Southern Regional Council, Atlanta; the National Archives, Washington, D.C.; the Legal Defense Fund, Inc., New York City; the Southern Christian Leadership Conference, Atlanta; and Columbia University, in particular Butler Library and the Law School Library.

During six years of research and writing, we were aided greatly by talented research assistants: Helene Toiv, Caryn Leland, Robert Belair, Julie Heilman Habers, Lucinda White, and Ellen Josephson. For secretarial assistance, our primary debt is to Lorene Cox and Mary Christiano, with additional support from Joanne Brown, Nancy Demmon, and Toby Cohen.

Once the manuscript was finished and moving through successive drafts, we profited from critical readings by James Nabrit, Norman Amaker, Charles Morgan, Jr., Andrew Young, Ramsey Clark, Harry Wachtel, Christopher Pyle, Sanford Rosen, Cheryl Johnson, Rod Davis, Stephen and Faith Williams, Helene Toiv, and Anne Rankin Mahoney.

We owe a special debt for creative and patient effort to our editor at Thomas Y. Crowell, Hugh Rawson, and to other Crowell editors who helped the project along: Herbert J. Addison, Peter Stillman, James Bergin, and Robert L. Crowell.

To our wives, Anne Rankin Mahoney and Bea S. Westin, we apologize for having taken so long, and offer by this proof of bound copies the final evidence that, this time, we are really done with the revision.

ALAN F. WESTIN
BARRY MAHONEY

February 1974

Contents

1

"Even a King
Is Under the Law"

ON OCTOBER 30, 1967, the midmorning flight from Atlanta, Georgia, to Birmingham, Alabama, taxied up Runway 7 at the Birmingham airport and stopped in front of a small waiting room. Six plainclothes detectives, four city policemen, and one sheriff's deputy (wearing a belt lined with shotgun shells) stood by the door. After most of the passengers disembarked, the police officers took up positions at the foot of the aircraft's stairway. Then out came the passengers the police were waiting to take to jail: four black ministers named Wyatt Tee Walker, Ralph Abernathy, A. D. King, and Martin Luther King, Jr.

In downtown Birmingham about a hundred members of the Southern Christian Leadership Conference and the Alabama Christian Movement for Human Rights were gathered outside the Jefferson County Jail to greet the four ministers when they arrived. They never did. Piling their prisoners into two cars, the police officials drove off at high speed to nearby Bessemer, running several stoplights in the process. "We have two county jails," Sheriff Mel Bailey explained later to protesting friends of Dr. King, "and I can choose either one. It's just plain routine."

In the Bessemer jail, King and his associates began serving a five-day sentence for contempt of court. Originally ordered in 1963, the jailing had been imposed for defying a state court injunction that forbade the protest demonstrations that King was leading that spring against Birmingham's segregation policies. The conviction was upheld by the United States Supreme Court in June 1967, in a case known as *Walker v. City of Birmingham*, and October had been set for serving the sentence.

This was not King's first time in jail, of course. "Actually, it's my nineteenth," he had remarked to reporters. He arrived wearing his "regular jail outfit" of faded blue denim work shirt and pants and an old brown cardigan sweater. He also carried three books: the Bible, John Kenneth Galbraith's *The New Industrial State,* and William Styron's novel *The Confessions of Nat Turner.* It had been a raw, drizzling day, and it continued to rain for the first two days the ministers were in jail. Dr. King developed a virus infection, was seen by a prison doctor, and then was moved to the main county jail in Birmingham. On the fourth day of his sentence, he was released. "We don't want to work a hardship on anyone," said Alabama circuit judge William C. Barber, who ordered King freed. "He's served enough time."

Before flying to Birmingham from Atlanta, King had told reporters that he was returning to Birmingham with "mixed emotions." The 1963 demonstrations, he noted, had led to the enactment of the Civil Rights Act of 1964, which guaranteed service in public accommodations to all Americans, black as well as white. Five days in jail, King said, "is a small price to pay for that." But, he added,

> I am sad that the Supreme Court of our land . . . could not uphold the rights of individual citizens in the face of deliberate use of the courts of Alabama as a means of oppression. . . . Perhaps these five days will afford all of us an opportunity for a more intense and serious evaluation of our situation, for all the signs of our times indicate that this is a dark hour in the life of America. . . . The Supreme Court has placed a

weapon for repression—an injunction against legitimate protest, granted in a one-sided hearing—in the very hands of those who have fostered today's malignant disorder of poverty, racism, and war.

That King and his associates were saddened by the decision in *Walker v. Birmingham* was understandable. For the liberal Supreme Court of the 1960s—the court that had so often supported the equality demands of black Americans—to uphold an Alabama court injunction against peaceful antisegregation demonstrations and approve Dr. King's jailing was a particularly bitter pill to swallow. And the moment when the court finally made its decision was a troubled one for the nonviolent civil rights movement. The urban communities were in eruption, and black-power advocates were capturing headlines across the nation; peaceful protest was out of fashion. King himself was under attack from both conservatives and radicals within the black community, and his organization, the Southern Christian Leadership Conference, was searching anxiously for a new role in the bitter confrontation-dominated setting of 1967–68.

The week before the opinion was announced, shooting, looting, burning, and street fighting had been triggered by a noisy welfare rights sit-in in Boston's racially tense Roxbury district. Between June 11 and 15 riots broke out in Tampa and Cincinnati requiring the governors of Florida and Ohio to call out National Guard troops. A week later racial violence exploded in Atlanta. These events were only the prelude to greater tragedy, however. In early July, Newark was convulsed with racial violence that left twenty-six persons dead and caused property damage of $10 million. Two weeks later Detroit's black ghetto erupted in a holocaust that killed forty-three persons and produced almost $50 million in property damage.

To many white Americans, Dr. Martin Luther King bore

major responsibility for these conflagrations. As one commentator, Lionel Lokos, expressed this judgment: the "criminal disobedience" that flared up in Newark and Detroit was the inevitable result of the "civil disobedience" taught by King; when one leader says he can flout laws that he considers unjust, the structure of government under law is cracked and others inevitably rush in to widen the assault.

It was in that spirit that Justice Potter Stewart had written his concluding paragraph for the Supreme Court majority in the *Walker* decision:

> [N]o man can be judge in his own case, however exalted his station, however righteous his motives, and irrespective of his race, color, politics, or religion. This Court cannot hold that the petitioners were constitutionally free to ignore all the procedures of the law and carry their battle to the streets. One may sympathize with the petitioners' impatient commitment to their cause. But respect for judicial process is a small price to pay for the civilizing hand of law, which alone can give abiding meaning to constitutional freedom.

The court's ruling, and its lecture to Martin Luther King, Jr., was heartily approved at the time by constitutional fundamentalists and political conservatives, North and South. But many Northern liberals also applauded it. "Obedience to the law and to the normal procedures," *The New York Times* declared, must be held "paramount." To have denied that principle, in an effort to "exculpate Dr. King," would have been "to make new law for this particular case." For the *Times,* the Supreme Court's ruling pronounced "doctrine absolutely basic to a democratic society."

Not everyone shared these views. Four justices of the Supreme Court—Chief Justice Earl Warren and Justices William O. Douglas, William J. Brennan, Jr., and Abe Fortas—had dissented in the *Walker* case, and had filed unusually strong dissenting opinions. Chief Justice Warren condemned the Supreme Court for giving its "seal of approval" to "a gross misuse of the judicial process" in Alabama, and said that the ruling would not lead to greater respect for the law. Justice Brennan saw the decision as "elevating a state rule of judicial administration above the right of free expression guaranteed by the Federal Constitution." The court, he charged, was "letting loose a devastatingly destructive weapon for suppression of cherished freedoms heretofore believed indispensable to maintenance of our free society." It was utterly wrong for the court to permit "fears of 'riots' and 'civil disobedience' generated by slogans like 'Black Power' " to overcome the fact that Dr. King's Birmingham march was a peaceful exercise of constitutionally protected rights of expression and that the state court injunction forbidding demonstrations was an unconstitutional order. In Brennan's view, King and his followers had no duty to obey such an order—especially at the price of abandoning their long-planned campaign to bring racial justice to Birmingham.

The Birmingham trial with its subsequent *Walker* appeals was the most celebrated case in which King was personally involved in his career as a civil rights leader. The trial was also the stimulus for his most famous piece of writing, *Letter from Birmingham Jail.* In both the literal and figurative senses, though, King was continually on trial. His campaigns against racial injustice always brought him into conflict with local public officials, who would arrest and prosecute him for a wide variety of offenses, all of which rested on disturbing the peace of segregated society. He was always "on trial" too in the court of elite and public opinion, charged by some whites as being too radical and by some blacks as being too conservative. His response to injunctions forbidding protest activity was frequently the focus for such judgments about his capacities as a leader, as in his famous protest campaigns in Selma, Alabama, in 1965 and Memphis, Tennessee, in 1968, as well as in Birmingham.

Walker v. Birmingham also stands as a microcosm of the larger civil rights struggle of the late 1950s and 1960s, illustrating the pivotal role played by "the law" in that epochal conflict over the redefinition of status in contemporary America. *Walker* brought together the four main protagonists in this struggle: Martin Luther King and the black protest movement; Southern white officialdom; the U.S. Department of Justice under Presidents Kennedy and Johnson; and the Supreme Court of the United States, in its famous "Warren Court" era.

The fundamental issues around which these four protagonists were gathered in the *Walker* case—the limits of lawful protest and the nature of the duty to obey the courts—are still major concerns of American life. They are involved in the struggles for social change, where minority racial, political, or social groups are demanding that American practices move closer to the society's professed ideals. They are also involved in battles over freedom of the press. Newspapers have found themselves faced with court orders prohibiting publication of stories about court proceedings; if the newspapers print such stories while they are hot and newsworthy, rather than delaying publication to contest the injunction, the reporters and publishers face punishment for contempt.

American society's commitment to the principle that court orders must be respected was recently manifested in striking fashion in the controversy over the Watergate tapes that occurred in October 1973. At that time President Nixon announced that he would not comply with the order of federal district judge John Sirica to produce nine tapes of presidential conversations sought by Special Prosecutor Archibald Cox. The President did so even though Judge Sirica's order had been confirmed by the U.S. Court of Appeals and the President had elected not to carry the case to the Supreme Court. At that moment the words that Justice Stewart had directed at Martin Luther King in 1967 seemed exactly the answer to the

President's claim that executive prerogative stood above the rule of courts: "In the fair administration of justice, no man can be judge in his own case, however exalted his station, however righteous his motives. . . . [R]espect for judicial process is a small price to pay for the civilizing hand of law, which alone can give abiding meaning to constitutional freedom." President Nixon quickly retreated from his declaration of noncompliance under what one of his aides called a "firestorm" of public outcry, providing admirers of the *Walker* ruling with further proof of its wisdom and merit.

The story of the *Walker* case is important not just because of the significance of the actors involved and the principle of law that it enunciates for political life today, but also because of what it reveals about how law is made and used in the American constitutional system. An analysis of this famous episode shows how groups, institutions, and individuals work to extend their political efforts by legal means: weighing their strategic and tactical choices in a concrete social conflict, moving back and forth between the political and legal arenas as a "dispute" becomes a "case," and trying to shape the scope and meaning of the "basic issues" as the case makes its way from a local court through the appellate courts and into the highest tribunal in Washington. It also shows how cases are presented to the nine lawyers who sit on the Supreme Court; how the justices arrive at their decision; and how the Supreme Court ruling then goes back into the political process, setting new norms of conduct in the particular area of political life involved.

2

Birmingham: The Magic City

FOR MOST AMERICANS, April 1960 was a good month in a good year. Under the presidency of Dwight D. Eisenhower, the nation was at peace, with none of its troops engaged in foreign combat. Though cold-war rhetoric still dominated American foreign policy and Castro's continued presence in Cuba rankled national sensibilities, Eisenhower had ended the Korean War in 1952, refused to embroil the United States in South Vietnam when Dien Bien Phu fell, and kept our military intervention in Lebanon in 1957 to a carefully brief (and successful) interlude. With the thaw in East-West relations during 1958–59 having made "détente" a fashionable word in Washington, the Pentagon budget for 1960 was mercifully moderate.

After several brief recessions during the 1950s, inflation was finally brought under control and the American economy was booming in early 1960. Production of goods and services was high, real income was up, and unemployment figures were low. As historian William O'Neill observed: "Nearly everyone was better fed and housed than before. Schools expanded rapidly enough to keep up with the baby boom. It was true that the popular culture was unexciting, the new subdivisions ugly and poorly planned, and the family-oriented, suburban style of living wanting in charm or distinction. The fact remains that these were years of real progress for ordinary Americans.''

There was progress on other fronts as well. With the censuring of Joseph McCarthy by his Senate colleagues (and his death soon after), the venomous loyalty/security issue was drained from American politics. Major reforms of American education and an ambitious space program were launched in response to the Soviet Union's sputnik achievement. Universities were entering what would come to be called their golden era, with enrollments soaring, campuses expanding, and faculty salaries and prestige rising. There was also an outpouring of vigorous popular writing that urged the nation to use its wealth and energies to fight poverty and discrimination at home and increase aid to underdeveloped nations abroad. Predictably, the major contenders for the Democratic presidential nomination in 1960—Senators Hubert H. Humphrey, Lyndon B. Johnson, and John F. Kennedy—vied with each other in calling for such new policies and attacking the Eisenhower Administration for its complacency and inertia. Meanwhile, Ike's heir apparent, Vice-President Richard M. Nixon, offered to continue his mentor's eight-year record of ''peace and prosperity.''

Race relations in early 1960 was one of the dozen major issues on the domestic front. According to public opinion polls, most white Americans felt that the Negro had made ''great strides'' in the late 1950s and that the pace of progress toward full legal equality was just about right. As these white Americans saw it, the Supreme Court's school desegregation ruling of 1954, in *Brown v. Board of Education,* was proper and was being pressed with appropriate firmness by the federal judiciary against the resistance of Southern diehards. Though President Eisenhower had shown no enthusiasm for racial integration (expressing doubts that laws could change men's prejudices), he had finally sent federal troops to Little Rock, Arkansas, to enforce a federal school desegregation order that had been blocked by the segregationist governor, Orval Faubus. And passage of the federal Voting Rights Acts of 1957 and 1960, though these were very limited measures, marked the first civil rights laws to be enacted by Congress since the days of Reconstruction.

Few Negroes or white civil rights advocates shared this satisfied view of racial progress. They regarded Southern defiance of desegregation orders and the passivity of Congress and the Eisenhower Administration as shameful evasions of the Supreme Court's equality rulings. As they kept pointing out, the rule of Jim Crow still prevailed in most of the South, protected by a combination of official action, economic sanctions, and vigilante terror. This had prompted the development of some new protest activities by Negroes, such as the Montgomery bus boycott of 1956, led by a young Baptist minister, Martin Luther King, Jr., and the lunch-counter sit-ins that black college students had begun in the early months of 1960. But to the well-satisfied nation in the last year of the Eisenhower reign, no sense of impending crisis hung over the race relations issue.

Except in Birmingham, Alabama.

On April 9, 1960, a front-page story on Birmingham appeared in *The New York Times,* written by Harrison Salisbury. Salisbury, a Pulitzer Prize–winning foreign correspondent, had recently returned from two decades of reporting on Russia under Stalin and Khrushchev, and was then on a tour of American cities. Birmingham, said Salisbury, is a city of "fear, hatred, and terror":

> No New Yorker can readily measure the climate of Birmingham today. Whites and blacks still walk the same streets. But the streets, the water supply and the sewer system are about the only public facilities they share. Ball parks and taxi-

cabs are segregated. So are libraries. A book featuring black rabbits and white rabbits was banned. A drive is on to forbid "Negro music" on "white" radio stations.

Every channel of communication, every medium of mutual interest, every reasoned approach, every inch of middle ground has been fragmented by the emotional dynamite of racism, reinforced by the whip, the razor, the gun, the bomb, the torch, the club, the knife, the mob, the police, and many branches of the state's apparatus.

In Birmingham, neither blacks nor whites talk freely. A pastor carefully closes the door before he speaks. A Negro keeps an eye on the sidewalk outside his house. A lawyer talks in the language of conspiracy.

Telephones are tapped, or there is fear of tapping. Mail has been intercepted and opened. Sometimes it does not reach its destination. The eavesdropper, the informer, the spy have become a fact of life.

Volunteer watchmen stand guard twenty-four hours a day over some Negro churches. Jewish synagogues have floodlights for the night and caretakers. Dynamite attempts have been made against the two principal Jewish temples in the last eighteen months. In eleven years there have been twenty-two reported bombings of Negro churches and homes. A number were never reported officially.

To illustrate the "almost reflexive" nature of Birmingham's repression of civil rights activity, Salisbury related a series of incidents that had taken place during the previous months. On April 2, for example, ten Negro students had gone in pairs into five downtown stores, made small purchases, and sat down at the "whites only" counters to be served. They were swiftly arrested on charges of trespassing and held for eighteen hours. Meanwhile, Public Safety Commissioner Eugene ("Bull") Connor and the Birmingham police swung into what Salisbury called some of their "favorite techniques." They arrested three local Negro ministers and two college students, one of the ministers being taken from his home to the police station barefooted and in his bathrobe. Despite their having homes, jobs, and funds, each was charged with "vagrancy," a crime for which "by Birmingham custom, persons . . . are not admitted to bail. They are held incommunicado for three days." For one of the ministers, Rev. Fred L. Shuttlesworth, Salisbury noted, this was only the latest of a long series of official and terrorist reprisals for his advocacy of Negro civil rights. "He has three cases on appeal. His church has been bombed twice. In one bombing, his home was destroyed. Both he and his wife were injured and a white pastor was badly manhandled by a Birmingham mob when the three of them sought to use the white waiting room of the local bus depot."

For those who knew Birmingham's stormy evolution from a rough-and-ready mining town, Harrison Salisbury's shocked report came as no surprise. Far from being one of the South's surviving cities of the Old Confederacy, as was Montgomery, Birmingham was not founded until 1871. In that year a group of railroad promoters took options on a large tract of forest and farmland at the junction where their North-South route would join an existing East-West line. Knowing that vast stores of mineral wealth lay untapped in the hills of north-central Alabama, they named their tract after England's great coal and iron center.

By the 1880s exploitation of Birmingham's rich coal, iron, and limestone resources, the building of huge furnaces, and the making of Birmingham's first steel were under way, and the area became a classic boomtown. Though many independent entrepreneurs made their fortunes in the mines and mills of what was called the "Magic City," most of the money for the consolidation of Birmingham's industry came from Northern capital. By the early 1900s Northern absentee ownership dominated the region, making Birmingham a site of "branch banks, captive mines, and chain stores," with

United States Steel's giant Tennessee Coal, Iron, and Railroad Company the most powerful operator.

As one leading history of Alabama noted, "Violence was an accepted part of life in the city's early days, when rough men from all sections of the country came to an overgrown mining camp. Physical clashes were common, and killings were so frequent that law enforcement officials spoke of the place as Bad Birmingham."

Violence also marked the area's labor relations. Strikes for better wages and working conditions in the mines and mills often led to bloody clashes between strikers and strike-breakers, and the National Guard was called in repeatedly between 1890 and the 1930s. Often the labor violence had racial overtones. While the unions organized in the 1880s by the Knights of Labor, and later by the United Mineworkers, were originally racially integrated, these unions were destroyed when they went on strike and employers brought in convict labor and National Guardsmen. With wages depressed in the 1920s and early 1930s, angry white workers added conflicts with blacks over jobs to the other sources of Birmingham's violent tradition. It was not until the mid-1930s that, with the help of favorable New Deal legislation, the mines and mills of Birmingham became unionized and the labor strife slackened.

By the early 1950s "modern Birmingham"—a city of 200,000 whites and 80,000 blacks, and the South's iron and steel center—had emerged from this turbulent past. The city was dominated by its white working class, primarily blue-collar employees and their families. The men were a rough "up from the country" corps, said by one local journalist to include "more freckle-eared sorghum-fed toughs than most large cities in the South."

Only a few of the Magic City's economic elite—bankers, corporation executives, local merchants, and successful professionals—lived within the city limits; most built handsome estates in the surrounding suburbs. Because of this, and because it was traditional for the "Big Mules" (the Northern company owners and financiers) to stay out of local politics unless their interests were directly threatened, the official government of Birmingham was run largely by the kind of white "rural populist" leaders that had dominated state politics in Alabama ever since the 1890s. The three-member City Commission, the police force, the courts, the school board, and other city agencies were all in the hands of these men, who were openly and fervently anti-Negro. Such men saw it as weakness to consider even the most modest steps toward improved race relations. Happily for them, black voters posed no threat to their rule. The full range of legal and coercive measures had been applied to limit voting by blacks: only 12 percent of Birmingham's eligible Negro voters were registered.

Economically, the Negro population of Birmingham was not badly off compared to blacks in many Southern cities. Though Negroes were confined to unskilled or semiskilled jobs in industry, those who worked in the factories received union-scale wages. There was a significant Negro middle-class element—college-educated professionals, teachers, ministers, and a few businessmen. The desperation in black Birmingham was not basically a matter of economics. It was more a matter of citizenship and dignity.

The result of "redneck" domination in city politics was that Birmingham in the early 1950s was a living monument to Jim Crow. Every public facility was racially segregated: schools, parks, playgrounds, swimming pools, golf courses, courtrooms, hospitals, libraries, and orphanages. On the private side, every place of public accommodation was similarly segregated: theaters, restaurants, waiting rooms in stations and depots, ambulances, taxicabs, buses, and the lunch counters and rest rooms in stores.

Behind these vigorously enforced legal rules lay Birmingham's apparatus of violence and terror: the Ku Klux Klan, with its night rides, whippings, and fires, and the city's "dynamite boys." Journalist Joe David Brown called them the "millbilly hoodlums"—men who did not bother to join the Klan but who kept Birmingham "perpetually on edge" with their explosive reprisals against any Negro—or white—who challenged the iron boundaries of racial place.

The Supreme Court's school desegregation decision of 1954 and the "all deliberate speed" ruling of 1955 had set new forces in motion. While some border states moved to comply with the ruling, government and political leaders in the Deep South, especially Mississippi and Alabama, were intransigent. In Alabama virtually the entire state political establishment declared that segregation would be preserved. The state legislature passed a resolution saying that it "nullified" the Supreme Court's 1954 ruling and, more concretely, enacted school pupil-placement laws designed to sidestep integration requirements. Public officials and white civic leaders in Birmingham were second to none in declaring their intention to keep every rule of their segregated society. "We're not going to have white folks and nigras segregatin' together in this man's town," Bull Connor announced, in his inimitable style.

The main voice of Alabama Negroes seeking to implement the Supreme Court's integration rulings in the mid-1950s was the state chapter of the National Association for the Advancement of Colored People, which had fifty-eight branches throughout Alabama and a membership of over fourteen thousand. The Southeastern Regional Office of the NAACP, covering seven states, had been opened in Birmingham in 1951. The Alabama NAACP employed a wide range of tactics: negotiations with local political and business groups, wherever possible; lawsuits to challenge denials of constitutional rights; and cooperation with the new boycott campaigns, such as the Montgomery bus boycott of 1955–1956.

Because of the NAACP's vigorous advocacy of Negro rights, Alabama's attorney general, John Patterson, moved in 1956 to force the NAACP to register as an out-of-state corporation and furnish lists of its officers, employees, and members to the state. The NAACP refused to expose its officers and members to the kind of reprisals that such disclosure would surely have led to, relying on Supreme Court decisions protecting freedom of association. The State of Alabama quickly obtained an injunction from a state court restraining the NAACP from conducting any activities within the state. From June 1, 1956, when this injunction was obtained, until 1965 the NAACP was caught up in continuous litigation with the state, during which it was barred from operations in Alabama. (Ultimately, the Supreme Court upheld the NAACP members' right of association and ordered Alabama to permit the organization to operate.)

In Birmingham during the 1950s the policy of enforcing segregation to the hilt had silenced almost all the white moderates who might have wished to see gradual integration. Most of the city's Negroes also accepted, painfully, the fact that integration would be a long time coming to the Magic City. But a small group of Birmingham Negroes associated with the banned NAACP chapter met in June 1956 to form a new group, the Alabama Christian Movement for Human Rights (ACMHR). Their leader was Rev. Fred L. Shuttlesworth, pastor of the Bethel Baptist Church. Shuttlesworth, a thin, wiry man about five feet ten with close-cropped hair, was a fervently religious minister and civil rights activist who had been membership chairman of the state NAACP.

The ACMHR began by seeking to get Negroes into "whites only" jobs in the municipal government; when they were rebuffed, they brought a lawsuit against the city's Personnel Board to open all civil service examinations to Negroes. In December 1956, after the U.S. Supreme Court decision holding bus segregation in Montgomery to be unconstitutional, Shuttlesworth announced that ACMHR members would ride in the front of Birmingham buses on December 26. On Christmas night a bomb destroyed his home, injuring several persons but leaving Shuttlesworth unhurt. On the 26th, 250 ACMHR members boarded buses and refused to sit in the rear. Twenty-one persons were arrested and convicted in the city recorder's court for violating local segregation ordinances.

In September 1957 the Shuttlesworths took their two daughters to the all-white Phillips High School and attempted to enroll them. A white mob with chains and brass knuckles beat Shuttlesworth, his wife was stabbed in the hip, and one of the children was also injured. A grand jury refused to indict three men charged with attempting to murder Shuttlesworth at the school. Shuttlesworth and other Negro parents then filed suit in federal court to desegregate the Birmingham schools, a lawsuit that would take six years to be completed. In June 1958 Shuttlesworth's church was bombed again.

The weekly meetings of the ACMHR were attended by city detectives who not only took notes and made tape recordings but also searched people leaving the meeting. Some ACMHR members were fired from their jobs when employers were told of their participation. One minister, Rev. Charles Billups, was kidnapped by the Klan, tied to a tree, and beaten. Any white person who visited Shuttlesworth was likely to be stopped and questioned by the police.

In October 1958, facing the ACMHR's lawsuit attacking the local bus-segregation ordinance, the city repealed its law and substituted an ordinance giving drivers the power to seat passengers and making it a breach of the peace to disobey their assignments. When thirteen ACMHR members rode the buses to test this law, they were arrested; Shuttlesworth was charged with inciting the disobedience. All of them were held in jail incommunicado for five days, then convicted in the

local courts. At that point the ACMHR not only filed a lawsuit in federal court but also initiated its first boycott. This
was in effect in 1959 when the federal district court finally
struck down the previous convictions of Negro bus riders and
of a couple who had disregarded whites-only seating in the
railway station. But the segregation signs were still up, and
Fred Shuttlesworth was beoming convinced that "court rulings only come to life when people put their bodies on the
line in a challenge to the old ways."

This was the tense racial situation that Harrison Salisbury
found in 1960, when he wrote his report for *The New York
Times.* So far, Fred Shuttlesworth and the ACMHR had
waged their four-year fight without active support from the
general Negro community, or from the Negro business and
professional elite. Nor had they any allies in the white community. Although there had been some unofficial biracial
committees in the city prior to the Supreme Court's 1954
decision in *Brown v. Board of Education,* these had been dis-
banded as racial tensions increased in the 1950s.

The federal government provided no assistance either. The
FBI, adopting a narrow view of the federal government's authority to investigate claims of violations of citizens' civil
rights, took the position that the numerous bombings and as-
saults on blacks in the Birmingham area were matters solely
for local law enforcement officials to handle. And local law
enforcement in Birmingham was personified by Bull Connor,
a man who had no use for blacks or for niceties of federal
constitutional law. In 1958, for example, he ordered three
Negro ministers from Montgomery arrested on charges of
vagrancy when they came to Birmingham to talk with Fred
Shuttlesworth and others. Questioned about the legality of the
arrests, Connor replied, "We don't give a damn about the
law. Down here we make our own law. . . . I had them
picked up on a charge of vagrancy until we could find out

what they were doing here. We're not going to have outsiders coming in and stirring up trouble. If they come here and do the wrong kind of talking, they'll see the inside of our jail.''

The Salisbury article and reports by other journalists who visited Birmingham brought the racial tensions in the city to the attention of national audiences. But the publicity produced no change in Birmingham's racial policies. A strong segregationist stance was good politics in Birmingham in 1961, as it was throughout the state of Alabama. Bull Connor was reelected for a four-year term as a city commissioner in 1961, along with two other arch-segregationists. In the same year George Corley Wallace was elected governor of Alabama after a tough-talking campaign during which he said that the U.S. Supreme Court ''did not have the brains to try a chicken thief'' and pledged to ''stand in the schoolhouse door'' in order to resist school integration.

In Birmingham the city officials elected in 1961 continued their adamant resistance to any form of integration. For example, after a federal district court ruled in December 1961 that the city would have to desegregate its recreational facilities, city officials closed sixty-seven parks, thirty-eight playgrounds, and four golf courses. The closings angered many whites, and more than twelve hundred of them signed an open letter of protest published in the Birmingham *News*. It was one of the first indications that the power of the Bull Connor forces might be weakening.

Some Birmingham blacks also began to be more active. In March a group of students from all-black Miles College initiated a boycott of stores in Birmingham's downtown business district. Termed a ''selective buying campaign'' by its leaders, this boycott had three objectives: desegregation of lunch counters, rest rooms, and drinking fountains; hiring of

Negroes as clerks and sales personnel; and general upgrading of black employees from solely menial jobs. The boycott quickly received the support of students at two other all-black colleges in Birmingham, as well as the backing of some students at all-white Birmingham Southern College. The students were joined by the ACMHR and other groups in the black community.

The city government's response was in keeping with its past policies. On April 3, 1962, at the suggestion of Commissioner Connor, the City Commission voted to cut off Birmingham's appropriation to Jefferson County's surplus food program. The next day Shuttlesworth was arrested on a downtown street, allegedly for blocking the sidewalk and failing to obey the command of a police officer to move on. However, not all of Birmingham's white community was pleased with this way of handling the situation. On April 5 the highly conservative Birmingham *News* published a front-page editorial stating that it was "time for Birmingham citizens to sit down and talk together."

No sitting down and talking was actually done until the Southern Christian Leadership Conference (SCLC), the association of Southern black ministers formed in 1957, indicated it might join the ACMHR in a massive campaign aimed at segregation in Birmingham. The SCLC had already announced plans to hold a convention in Birmingham in September 1962. The possibility of such expanded protest brought some white and black community leaders together for the first time. After a series of talks, agreements were reached in which some merchants promised to remove Jim Crow signs from their stores and to join the ACMHR in a lawsuit seeking the nullification of city ordinances that prohibited integrated lunch counters.

After the agreements had been reached, Shuttlesworth announced that a moratorium had been declared on boycotts

the Supreme Court's ruling: it seemed, in
54, to promise a speedy dismantling of the
that he had known and chafed under in his
black child, even in the prosperous Sugar
lanta, he had learned what it meant to be
lace was in the colored part of the city, in
nd colored parks, in the colored section of
way stations, courtrooms, and libraries. The
od'' and dignity was terrible, King wrote
"abhorring not only segregation but also
d barbarous acts that grew out of it.''

d spots where Negroes had been savagely
had watched the Ku Klux Klan on its rides at
seen police brutality with my own eyes, and
oes receive the most tragic injustices in the

reme Court ruling promised an end to this
zed discrimination. But as a young minister
King saw most of Southern officialdom
ccept the judicial mandate. First came open
efiance by governors, legislators, mayors,
nen, police, and school boards, memorial-
c resolutions of nullification and interposi-
the organic nature of the American federal
ne the concrete actions of resistance: pupil-
nd other measures to avoid school integra-
nforcement of segregation in transportation,
lations, and governmental facilities; adher-
preventing voter registration and exercise of
roes; exclusion of blacks from local-govern-
t opportunities; intensified racial discrimi-
forcement and the administration of justice,
risal for any efforts to press for integration;

and demonstrations. He added that if the commitments
of the business leaders were not honored, the SCLC would be
asked to undertake an action campaign in Birmingham. Some
merchants actually did remove Jim Crow signs when the
SCLC convention was held in September, but the signs reappeared after the convention ended; Bull Connor had allegedly
threatened the merchants with loss of their licenses if the
signs were not restored.

But even as Bull Connor was pressuring the merchants to
back down on their agreement, a significant segment of Birmingham's socioeconomic elite was mounting a serious challenge to his rule. For some time a group of young white lawyers and businessmen interested in bringing change to
Birmingham had been working on a plan to alter the city's
form of government from the city-commission system to a
mayor-council system. In August they succeeded in getting a
referendum on the proposed change placed on the November
1962 ballot. During the fall of 1962 the issue of governmental reform became the focal point of division between
these "moderates" and the supporters of the Bull Connor
regime. After a stormy campaign the proposal for adoption of
the mayor-council system was approved by a 2,500-vote
margin. In the eyes of the white moderates the referendum
victory marked a major turning point for Birmingham: Bull
Connor, the personification of extreme racism in the city, had
opposed the proposal for change and had been beaten convincingly.

An election to choose the new mayor was set for March 5,
1963. For the moderates, it was an opportunity to install an
administration that would work to change Birmingham's
image.

But Fred Shuttlesworth and the ACMHR leaders did not
believe that a change in Birmingham's form of government,
or even the election of a "moderate" city administration,

would produce basic changes in the city's racial policies. Only a direct campaign against official segregation policies, they felt, could do that. Sensing that the time was ripe for such a campaign, Shuttlesworth turned for assistance to an old friend and SCLC associate, Martin Luther King.

Mart

ALMOST EVERYT
perspective today
confrontation in E

King was born
was a Baptist mir
a strict but loving
Atlanta's racially
black community
schools, he grad
Negro Morehouse
arts degree and a
for three years (ai
Theological Semi
first in his class. I
ing a Ph.D. in sy
completing his the
the Dexter Avenue
moving there with

When the new
job, the U.S. Sup
that public schoo
guarantee of the F
stitution. As King

was "elated"
the summer of
Jim Crow syste
youth. Like ev
Hill section of
"colored." His
colored schools
buses, stores, ra
blow to "self
later. He grew
the oppressive a

I had pa
lynched, and
night. I had
watched Ne
courts.

The 1954 Su
structure of lega
in Montgomery
flatly refuse to
declarations of
judges, busines
ized in tragicon
tion that mocke
system. Then ca
placement laws
tion; continued
public accomm
ence to policies
the ballot by Ne
ment employme
nation in law e
especially in re

and effective bars against Negroes serving on juries in most Southern communities.

Montgomery, capital of Alabama and site of the segregationist state government, was a stronghold of the "Never!" forces. King found life for its forty-two thousand Negroes one of strict segregation in all the institutions of daily life. Though he busied himself with the affairs of his small, prosperous church, he also adopted an activist civil rights stand— calling on his parishioners to join the NAACP, to register as voters, and to participate in social action through the church. He joined the local NAACP chapter himself, as well as the Alabama Council on Human Relations, the one interracial group in Alabama seeking to promote equal opportunities for Negroes. As yet, he had formulated no special program to deal with the problem of racial justice, but events found him, as they so often did in his career. It was King's special gift that he grasped such moments and transformed crisis into opportunity.

In Montgomery, it was the buses. The Montgomery Bus Line, a private company franchised by the city, followed standard Southern practice: blacks seated from the rear, whites from the front. Whites received preference for all seats, and drivers often engaged in acts of calculated discourtesy and insult to Negro riders. Negro protests against these policies were rejected.

On December 1, 1955, a slender, middle-aged black woman, Mrs. Rosa Parks, boarded a bus and sat in a vacant seat in the middle section. A seamstress, and secretary of the local NAACP chapter, Mrs. Parks had put in a long hard day. Her feet were aching, and she settled down to the ride home. As the bus became filled up, the driver called out to her to get up and move to standing room in the back. "No," she replied quietly, "I won't." She was well versed in the city's racial etiquette, and did not intend to become a test case. But her feet hurt, and she would not move. Following standard procedure, the driver called the police, who took Mrs. Parks to the station and charged her with violating the bus-segregation ordinance.

News of Mrs. Park's arrest galvanized E. D. Nixon, the local representative of the Brotherhood of Sleeping Car Porters, to call a meeting of prominent black leaders. They agreed to organize a one-day boycott of the buses on December 5, to coincide with the day of Mrs. Parks's trial. King was on the committee.

The one-day boycott went extremely well, but Mrs. Parks was still convicted and fined. The black leaders decided to form an ad hoc organization to keep the boycott going until the bus company agreed to "fair seating" policies, basic courtesy to Negro riders, and the hiring of some black drivers. The Montgomery Improvement Association (MIA) was formed, and King was chosen to serve as its president.

At an evening mass meeting at the Holt Street Church on December 7, four thousand Montgomery blacks heard Martin Luther King lay out the issues confronting them. In a speech that mixed sharp social analysis with an eloquence that reached every listener, King sounded a message of new commitment: "There comes a time when people get tired—tired of being segregated and humiliated, tired of being kicked about by the brutal feet of oppression." Now, "we have no alternative but to protest . . . we come here tonight to be saved from that patience that makes us patient with anything less than freedom and justice." He invoked the constitutional right "to protest for right"; distinguished boycotts by Negroes in behalf of civil rights and justice from the White Citizens Councils' boycotts to defeat the supreme law of the land; and called for loving persuasion and Christian faith to overcome oppression by whites. He also insisted that "we must not become bitter and end up by hating our white broth-

and demonstrations. He added that if the commitments of the business leaders were not honored, the SCLC would be asked to undertake an action campaign in Birmingham. Some merchants actually did remove Jim Crow signs when the SCLC convention was held in September, but the signs reappeared after the convention ended; Bull Connor had allegedly threatened the merchants with loss of their licenses if the signs were not restored.

But even as Bull Connor was pressuring the merchants to back down on their agreement, a significant segment of Birmingham's socioeconomic elite was mounting a serious challenge to his rule. For some time a group of young white lawyers and businessmen interested in bringing change to Birmingham had been working on a plan to alter the city's form of government from the city-commission system to a mayor-council system. In August they succeeded in getting a referendum on the proposed change placed on the November 1962 ballot. During the fall of 1962 the issue of governmental reform became the focal point of division between these "moderates" and the supporters of the Bull Connor regime. After a stormy campaign the proposal for adoption of the mayor-council system was approved by a 2,500-vote margin. In the eyes of the white moderates the referendum victory marked a major turning point for Birmingham: Bull Connor, the personification of extreme racism in the city, had opposed the proposal for change and had been beaten convincingly.

An election to choose the new mayor was set for March 5, 1963. For the moderates, it was an opportunity to install an administration that would work to change Birmingham's image.

But Fred Shuttlesworth and the ACMHR leaders did not believe that a change in Birmingham's form of government, or even the election of a "moderate" city administration, would produce basic changes in the city's racial policies. Only a direct campaign against official segregation policies, they felt, could do that. Sensing that the time was ripe for such a campaign, Shuttlesworth turned for assistance to an old friend and SCLC associate, Martin Luther King.

3

Martin Luther King, Jr.

ALMOST EVERYTHING IN KING'S CAREER, viewed from our perspective today, seemed to have been preparing him for a confrontation in Birmingham.

King was born in 1929, in Atlanta, Georgia. His father was a Baptist minister and his mother a schoolteacher. It was a strict but loving family, with his father a leading figure in Atlanta's racially segregated but prosperous middle-class black community. After attending the local (black) public schools, he graduated at fifteen and entered Atlanta's all-Negro Morehouse College, emerging in 1948 with a liberal arts degree and a major in sociology. King then went North for three years (and a Bachelor of Divinity degree) at Crozer Theological Seminary in Chester, Pennsylvania, graduating first in his class. In 1951 he entered Boston University, earning a Ph.D. in systematic theology in 1955. While he was completing his thesis, he accepted a call to become pastor of the Dexter Avenue Baptist Church in Montgomery, Alabama, moving there with his wife, Coretta, in June 1954.

When the new minister returned South to take up his first job, the U.S. Supreme Court had just held (a month earlier) that public school segregation violated the equal protection guarantee of the Fourteenth Amendment to the Federal Constitution. As King was to relate later in one of his books, he was "elated" at the Supreme Court's ruling: it seemed, in the summer of 1954, to promise a speedy dismantling of the Jim Crow system that he had known and chafed under in his youth. Like every black child, even in the prosperous Sugar Hill section of Atlanta, he had learned what it meant to be "colored." His place was in the colored part of the city, in colored schools and colored parks, in the colored section of buses, stores, railway stations, courtrooms, and libraries. The blow to "selfhood" and dignity was terrible, King wrote later. He grew up "abhorring not only segregation but also the oppressive and barbarous acts that grew out of it."

> I had passed spots where Negroes had been savagely lynched, and had watched the Ku Klux Klan on its rides at night. I had seen police brutality with my own eyes, and watched Negroes receive the most tragic injustices in the courts.

The 1954 Supreme Court ruling promised an end to this structure of legalized discrimination. But as a young minister in Montgomery, King saw most of Southern officialdom flatly refuse to accept the judicial mandate. First came open declarations of defiance by governors, legislators, mayors, judges, businessmen, police, and school boards, memorialized in tragicomic resolutions of nullification and interposition that mocked the organic nature of the American federal system. Then came the concrete actions of resistance: pupil-placement laws and other measures to avoid school integration; continued enforcement of segregation in transportation, public accommodations, and governmental facilities; adherence to policies preventing voter registration and exercise of the ballot by Negroes; exclusion of blacks from local-government employment opportunities; intensified racial discrimination in law enforcement and the administration of justice, especially in reprisal for any efforts to press for integration;

and effective bars against Negroes serving on juries in most Southern communities.

Montgomery, capital of Alabama and site of the segregationist state government, was a stronghold of the "Never!" forces. King found life for its forty-two thousand Negroes one of strict segregation in all the institutions of daily life. Though he busied himself with the affairs of his small, prosperous church, he also adopted an activist civil rights stand— calling on his parishioners to join the NAACP, to register as voters, and to participate in social action through the church. He joined the local NAACP chapter himself, as well as the Alabama Council on Human Relations, the one interracial group in Alabama seeking to promote equal opportunities for Negroes. As yet, he had formulated no special program to deal with the problem of racial justice, but events found him, as they so often did in his career. It was King's special gift that he grasped such moments and transformed crisis into opportunity.

In Montgomery, it was the buses. The Montgomery Bus Line, a private company franchised by the city, followed standard Southern practice: blacks seated from the rear, whites from the front. Whites received preference for all seats, and drivers often engaged in acts of calculated discourtesy and insult to Negro riders. Negro protests against these policies were rejected.

On December 1, 1955, a slender, middle-aged black woman, Mrs. Rosa Parks, boarded a bus and sat in a vacant seat in the middle section. A seamstress, and secretary of the local NAACP chapter, Mrs. Parks had put in a long hard day. Her feet were aching, and she settled down to the ride home. As the bus became filled up, the driver called out to her to get up and move to standing room in the back. "No," she replied quietly, "I won't." She was well versed in the city's racial etiquette, and did not intend to become a test case. But her feet hurt, and she would not move. Following standard procedure, the driver called the police, who took Mrs. Parks to the station and charged her with violating the bus-segregation ordinance.

News of Mrs. Park's arrest galvanized E. D. Nixon, the local representative of the Brotherhood of Sleeping Car Porters, to call a meeting of prominent black leaders. They agreed to organize a one-day boycott of the buses on December 5, to coincide with the day of Mrs. Parks's trial. King was on the committee.

The one-day boycott went extremely well, but Mrs. Parks was still convicted and fined. The black leaders decided to form an ad hoc organization to keep the boycott going until the bus company agreed to "fair seating" policies, basic courtesy to Negro riders, and the hiring of some black drivers. The Montgomery Improvement Association (MIA) was formed, and King was chosen to serve as its president.

At an evening mass meeting at the Holt Street Church on December 7, four thousand Montgomery blacks heard Martin Luther King lay out the issues confronting them. In a speech that mixed sharp social analysis with an eloquence that reached every listener, King sounded a message of new commitment: "There comes a time when people get tired—tired of being segregated and humiliated, tired of being kicked about by the brutal feet of oppression." Now, "we have no alternative but to protest . . . we come here tonight to be saved from that patience that makes us patient with anything less than freedom and justice." He invoked the constitutional right "to protest for right"; distinguished boycotts by Negroes in behalf of civil rights and justice from the White Citizens Councils' boycotts to defeat the supreme law of the land; and called for loving persuasion and Christian faith to overcome oppression by whites. He also insisted that "we must not become bitter and end up by hating our white brothers," for "we are tied together. The Negro needs the white man to free him from his fear; the white man needs the Negro to free him of his guilt."

Once organized, the Montgomery Improvement Association proceeded to set up taxi shuttles and car pools, which produced a bus boycott that was 99 percent effective, cutting off most of the bus company's revenues and a major part of downtown Christmas shopping. Negotiations with the bus-company manager and police commissioner got nowhere; their position was that the city's segregation ordinance required racial seating and that the law must be obeyed. As the boycott continued, the national press and television reported the story, and financial contributions and support from national civil rights leaders began to flow in.

Montgomery whites tried all the customary techniques for getting "their" Negroes back into line. Some Negro domestic workers who would not ride the buses were fired, but white households learned that they could not manage without the "help," and this fizzled out. Threatening telephone calls echoed night after night, and the Klan issued its traditional warnings of night rides and bloodshed. Over the next few months bombs struck King's home, the home of fellow-minister Ralph Abernathy, four churches, and the homes of other MIA leaders.

But the primary attack on the boycott came through the city's use of police power and the law. On January 26, 1956, a policeman who had been trailing King's car stopped him, arrested him on a charge of driving thirty miles an hour in a twenty-five-mile zone, and took him directly to jail in a patrol car. Though he offered no resistance, his arm was twisted behind his back. He was booked on the speeding charge and was refused release on bond. Only after hundreds of Montgomery residents went to the jail grounds and the officials saw the mounting crowd was King released on his own recognizance. Two days later, after a hearing in Montgomery police court in which the police officer's word was taken as entirely true, King was fined ten dollars.

Two days later a bomb exploded on the front porch of King's home, ripping out portions of the housefront but, luckily, causing no injuries to the family. The next day, to the surprise of the Negro community, seven white men were arrested for the bombing, and two were indicted. The work of one city detective had been outstanding, and the two men even signed confessions. Despite both physical evidence and the confessions, however, the two men were acquitted by an all-white jury. "With their friends crowding around them," King recalled, "Raymond D. York and Sonny Kyle Livingston walked grinning out of the courtroom. Justice had once more miscarried."

In February the city secured a grand jury indictment against King and eighty-nine other participants in the boycott movement for violating an Alabama statute making it a misdemeanor to hinder lawful business "without just cause or legal excuse." A battery of black lawyers, drawn from Alabama and the New York office of the NAACP, defended the MIA leaders at a four-day trial held in March, but the defendants were found guilty. King was sentenced to pay a fine of five hundred dollars plus court costs, with the alternative of spending a year in jail. King's lawyers filed an appeal.

About the same time that the city initiated its state court prosecution of the boycott leaders, Montgomery Negroes turned to the federal courts for assistance. In February a suit against the city was filed in U.S. District Court in Montgomery by several black residents, aided by NAACP lawyers, to have the racial-seating ordinance declared unconstitutional. A hearing was held before a special three-judge court, and on June 4, 1956, a 2–1 decision relying heavily on the Supreme Court's 1954 school desegregation ruling held that city and state laws requiring segregation on buses violated the Fourteenth Amendment. The ruling did not result in immediate desegregation of the buses, however, because city officials obtained a stay of the court's order pending the outcome of an appeal to the U.S. Supreme Court.

During the fall of 1956, before the Supreme Court had taken any action on the city's appeal, city officials moved along a new track. They began a lawsuit in state court, seeking an injunction against the operation of the MIA's car pools—the lifeblood of the boycott movement. It was a move that King and the MIA leaders had expected the city to make long before, since an injunction could have a devastating effect on a protest campaign.

An injunction is a court order that directs individuals named in it to do (or refrain from doing) the acts specifically described in the order. A party against whom an injunction is issued cannot violate any of its terms, or he will be subject to punishment for contempt of court. If the injunction against the car pools was granted, it could break the back of the Montgomery campaign. Most black workers could not walk the long distances between their homes and their places of employment. On November 13, 1956, the case came up in court before Judge Eugene Carter, the same man who had previously convicted the MIA leaders of participating in an unlawful boycott. In the midst of the hearing, a reporter rushed in with word that the U.S. Supreme Court had unanimously upheld the federal court ruling declaring segregation on the city's buses unconstitutional. Even though Judge Carter went on to enjoin the use of car pools, the larger battle had been won. On December 21, 1956, with national television cameras recording the event, King and the other MIA leaders rode in the front of Montgomery's buses.

The MIA handled its victory in a special way. King and his colleagues distributed leaflets calling on blacks to refrain from trumpeting their success or acting defiantly when they rode the buses. Elaborate training sessions were held in the churches to teach people how to remain nonviolent even when insulted or physically provoked by whites trying to start trouble on the buses. Several instances of physical mistreatment of Negroes along with other acts of violence did take place on buses following the change in policies. A shotgun blast ripped through King's front door, and a packet of fourteen sticks of dynamite with a smoking fuse was thrown onto his porch but failed to explode. But the buses were never resegregated. King and the MIA had not only ended bus segregation in Montgomery, but their campaign had also produced a new judicial ruling against bus-segregation laws anywhere in the nation.

With the victory of the Montgomery bus-boycott campaign, King had become an internationally known public figure, his stature certified by a favorable cover story in *Time* magazine in early 1957. He hoped that the example of Montgomery's nonviolent mass action would be picked up throughout the South, and he devoted himself to spreading that message. *Jet* magazine reported that he gave 208 speeches in 1958, flying over 750,000 miles around the country. In 1958 he published *Stride Toward Freedom,* a movingly written account of the Montgomery campaign that sketched out the Negro people's long suffering under discrimination, explained their determination to have equality *now,* and argued that it was essential to add nonviolent community-based protest to the classic, and still vital, techniques of legal, political, and educational effort.

But the Montgomery model did not spread through the South. Some imitative efforts were made in other Southern communities, including Birmingham, and in several campaigns attempted by the Congress for Racial Equality, a small, essentially Northern-based interracial group founded in 1942. None of these proved successful, though, and even the larger legal victory that had seemed to be won in Montgomery proved illusory. Though the Supreme Court ruled that legally required bus segregation was unconstitutional, most cities and towns of the Deep South continued segregated seating, enforced by the police (as a matter of "public safety") and by community pressures.

In this inhospitable climate King spent the next three years trying to find an organizational base for himself and then to discover how nonviolent protest could be made into a practical force for community action. The organizational base began to be developed in 1957. A two-day meeting of Southern Negro ministers active in civil rights was called by Rev. E. K. Steele of Tallahassee, Florida, to be held at the church of Martin Luther King, Sr., in Atlanta. Martin Jr. and Ralph Abernathy were invited from the Montgomery Improvement Association. The ministers who attended the meeting hoped to find a way to coordinate local efforts and also to formulate plans for persuading the Eisenhower Administration to support civil rights in the South, at least by presidential speeches calling on Southern officials to obey the Supreme Court's mandates. A second planning meeting was held in New Orleans, and resulted in the decision to found a permanent organization, the Southern Christian Leadership Conference. Martin Luther King, Jr., was selected to be the group's president. The Alabama Christian Movement for Human Rights became an SCLC affiliate, and Fred Shuttlesworth an SCLC board member. The SCLC was to be, as its name said, an organization of leaders and affiliated groups, not a general membership association. From that point on, King conducted most of his civil rights work through the SCLC.

From 1957 through 1959 this activity primarily involved efforts to spur Negro voting registration following the 1957 Voting Rights Act and to force the Eisenhower Administration to abandon its neutrality on civil rights. In May 1957 King addressed a national Prayer Pilgrimage in Washington, an idea he conceived and the NAACP sponsored. He delivered an eloquent speech, "Give Us the Ballot," to thirty thousand people (about 10 percent white) assembled outside the Lincoln Memorial. In February 1958 King coordinated the mass civil rights meetings held in twenty-one Southern cities on Lincoln's Birthday. By June enough pressure had been generated that Eisenhower agreed to meet with a delegation of Negro leaders: King; Roy Wilkins of the NAACP; Lester Granger of the Urban League; and A. Philip Randolph, head of the Brotherhood of Sleeping Car Porters. The meeting was intensely discouraging. Eisenhower spoke of the complexity of the race problem and the need to change men's hearts; he promised no federal action, or even public expressions of support for desegregation. Angry at this cool response, King proposed a campaign of student "study-ins" at white schools, but his colleagues considered it unwise and dangerous to send children in to do the work of adults.

As 1959 ended, a sense of frustration hung over King and the SCLC. The NAACP, Urban League, and other main-line Negro organizations were pressing ahead with their regular efforts, but the SCLC was floundering. Most of the Southern ministers wanted to spur immediate community action, not commit themselves to the slow, painful, and future-oriented work of voter registration. Tremendous pressure was building up in the black community, especially among young people who had come of age after the 1954 Supreme Court decision and now saw its command flouted everywhere. But during the late 1950s, King and his associates had not found the right protest instrument for harnessing this growing pressure.

Then, in 1960, the civil rights scene suddenly exploded in new directions. At 10 A.M. on February 1, 1960, four students from the all-Negro Agricultural and Technical College of North Carolina, in Greensboro, walked into the local Woolworth's and sat down at the "whites only" lunch counter. They were refused service, but they sat quietly all day on the counter stools and then left. The next day they were back, and for several more days. A reporter called the action a "sit-in'' and from then on, the tactic spread like wildfire. Within the next few weeks, black college students and white allies sat-in at lunch counters elsewhere in North Carolina and in four other Southern states. There had been some efforts at sit-ins in the South earlier, but these had never attracted much national attention. This time, however, the actions by students in Greensboro took hold, especially when the police were called and they began to haul the nonresisting students to jail. In many communities, store owners removed the stools or closed the lunch counters. Whenever the sit-in students were insulted, pushed, or punched, they remained nonviolent, refusing to be provoked or to respond with force. All this made exciting press copy, and within two months the lunch-counter sit-ins had spread to ten states.

The sit-ins had been entirely spontaneous, their rapid spread not unlike the swift dissemination of other trends among college students and through the mass media. King read about the students' action, saw it as nonviolence in its best form, and offered the SCLC's support. He had just moved to Atlanta, leaving Montgomery to be able to spend more time at SCLC headquarters and to take over the less time-consuming church post of co-pastor at his father's Ebenezer Baptist Church.

By now the SCLC had assembled some of the dedicated black aides who would be working alongside King during the rest of his life. Rev. Wyatt T. Walker, a thin, intense man with strong organizational talents, cracked the whip in Dr. King's name to get things moving more efficiently in SCLC affairs. Rev. Andrew Young, a graduate of Howard University, had worked as a youth organizer for the National Council of Churches, and was one of the more intellectual activists on King's staff. Rev. Bernard Lee served as Dr. King's traveling companion, bodyguard, and general amanuensis. Rev. Ralph Abernathy, the old comrade from Montgomery days who was King's closest personal friend, complemented

King's intellectual gifts with some shrewd, plain-folks understanding of Southern blacks and considerable rhetorical skill. Also in King's entourage was Bayard Rustin, a tall, handsome radical whose socialist ideas and pacifist philosophy had been deepened with Gandhi in India, and whose capacities for social analysis and organizational politics were a great strength to King. Interestingly, the SCLC was an organization led, governed, and staffed almost exclusively by blacks. Though Dr. King was a firm supporter of interracial goals and interracial movements, the role played by whites in his own movement was to give money, provide advice when sought, and supply some special services such as legal help.

After the sit-ins began to gather momentum in the winter of 1960, King spoke at several sit-in rallies at Southern colleges. The SCLC called a conference of sit-in leaders from ten Southern states, held at Shaw University in Raleigh, North Carolina, at which King called for a "continuing organization" to promote the sit-in effort. This was formed, and took the name Student Nonviolent Coordinating Committee (SNCC). King agreed to serve as one of its advisers, and he continued to teach nonviolent principles and tactics at sit-in training sessions during 1960.

If linking up with the student-generated sit-in movement was one important theme of King's life in 1960, another was his personal experiences with the punitive use of law by Southern officials. In February 1960 a Montgomery grand jury indicted King for perjury, charging that he had willfully lied in the filing of his 1956 and 1958 state income tax returns. Basically, the Alabama authorities alleged that he had failed to report as personal income amounts that various groups had spent to pay his transportation, hotel accommodations, and other expenses in connection with civil rights work during those years. King was deeply disturbed by the indictment. He knew that he had filed honest returns, but the thought of a lengthy and complicated trial before an all-white jury, and the effect on his standing as a moral spokesman, caused him intense dismay.

In May, King's perjury case came to trial in Montgomery. Fortunately, the lawyers defending him had done an excellent job of preparation and were able to subject the tax auditors to a withering cross-examination on the procedures by which they had arrived at their conclusions about Dr. King's income. The state's principal witness, a tax agent named Lloyd Hale, admitted under questioning that he had found "no evidence of fraud" in King's returns, that he had actually said this to Dr. King when the matter first came up, and that there were errors in the state's computation of tax owed. The jury went out, and came back four hours later with a verdict of "not guilty." The ordeal was over, and while King always felt that "something had happened to that jury" to make it rule so unexpectedly, the power of the Alabama prosecutors to subject him to that ordeal was never forgotten. Very few Southern blacks could have afforded the battery of lawyers and the costs of investigation that made it possible to expose the weakness of the indictment to public view.

While the perjury case was in progress during the spring of 1960, King and the SCLC were hit with a second legal blow. King's colleagues had organized a defense committee to help raise money to defray the expenses of defending against the perjury charges. On March 29, 1960 the defense committee published a full-page advertisement in *The New York Times*. The ad described the nonviolent protest movement and charged that it was being met with "an unprecedented wave of terror." Among the incidents discussed in the text of the ad were the institution of the perjury charges against King, the deployment of police armed with shotguns and tear gas around the campus of all-black Alabama State College in Montgomery, and the padlocking of the college's dining hall. The Montgomery City Commissioner who supervised the police department, L. B. Sullivan, brought a libel suit against Ralph Abernathy, Fred Shuttlesworth, two other black ministers who had signed the ad, and *The New York Times*. Sullivan asked $500,000 in damages, claiming that false statements in the ad about "police" and "Southern violators" would be read to reflect adversely on him and injure his professional reputation. After a trial in Montgomery circuit court, a jury awarded Sullivan the full $500,000 against all the defendants.

The libel judgment obtained against Ralph Abernathy and the other Alabama churchmen was a tremendous threat to the SCLC. If the money could not be collected against *The New York Times,* as an out-of-state corporation, the Negro ministers would be bankrupted to pay it. Furthermore, if solicitations for funds in Northern newspapers could be made the subject of successful libel suits before all-white Southern juries, the ability of the civil rights movement to obtain funds—or even to place ads—would be crippled. Even though King had not been sued personally by Sullivan, since he had not signed the ad seeking funds for his defense, he was deeply distressed at the situation in which Ralph Abernathy and the other Alabama ministers had been placed. Possibly the verdict could be reversed on appeal, but the case would have to be taken all the way to the U.S. Supreme Court, with no assurance of success. Whatever the outcome, the litigation would be long and costly, putting a severe drain on the SCLC's financial resources.

King's final encounter with the law in 1960 was a two-part drama. When he moved to Atlanta in early 1960, he neglected to obtain a Georgia license plate for his car, continuing to drive with his Alabama plates. This was discovered by a policeman in rural De Kalb County who stopped King on a routine license check in May. The officer could have dismissed him with a warning that since he had been a permanent resident of the state for more than three months, he had to change the registration. However, he arrested King, and at

a trial before De Kalb County judge Oscar Mitchell in September, the judge imposed a fine of twenty-five dollars and
placed King on a year's probation. King paid the fine immediately, changed his registration, and gave no further thought
to the probation, assuming that it related only to his driving
privileges.

In early October he joined students in Atlanta at a lunch-
counter sit-in at Rich's department store. As more or less expected, he was arrested and booked, though no one expected
that charges would be pressed very vigorously by the sophis-
ticated Atlanta officials. The arrest was well reported, however, and on October 20 De Kalb County officials called the
Atlanta police to apprehend King and deliver him to De Kalb
for violating the condition of his probation—that he "stay out
of trouble with the law" for a year. He was taken in hand-
cuffs to De Kalb County, and even though his arrest had not
resulted as yet in a conviction, Judge Mitchell held that his
conduct in "trespassing" at Rich's department store violated
the probation. King was sentenced to four months at hard
labor in Reidsville state prison, and ordered to be taken there
the next morning.

King's friends were deeply concerned. There was no telling what might happen to him in the prison, and the thought
of his having to serve four months at hard labor because of a
license-plate oversight was outrageous. The story was given
to the press and widely reported. With the presidential election of 1960 in its closing weeks, advisers in both the Nixon
and Kennedy campaign camps considered whether their can-
didate should say or do anything about King's imprisonment.
Vice-President Nixon decided on "no comment." On the
night of October 26, John F. Kennedy called Mrs. King to let
her know that he would try to help her husband. The next day
Robert Kennedy called Judge Mitchell to inquire about bail
for Dr. King, and by midday King was freed from Reidsville
on two thousand dollars bail. Back in Atlanta, the mayor or-

dered the trespassing charge against King and the others to be dropped, and this was done in municipal court. With no charges in Atlanta, the De Kalb County authorities had no case, and the probation violation was withdrawn.

The reaction of the two presidential candidates to King's jailing was well publicized. Rev. Martin Luther King, Sr., issued a strong endorsement of Senator Kennedy for the presidency, citing Kennedy's courageous action in behalf of his son. Election analysts credited the Kennedy telephone call with influencing a considerable number of Negro votes at the last minute, helping Kennedy achieve his razor-thin margin of victory over Nixon.

With Kennedy elected, a Democratic administration was in office that had made generous civil rights pledges in its 1960 platform. However, the Kennedy Administration followed a distinctly gradualistic course in civil rights during its first two years in office. It made a number of sympathetic gestures: several blacks were appointed to high offices in the federal government; the Committee on Equal Employment Opportunity was organized with a mandate to improve employment opportunities for Negroes in government and with companies doing business with the government; and the Justice Department made appreciably greater use of its limited powers to participate in voting rights cases under the Civil Rights Act of 1957. However, the Administration did not seek the passage of any major civil rights legislation during 1961 or 1962.

A major reason for the Administration's posture was the composition of Congress, where many of the President's "New Frontier" legislative programs were meeting strong opposition from a coalition of conservative Republicans and Southern Democrats. The Administration felt that a fight for civil rights legislation was unlikely to be successful, and might adversely affect the President's ability to achieve other goals. Even where the President had executive power to end discrimination and had promised to do so, in federally assisted housing, it was not until late 1962 that Kennedy signed such an order. Even then, the executive order was written to reach discrimination in only a small percentage of the housing units in the country.

Civil rights leaders tried repeatedly to prod the federal government into taking stronger action. In the spring of 1961, CORE decided to dramatize Southern noncompliance with Supreme Court rulings outlawing segregation in interstate transportation and terminal facilities by sponsoring a series of "Freedom Rides." The idea was quickly endorsed by SNCC and SCLC, and King served as chairman of the Freedom Ride Coordinating Committee. SCLC also helped finance the venture. The rides began early in May, with groups of Negroes and whites buying tickets on interstate buses which took them into the Deep South. They met repeated refusals of service in terminal facilities as they got farther into the South, and in some instances encountered considerable violence. On May 14, 1961, just outside Anniston, Alabama, one of the buses was set on fire by angry whites. In Birmingham the same day, a busload of Freedom Riders was severely beaten by a waiting mob which descended upon them as soon as the bus arrived at the terminal.

Before the Freedom Rides started, Justice Department officials had taken the position that the federal government could not provide protection for the riders if they met with violence. To do so, they felt, would be intruding into an area that was the responsibility of local law enforcement authorities. Only if it was clear that local authorities could not provide adequate protection would there be any basis for federal intervention. After the incidents in Anniston and Birmingham, however, Attorney General Robert Kennedy met with several of his top aides to formulate contingency plans should Alabama authorities be unable to prevent violence to the next group of Freedom Riders. Deputy Attorney General Byron White, together with key Justice Department aides Louis Oberdorfer, Burke Marshall, Joseph Dolan, and a few others, devised a plan for assembling a special force of U.S. marshals, transporting them to Alabama, and deploying them to cope with violence. Another Justice Department official, John Siegenthaler, was dispatched to Montgomery on Friday, May 19, as President Kennedy's personal representative. After meeting with Governor John Patterson for two hours, Siegenthaler called Attorney General Kennedy from the governor's office to say that he had been assured that Alabama authorities had "the means, the ability, and the will to keep the peace without outside help."

The next morning, a busload of Freedom Riders set off from Birmingham, bound for New Orleans by way of Montgomery. When they arrived at the Montgomery bus terminal, a crowd of about a thousand whites had gathered, and no policemen were anywhere to be seen. As the passengers started to get off the bus, they were attacked with fists, clubs, sticks, and pipes. Several of them were badly injured, and so were four out-of-town newsmen. John Siegenthaler was knocked unconscious when he tried to help one of the riders escape into a car; he lay on the pavement for twenty-five minutes before the police finally took him to a hospital.

John Doar, Burke Marshall's chief assistant in the Justice Department's Civil Rights Division, was watching the scene from a window in the U.S. Attorney's office in Montgomery and describing it over the phone to Robert Kennedy in Washington. Hearing his report, the Attorney General acted immediately, telling Byron White to organize his force of marshals immediately and have them in Alabama as quickly as possible. By nightfall the men he had selected were streaming into Montgomery from all over the nation, assembling at an air force base just outside Montgomery. At the same time,

Kennedy asked FBI Director J. Edgar Hoover to send additional agents to Montgomery to investigate the violence. He also directed John Doar to seek a federal court injunction restraining the Ku Klux Klan, the National States Rights Party, and the Birmingham and Montgomery police from interfering with interstate travel. Doar prepared an application for an *ex parte* injunction, presented it to federal district judge Frank Johnson that afternoon, and Johnson signed it.

Once the court order had been obtained, the Justice Department officials felt that they had a firm basis for using the federal marshals. White deployed them as soon as he heard from Doar that the order had been signed, and by late afternoon they were patrolling at the bus terminal, the railway station, along the highways, and in the black neighborhoods of the city. That evening about a hundred of the marshals formed a protective cordon around Rev. Ralph Abernathy's First Baptist Church, where a mass rally was being held to support the Freedom Riders. Outside, a howling mob of several thousand whites was hurling rocks and bottles at the church and shouting that it would be burned down. Inside, Martin Luther King was addressing a crowd of twelve hundred. Referring to the marshals outside the building, King told the crowd, "The law may not be able to make a man love me, but at least it can keep him from lynching me."

Order was finally restored in Montgomery, though only after Governor Patterson had declared martial law and called out the National Guard. The Freedom Rides continued during the summer, but before the end of June the riders had achieved one of their principal objectives: Attorney General Robert Kennedy initiated a special proceeding before the Interstate Commerce Commission requesting an ICC order barring segregation in interstate bus terminals. His move confirmed the judgment of many civil rights leaders: that the Kennedys were basically decent men, sympathetic to the civil

rights cause, who would intervene in the battles between protest groups and Southern officialdom if enough pressure was
generated. In September the ICC issued the requested order.

The handling of the Montgomery crisis was a good illustra-
tion of the way the Justice Department operated during the
1961–63 period. With John Kennedy in the White House and
Robert Kennedy heading Justice, the Justice Department became an extension of the presidency to a far greater extent
than ever before. Other Presidents, knowing the critical role
the Justice Department can play in advancing an administration's political objectives and guarding its flanks, had also
appointed their campaign managers or other close advisers as
Attorney Generals, but the relationship between John and
Robert Kennedy was uniquely close. Civil rights leaders
knew that when they talked with Robert Kennedy, they were
talking with the White House.

The Justice Department during this period had talent at the
top levels that had not been seen in the department since the
New Deal days of the 1930s. White and his aides in the Deputy's office, in addition to being Kennedy-style activists,
were all exceptionally shrewd lawyers. Complementing them
was a cadre of extraordinarily able lawyers recruited (mainly
by White) from the nation's leading law firms. As Victor
Navasky has documented, these men were remarkably alike
in their backgrounds—almost all were graduates of leading
Eastern law schools (principally Yale), all had had years of
experience in handling complex legal problems that required
skillful negotiation, and all had developed an instinct for an-
ticipating and avoiding troublesome problems.

From the outset Robert Kennedy and Byron White had
seen civil rights as an area that would require particularly
skillful handling. Knowing that John Kennedy would leave
his administration's handling of civil rights issues primarily
to the Justice Department, they gradually developed a strat-

egy for coping with the civil rights crises that unfolded in the 1960s.

Their strategy had two basic elements. First, it sought to spur the registration of Negro voters in the South, using the federal Voting Rights Acts of 1957 and 1960 as a basis for participation by the department in litigation designed to increase black voter registration. Second, it stressed the use of the courts to chip away at segregation. The lawyers in Justice anticipated that court decisions—particularly decisions of the U.S. Supreme Court, which lower courts would be bound to follow—would continue to go in the direction charted by the 1954 school desegregation case. With a court order to lend legitimacy to their actions, Justice Department lawyers could take a position on the side of the civil rights forces while still maintaining the posture of only enforcing the law—not making it. Robert Kennedy outlined the department's policy position in a speech at the University of Georgia on June 6, 1961, just as the first Freedom Rides were getting started:

> [I]f one man's rights are denied, the rights of all are endangered. In our country the courts have a most important role in safeguarding these rights. The decisions of the courts, however much we may disagree with them, in the final analysis must be followed and respected. If we disagree with a court decision and thereafter irresponsibly assail the court and defy its rulings, we challenge the foundations of our society. . . .
>
> Our position is clear. We are upholding the law. . . . I say to you today that if the orders of the court are circumvented, the Department of Justice will act. We will not stand by or be aloof. We will move.

In Montgomery the sweeping *ex parte* injunction that John Doar had obtained from Judge Johnson was a critical element in the action taken by the Justice Department in support of the civil rights protesters. It also set an important precedent: having insisted in Montgomery that federal court orders must be respected by belligerent white segregationists, the officials in Justice felt they could not take a different position when a federal court order was directed at civil rights protesters.

Late in 1961 King committed himself and the SCLC to a major campaign to desegregate public facilities in a single small city: Albany, Georgia. Albany, with a population of fifty-six thousand (40 percent black), is in southwestern Georgia, in "peanut, pecan, and corn country." The Albany Movement, an amalgam of SNCC organizers, local college students, and leaders of Albany's older black organizations, had been formed in November, following the arrest of several students who had tried to integrate the Albany bus terminal. The city responded with an unyielding defense of its totally segregated institutions. By December 15, when the Movement's president, Dr. William G. Anderson, a local osteopath, called King and asked that he come to Albany, more than five hundred people had been arrested in protest demonstrations. The Albany police chief, Laurie Pritchett, applied a shrewd policy toward demonstrators: politeness and no police brutality in public but a firm, "fill the jails" arrest policy. He "killed them with kindness," one city official told reporters.

King himself was in jail three times during the Albany campaign, which stretched out over the next ten months. For King and the Movement, the jailings (on charges such as obstructing a sidewalk and parading without a permit) were an opportunity: they provided a cause around which national pressure could be mounted against the city's public officials. But each time, just when it seemed that the city would have to alter its intransigence under the glare of national publicity, something would happen to bring King out of jail. Once it was a promise by city officials (later rescinded) to open meaningful negotiations. Another time it was the need to get medical attention for one of the imprisoned local leaders who refused to leave jail as long as King remained behind bars. The third time an "anonymous" person paid King's fine in order to obtain his release. Each time he emerged from jail, the effect was to diffuse the Movement and lighten the pressure on the city.

In July 1962, after many false starts, the Albany campaign at last seemed to be gathering some momentum. "Daily," historian David Lewis recounts, "small groups of blacks and some non-resident whites sought service at lunch counters, cinemas, libraries, parks, and bowling alleys." On Sundays, delegations tried to integrate the local churches. All these activities produced further mass arrests, and the pressure on the city began to build toward a climax. At this point city officials went before federal district judge J. Robert Elliott to ask for an injunction against the demonstrations. The demonstrators, they said, were preventing residents of Albany from exercising their rights and were disturbing the public peace. At midnight on July 20 Judge Elliott—an acknowledged segregationist who had been appointed to the bench a year earlier by President Kennedy—issued the order requested by the city. It enjoined King and the other Movement leaders from engaging in "unlawful picketing, congregating, or marching in the streets" and from doing anything else "designed to provoke breaches of the peace."

King's lawyers advised him that Judge Elliott's injunction—a temporary restraining order operative for ten days—was probably invalid, because of its sweeping curtailment of the demonstrators' constitutional rights to free speech and assembly. But it would take time to have it dissolved on appeal, and obedience to it would halt the Movement's momentum. On the other hand, defiance of the order could seriously alienate the Justice Department, which was completely committed to the principle that federal court orders must be obeyed by Southern officials or anyone else. Disobedience would also conflict with King's often-expressed philosophy of challenging local segregationist law but respecting federal law.

King decided that he and the others named in the injunction would not lead the scheduled march. He announced to the press that "out of respect for the leadership the federal judiciary has given" to the cause of civil rights, they had agreed to obey the order. King and his lawyers went to Atlanta to ask U.S. Court of Appeals judge Elbert Tuttle to overturn the temporary injunction.

Judge Tuttle vacated the Elliott injunction on July 24, but the delay had cost King dearly in terms of credibility in Albany's black community and among the SNCC organizers. After they agreed to abide by the injunction, King and his aides were never able to assume effective leadership of the campaign, and factional quarrels grew in intensity. More demonstrations were held, but the civil rights forces could not bring city officials into meaningful negotiations. In November, King announced that other commitments for civil rights required him to leave Albany for the time being and would not permit an early return.

At the close of 1962 racial conditions in Albany seemed to be no better than a year earlier. Despite repeated mass meetings, protest demonstrations, and arrests, the city leaders had not budged from their segregationist stance. Lunch-counter segregation remained unchanged in local department stores, no move was made to hire black policemen or bus drivers or to upgrade black employees of local businesses, and public facilities such as parks and swimming pools were either closed or "sold" to a group of Albany businessmen. Some civil rights leaders, including Slater King in Albany, felt that important progress had been made in raising the consciousness of the local black community and that the struggle would go forward to solid advances after 1962. But the view adopted in the Northern press, in many quarters of the civil rights movement, and by Southern white officials who had come to Albany to observe Chief Pritchett's containment policies was that the Albany Movement had been a gigantic failure.

Nor was the situation much better on other fronts. At Oxford, Mississippi, it had taken a huge force of federal marshals to overcome resistance to the admission of a single black student, James Meredith, to the University of Mississippi pursuant to a federal court order. Over 90 percent of the school districts in the Deep South remained totally segregated. The Kennedy Administration had not yet made the commitment to sweeping antidiscrimination legislation and executive action sought by civil rights leaders. To many in the movement, it seemed that the impetus provided by the direct-action programs of the early 1960s was being lost.

It was in this disappointing context that Martin Luther King, Jr., turned his attention to Birmingham, Alabama.

4

Project C—for Confrontation

PREPARATIONS FOR THE BIRMINGHAM campaign got under way in December 1962, when the SCLC held a three-day planning session at its training center near Savannah, Georgia. Several key decisions were made at that time, each of which reflected the hard experience of the Albany campaign.

First was the decision to go about making preparations both carefully and quietly. Given the sensitivity of the forthcoming Birmingham elections in early 1963, they didn't want to inject the SCLC project into those elections or to attract national publicity prematurely. Knowing that the Birmingham and state police regularly tapped the phones of ACMHR leaders, they dubbed the campaign "Project C" (for "confrontation") and used a variety of other code names for people, places, and events when talking about their plans on the telephone.

The second, and perhaps most important, decision was to concentrate on the Birmingham business community and to make the lunch counters at the downtown department stores the primary target. In Albany there had been no central focus to the demonstrations; the protesters' efforts had become widely scattered, covering buses, terminals, restaurants, and many other public places. By concentrating on the downtown stores with lunch counters, the Birmingham protesters would be exerting pressure on a limited number of white business-men who were already hurting because of the losses they had suffered during the March boycott. These stores were all located close to one another in the heart of a relatively small (twelve square blocks) business district, where the demon-strations would be bound to attract attention. Many of these merchants had already indicated that they would agree to black demands for desegregation of their facilities if the city authorities would permit them to do so. Since a number of the stores—such as Woolworth's, H. L. Green's, and J. J. Newberry's—were branches of nationwide companies, pres-sure on their national managements could also be generated in the North. If the merchants were squeezed sufficiently hard, at least some of them could be expected to pressure other elements in the white community to open negotiations with the blacks. There was also a symbolic value to the choice of department-store lunch counters as the primary target. As King later observed, "There is a special humilia-tion for the Negro in having his money accepted at every department in a store except the lunch counter." In deciding to focus on lunch-counter segregation, the protest leaders would gain wide support in the black community and thus help broaden the movement's base.

Third, the start of the campaign was timed to coincide with the beginning of the Easter season. Here too there was an ob-vious symbolic purpose, since participation in the protest movement required self-sacrifice for a larger cause. There was also a practical value—Easter is the second-biggest shopping period of the year. In 1963 Easter Sunday fell on April 14. It was decided to begin the campaign during the first week in March, the beginning of Lent.

Fourth, establishing close liaison with black leaders in Bir-mingham was made a top priority. In Albany a major cause of tension had been factional quarrels, fed by resentment at King and the SCLC for coming on the scene after SNCC organizers and local leaders had done much of the ground-work. Similar difficulties could be anticipated in Bir-mingham. Although ACMHR president Fred Shuttlesworth had asked King and the SCLC to come to Birmingham, Shuttlesworth represented the activist wing of the local Negro community, and other Birmingham Negroes could be ex-pected to oppose the campaign. The existence of such op-position was confirmed at a meeting that King and his chief aides had in Birmingham in early January with several local black leaders. A. G. Gaston, then seventy-three years old and one of the wealthiest men in the city, white or black, felt that the planned demonstration would hurt progress on the racial front in Birmingham. Rev. J. L. Wall, head of the local Bap-tist Ministers Conference, held a similar view. More than anything else, the local leaders were opposed to the date chosen by the SCLC to start the campaign. With mayoralty elections scheduled for March 5, they did not want anything to happen that would increase the chances of a Bull Connor victory.

Connor's two principal opponents, Tom King and Albert Boutwell, were both regarded in the black community as decidedly preferable to Connor. Both King and Boutwell were campaigning as "moderates," endorsing segregation but stressing the need for Birmingham to adapt to changing times; Tom King was the more liberal of the two. Connor was running on his record as a city commissioner dedicated to preservation of the status quo; he wore a button saying "Never" to make his position on the race question entirely clear.

As a result of objections raised at the January meeting in Birmingham, the SCLC leaders agreed to postpone the start of the demonstrations until mid-March. They also agreed to keep virtually all their staff members out of the city until after the election, to avoid giving Connor an opportunity to make political capital out of their activities. When the March

5 balloting resulted in a run-off between Boutwell and Connor being scheduled for April 2, the starting date was again set back, this time until April 3.

During most of January, February, and March, the protest leaders concentrated on preparations. Martin Luther King went on a nation-wide speaking tour to raise funds for the SCLC's activities in the South. In private meetings he solicited money and support for the coming Birmingham campaign from other civil rights organizations and from sympathetic business leaders, clergymen, and newspaper editors. Wyatt Walker was charged with organizing the operation, which included contacting local recruits, setting up workshops on nonviolent-action techniques, and mapping the locations of possible targets for sit-ins, marches, and other types of protest demonstrations.

Getting information from lawyers about the legal problems to be expected was a very important part of these organizational preparations. A number of different lawyers were associated with King and the SCLC at this time, among them New York City attorneys Clarence Jones, William Kunstler, and Harry Wachtel, Birmingham attorneys Arthur Shores and Orzell Billingsley, Jr., and the lawyers for the New York–based NAACP Legal Defense Fund, Inc. The "Inc. Fund," as it is known, was formed in 1938 as an offshoot of the NAACP. Under the leadership of Thurgood Marshall, it had led the fight in the courts for racial equality. In mid-1961 Marshall accepted an appointment to the U.S. Court of Appeals for the Second Circuit, and his place as head of the Inc. Fund was taken by a white lawyer, Jack Greenberg, who had been Marshall's chief lieutenant for many years. The Inc. Fund first began representing the SCLC during some of the early sit-in demonstrations in 1960, and by 1963 had become its principal legal adviser.

The Inc. Fund's role in the preparations for Project C was strictly a supporting one. The Fund's lawyers advised King and his aides on the state of the law, but the choice of strategy and tactics was always retained by the SCLC leaders. Whatever course of action was adopted, the Inc. Fund lawyers would work with cooperating attorneys in Birmingham and represent SCLC people in legal proceedings.

Briefing the SCLC leaders on what legal rights they had was not an easy assignment, for the law was in a state of considerable flux in late 1962 and early 1963. For example, though the sit-ins of 1960 and 1961 had produced several cases involving demonstrators' claims to First Amendment protection, the U.S. Supreme Court had not yet ruled on the scope of such "protest rights." The court had also not decided whether any orderly person had a constitutional right to receive service in a privately owned restaurant, motel, or other public accommodation facility despite the owner's wish to employ a racially restrictive policy.

Even if the nation's highest court were ultimately to decide that individuals did have rights to be served, the lawyers knew, there was no doubt that sit-in demonstrators would be arrested by the Birmingham police, probably on charges of trespass or breach of the peace. The lawyers hoped that the Supreme Court would overturn such convictions when they were used to enforce racial segregation ordinances, but that remained a hope for the future.

One of the protest leaders' traditional means of arousing support was the demonstration march, and here too the law in 1963 was unclear. Although a number of Supreme Court cases recognized the right of protest groups to express their grievances in demonstrations in public streets and parks, other high-court decisions had held that municipalities could impose reasonable regulations on the use of their public places and could take measures to protect the public peace. The court's decisions had repeatedly emphasized, however, that the regulations had to be reasonable and that public officials could not be given power arbitrarily to refuse permission for demonstrations.

In Birmingham the principal law governing demonstration marches was Section 1159 of the City Code, which provided:

> It shall be unlawful to organize or hold, or to assist in organizing or holding, or to take part or participate in, any parade or procession or other public demonstration on the streets or other public ways of the city, unless a permit therefor has been secured from the commission.
>
> To secure such permit, written application shall be made to the commission, setting forth the probable number of persons, vehicles and animals which will be engaged in such parade, procession or other public demonstration, the purpose for which it is to be held or had, and the streets or other public ways over, along or in which it is desired to have or hold such parade, procession or other public demonstration. The commission shall grant a written permit for such parade, procession or other public demonstration, prescribing the streets or other public way which may be used therefor, unless in its judgment the public welfare, peace, safety, health, decency, good order, morals or convenience require that it be refused. It shall be unlawful to use for such purposes any other streets or public ways than those set out in said permit.

The Inc. Fund lawyers felt that, on its face, Section 1159 did not provide the precise standards required by the Supreme Court for permit ordinances. The criteria mentioned— "public welfare, peace, safety, health, decency, good order, morals or convenience"—were so broad that the city commissioners really had no standards at all upon which to base the granting or denial of a permit. If the SCLC leaders were to hold a march without a permit, and were convicted by Birmingham of violating the ordinance (a misdemeanor carrying a maximum sentence of six months), the Inc. Fund lawyers believed the convictions would be reversed by the

U.S. Supreme Court. However, the SCLC leaders were less interested in test-case litigation than in holding effective protest marches in Birmingham that spring, and they decided that they would at least try to obtain a permit. By doing so, they would show an attempt to comply with the law, and if a permit were arbitrarily denied, they would be in a better legal position in any litigation that might follow.

A third critical area in which the law was in flux had to do with injunctions. As noted earlier, an injunction is a court order directing named individuals to do (or refrain from doing) specified acts. The usual method by which an injunction is obtained is for the party desiring it (the complainant) to present a judge with a sworn bill of complaint, accompanied by supporting affidavits of fact. On the basis of these papers, the complainant asks the judge to issue a temporary injunction that will be binding upon the parties until a hearing can be held to determine whether the injunction should be extended. When the papers are presented to the judge without the parties against whom the injunction is sought being present, any temporary injunction issued is known as an *ex parte* order. This was the procedure followed by the Justice Department in Montgomery in 1961 when John Doar obtained a federal court injunction from Judge Johnson forbidding police officials and Klan groups from interfering with the Freedom Rides.

Throughout most of its history, however, the injunction has not generally been used for such beneficent purposes. Widespread use of *ex parte* injunctions dates primarily from the 1890s, when employers sought such orders to halt picketing and other strike activities by labor unions. The injunctions were frequently decisive in breaking strikes. Like the mass demonstrations that the SCLC hoped to mount in Birmingham, the strike was generally the climax of a long and difficult organizational drive. Once the strike was stopped, the drive's momentum was usually lost forever. Even though *ex parte* injunctions were supposed to last only for a few days, it would often take weeks for hearings to be held, and these frequently resulted in a continuation of the temporary injunction until a full trial could be held on the question of whether the injunction should be made permanent. This, especially with appeals to higher courts, could take years. In the meantime, a party against whom such a "temporary" injunction was issued could not violate any of its terms or he would be subject to punishment for contempt of court.

Contempt of court comes in two different varieties in American law—civil and criminal. Criminal contempt arises from acts "done in disrespect of the court," obstructing the administration of justice or bringing the court into disrepute; it is generally punishable by fine and imprisonment. In civil contempt, the party fails to do something that he is ordered to do by the court, and the individual can be jailed until he performs the required action and "purges himself" of the contempt. Both types of contempt could be charged in a protest situation. A union leader who violated an antistrike injunction might, for example, be jailed for civil contempt until he ordered the strikers back to work, and he might also be held in criminal contempt for the act of defying the court's order.

Moreover, under the law of most states, Alabama among them, a person who violated an injunction could be held in contempt even if the injunction itself was invalid. In this respect, injunctions are significantly different from statutes passed by legislative bodies or administrative orders issued by executive-branch agencies. In our system of law, a citizen can decline to obey local statues or administrative orders and then assert his federal constitutional rights as a defense in a prosecution for the violation. Our test-case–oriented system of constitutional litigation has long assumed that such refusal is an important way to obtain a timely and authoritative judicial resolution of an alleged conflict between local and national law or between the actions of elected officials and the

Constitution. If the citizen is wrong about his claim of constitutional invalidity, he may go to jail; but if he is right, he will
suffer no punishment.

However, while statutes and administrative rules are generalized commands addressed to the world at large, injunctions
are directed to specific parties in a court order. Most courts
have felt that this is a crucial distinction and have required
persons so named to obey the injunction and test its validity
by legal motions. The SCLC lawyers knew that antidemon-
stration injunctions obtained by city officials against civil
rights protests were usually very broad and sweeping. Ultimately, they might be struck down because they abridged
First Amendment rights of expression. But until they were
vacated, they could be crippling to the movement—unless
they could be disobeyed from the outset on the ground that
they were "constitutionally void," in the same way that invalid statutes could be disobeyed.

In 1963 there were only a few Supreme Court cases on this
question of injunctions and federal constitutional rights. One
of these was in *In re Debs,* a case growing out of the labor
and farmer unrest that shook the nation from the late 1880s to
the early 1900s. In 1894 the American Railway Union, led
by Eugene Debs, called a strike in the Midwestern rail yards.
When it could not be ended by management through usual
strikebreaking techniques, President Grover Cleveland secured a federal court order enjoining Debs and the ARU
leaders from committing acts interfering with the flow of mail
and interstate commerce by railway transportation. Debs was
arrested and convicted for violating the injunction, and his
conviction was upheld by a unanimous Supreme Court. The
court's opinion noted the "earnest and eloquent appeal"
made on behalf of the oppressed railway workers, and said
that the justices "yielded to none in [their] admiration of
any act of heroism or self-sacrifice . . ." But, it continued,
court orders must be obeyed:

It is a lesson that cannot be learned too soon or too thoroughly that under this government of and by the people the means of redress of all wrongs are through the courts and at the ballot-box, and that no wrong, real or fancied, carries with it legal warrant to invite as a means of redress the cooperation of a mob, with its accompanying acts of violence.

It was in the tradition of the *Debs* case that the Supreme Court in 1922 decided a case called *Howat v. Kansas*. The *Howat* case, decided at the peak of the era when labor injunctions were in vogue, involved a state court injunction issued to enjoin a miners' strike in Kansas. The miners defied the injunction. In the contempt proceeding that followed, they argued that the court that issued the order had no power to do so, because the state statute authorizing such injunctions was void as a matter of federal constitutional law. The Kansas courts found the miners in contempt, however, taking the position that the miners could not challenge the validity of the injunction in the contempt proceeding. The U.S. Supreme Court dismissed the miners' appeal summarily, holding in a brief unanimous opinion that this Kansas rule of law was valid.

The leading Supreme Court precedent of relatively recent times was a 1946 decision in a case arising from a national coal miners' strike. In that case, *United States v. United Mine Workers,* the court by a 7–2 vote upheld the conviction of UMW leader John L. Lewis for violating a federal court injunction. Two of the justices, Hugo Black and William O. Douglas, found that the injunction was valid, so they did not reach the question of whether an invalid order could be punished by contempt. Three others, Chief Justice Fred Vinson and Justices Harold Burton and Stanley Reed, rested their votes for affirmance on alternative grounds: first, they agreed with Black and Douglas that the injunction was a valid order that had to be obeyed; second, they expressed the view that even if the injunction was not valid, disobedience of it was punishable as contempt of court. Vinson's opinion, joined by Burton and Reed, quoted approvingly from the court's 1920 opinion in *Howat*.

The other two justices who voted to uphold the contempt conviction in the *United Mine Workers* case, Felix Frankfurter and Robert Jackson, took the position that the district court did not have statutory authority to issue the labor injunction but that Lewis was nevertheless guilty of contempt for having violated the order. On this point Frankfurter commented in his concurring opinion that:

> Only when a court is so obviously traveling outside its orbit as to be merely usurping judicial forms and facilities, may an order issued by a court be disobeyed and treated as though it were a letter to a newspaper. Short of an indisputable want of authority on the part of a court, the very existence of a court presupposes its power to entertain a controversy, if only to decide, after deliberation, that it has no power over the particular controversy. Whether a defendant may be brought to the bar of justice is not for the defendant himself to decide. . . . There can be no free society without law administered through an independent judiciary. If one man can be allowed to determine for himself what is law, every man can. That means first chaos, then tyranny.

The decision in the *Mine Workers* case seemed to give new life to the judiciary's power to influence the outcome of social conflict through the use of the injunction.

However, in 1962 a Supreme Court decision in a case called *In re Green* seemed to indicate that the court was reconsidering the judiciary's power to punish violation of court orders even when they were invalid—a view that had by then come to be known as the *"Mine Workers* rule." In the *Green* case the court voted 7–2 to reverse a state court conviction of contempt arising out of the violation of a labor injunction. Green, the petitioner who had been held in contempt for his actions, argued that the state court had no power to issue the injunction because the National Labor Relations Board had exclusive jurisdiction over the labor dispute. Justice Douglas' opinion for the majority held that Green was entitled to a hearing at which he would have an opportunity to establish this claim. The implication of the opinion was that if Green could show that the state court had no jurisdiction over the dispute, he could not be held in contempt. As Justice Harlan noted in a dissent which Justice Clark joined, it was a decision that seemed inconsistent with the *Mine Workers'* rule.

The lawyers advising King concluded that violation of a sweeping state court injunction obtained by the city against the planned demonstrations would very probably result in a conviction for contempt of court. There would be only a slim chance that the constitutionality of the ordinance on which an injunction was based could be raised in the state courts. However, the recent Supreme Court decision in the *Green* case gave some hope that protesters who disregarded an injunction that deprived them of their First Amendment rights might ultimately be vindicated by the nation's highest court.

These were the legal considerations presented to King by Inc. Fund lawyers and other legal advisers in meetings during late 1962 and early 1963. King listened carefully to the advice and sought to understand his legal options. But he knew that he also had other policy matters to consider in determining how to respond to an injunction.

First was the Albany experience. SCLC aide Andrew Young recalled in an interview that King felt the injunction had "broken our backs" in Albany:

> It was a federal injunction, and Dr. King felt that the federal courts were our only real ally nationally. They had challenged segregated law schools, dining cars, etc., then the 1954 school decision, and had helped in Montgomery. Breaking a federal court injunction in Albany was a slap in the face of the federal courts that he couldn't bring himself to make. But after the Al-

bany campaign collapsed, Dr. King lamented the fact that he had abided by the injunction, and he entered the planning for Birmingham ready to defy even a federal court rather than see the Albany collapse repeated. And if he had allowed himself to be halted in his tracks in Birmingham, it would have become the technique used against the movement everywhere throughout the South.

By January 1963, Young said, "we had reached the decision that we couldn't let the courts be used to destroy our basic rights of expression and protest."

One hopeful feature of the situation, King realized, was that any injunction against demonstrations in Birmingham was likely to come from a state rather than a federal court. Defying an order of the Birmingham judiciary when, as Young recalls, "everyone knew that Birmingham justice was thoroughly racist," would give the movement a good cause with which to mobilize national support, and from which to appeal to the U.S. Supreme Court.

King's second political problem involved his relations with the Justice Department. A kind of uneasy, unspoken partnership had grown up between King and the key aides of Attorney General Robert Kennedy in charge of enforcing federal civil rights, primarily (at this point) Nicholas Katzenbach and Burke Marshall. The Justice Department's own focus in 1963 was on the enforcement of school desegregation orders against Southern officials and assistance for the registration of Negro voters in the South. The Justice Department officials reasoned that adding millions of Negro voters to the rolls would be the best way to win other legal rights for Negroes, through changes in the structure of local and state politics. At the same time, they recognized that federal jurisdiction to attack other local and state segregation policies or to deal with discrimination by private property owners was quite limited under existing federal statutes and judicial decisions and that there was little chance of enacting broader legislation in the near future. And, while Robert Kennedy and his aides were sympathetic with the equality aims of the movement, they were also concerned about the potential of mass-action campaigns for erupting into violence, and they had a strong commitment to the principle of respect for court orders.

"Fortunately," Nicholas Katzenbach recalls, "that position placed us in accord with Dr. King in many situations in the early 1960s. Since the Supreme Court had ordered an end to state-enforced segregation and it was Southern officials who were defying court orders, we could give support to the civil rights groups by taking legal actions to enforce the law of the land." It was this position that had been the basis for Justice Department action in numerous school desegregation situations, including the showdown over the admission of James Meredith to the University of Mississippi in the fall of 1962. It had also been the basis for the use of federal marshals in Montgomery in 1961 to protect King and the Freedom Riders.

For Justice Department civil rights strategists, the injunction was thus a weapon that could be of great value in breaking down segregation. Given this attitude of the Justice Department, King had to weigh whether disobedience of a state court injunction would create serious difficulties for the movement with the Kennedy Administration.

The final imponderable in the Birmingham injunction problem arose from within King himself. King was prepared to go to jail, and the planning for Birmingham was based on the likelihood of mass arrests, convictions, and efforts to make it difficult to obtain bail. But as Bayard Rustin recently noted, "There was a deep ambivalence in Martin. No matter how clearly we all would analyze what Southern officials did and would do, his Christian nonviolence wouldn't permit him to conclude that they would necessarily follow such a course. He always had to consider their possible redemption, and allow for that in the planning.'' This was directly involved in the concern over a court injunction in Birmingham, Rustin said.

> He agreed in the planning sessions that the courts would be used against us, as they always had been in the South. But he would say, ''Not every judge will issue an injunction; we can't assume that.'' And Fred Shuttlesworth answered him, ''Where are those converted judges? Where did niggers ever move and law was not used to beat our heads, with the judges helping?'' ''Well,'' King would repeat, ''we can't take that for granted.'' He really believed that sacrifice and cheerful acceptance of the consequences might lead some judges to be moral. It was often very confusing—and frustrating—to his followers, but that was Martin's faith, and he was always the leader.

Given this position by King, the movement came to Birmingham determined not to let a court injunction cripple its campaign for justice. But the tactical problems of precisely how to respond to an injunction were never resolved in advance.

5

Birmingham Gets an Injunction

THE RUN-OFF ELECTION for the Birmingham mayoralty was held on April 2, 1963, with Albert Boutwell defeating Bull Connor by 29,630 to 21,648 votes. The Boutwell
victory was the product of a tacit coalition of blacks and
those who were then called white "moderates." Although
Connor carried the blue-collar districts by substantial
margins, the coalition's strength was too great to overcome.

The next day the Birmingham *News* ran a front-page drawing showing a golden sun rising over the city. The caption
was "New Day Dawns for Birmingham," and under it was
Boutwell's first statement as mayor-elect. It closed with a
passage which suggested that the new administration would
be interested in serious discussions with black citizens about
their grievances:

> "I want to reiterate that I will meet with our citizens in all
> sections of our city—help them solve their problems—without
> their having to come to City Hall, although the doors there will
> be open to them.
> "Indeed, we are on our way to better things.
> "Yes, there's a new day for Birmingham."

A new day did indeed dawn for Birmingham on April 3,
1963, but it was far from what the white "moderates" sup-

porting Boutwell had hoped it would be. On that day, despite pleas from Justice Department officials to hold off the demonstrations and give Birmingham's new administration a chance, the SCLC's long-planned Project C got underway with sit-ins at lunch counters in five of Birmingham's downtown department stores. The protest leaders issued a "Birmingham Manifesto" announcing that demonstrations would continue until three demands were met: desegregation of facilities such as lunch counter and fitting rooms in downtown department stores; commitment to a policy of hiring and upgrading of Negroes on a nondiscriminatory basis by Birmingham businesses; and establishment of a biracial committee to work out a timetable for desegregation in other areas of the city's life. At four of the stores where demonstrators appeared, the management closed the lunch counters but did not call the police; at the fifth, Britt's, the police were called and twenty demonstrators were arrested.

Mayor-elect Boutwell issued a statement warning of outside agitators:

> Of one thing we are certain, the people of Birmingham, in vast majority, have a deep and abiding respect for law and order and for their fellow man.
>
> Believing in the orderly processes of government, I urge our local Negro citizens to think long and hard before following the questionable leadership of strangers, people whose sole purpose is to stir strife and discord here, and who will then leave our citizens to pay the penalty of this discord, once they have worked their mischief and have put upon us, whites and Negroes, an atmosphere of tension and violence. . . .
>
> I urge everyone, white and Negro, calmly to ignore what is happening in Birmingham.

Boutwell's problems were not confined to those presented by the black demonstrators. On the day the demonstrations began, the three city commissioners—Connor, Art Hanes, and J. T. Waggoner—announced that they would take legal action to prevent the new mayor-council government from taking office on April 15, the scheduled date. Hanes told a press conference that he and his fellow commissioners were elected in 1961 for four-year terms, had arranged their personal affairs so as to be able to serve the city during that period, and did not intend to relinquish their offices after only a year. An apparent conflict in statutes lent some legal support to the commissioners' position. Thus, from the time the demonstrations began, it was never altogether clear who would be speaking for City Hall after April 15. Although the Boutwell administration generally was expected to prevail in a court test of its right to take office, the outcome was not certain. Boutwell himself seemed acutely conscious of the possibility that an overly accommodating stance toward Negroes in Birmingham might jeopardize the new administration's position in the Alabama courts.

King's planning called for an attempt to secure a parade permit, however predestined to failure any such application might be, since it required the approval of the City Commission dominated by Bull Connor. As a *Newsweek* story of the Birmingham events put it:

> Eugene (Bull) Connor is an unprepossessing figure—a fleshy man of 63 with jug ears, nagging sinuses, a glass eye, and a bellowing style that dates back to an early job reading the baseball ticker aloud in a poolroom. But Connor is as much a giant in Birmingham as the cast-iron statue of Vulcan, god of the forge, atop Red Mountain, just outside town. Both are monuments—Vulcan to the city's steel economy and Connor to her standing as the biggest, toughest citadel of segregation left in the Deep South.

On the first day of the campaign, April 3, Rev. Fred Shuttlesworth sent Mrs. Lola Hendricks, a veteran member of the

Alabama Christian Movement for Human Rights, and Rev. Ambrose Hill, of the Lily Grove Baptist Church, to City Hall to apply for a parade permit. It wasn't long before they returned to ACMHR headquarters to report what had happened when they asked Public Safety Commissioner Bull Connor about getting a permit for picketing or parading. "No," Connor had said, "you will not get a permit in Birmingham, Alabama, to picket. I will picket you over to the City Jail."

Two days later Shuttlesworth himself sent a telegram to Connor requesting, on behalf of the ACMHR, a permit to picket "against the injustices of segregation and discrimination." Connor replied promptly by wire: "Under the provisions of the City Code of the City of Birmingham, a permit to picket as requested by you cannot be granted by me individually but is the responsibility of the entire Commission. I insist that you and your people do not start any picketing on the streets in Birmingham, Alabama."

The movement's leaders did not make any further attempts to obtain permits. The demonstrations continued nevertheless, with sit-ins at department-store lunch counters and picketing in front of the stores.

At the start the demonstrations involved only a small number of people, and they received little press coverage. The Birmingham *News* deliberately kept the events to their back pages, but a number of the out-of-state newspapers and national newsmagazines that were covering the demonstrations also failed to treat the marches as a major news event. The big story locally during the first week of the campaign was a speech critical of King given by Rev. Albert S. Foley, a white priest who had been active in community relations work in Alabama and was then chairman of the Alabama Advisory Committee of the U.S. Commission on Civil Rights. According to Father Foley, King's efforts had "broken up peaceful progress in race relations in Birmingham" by undermining behind-the-scenes negotiations between the

downtown business leaders and "responsible Negro citizens." These negotiations, he said, had been about to produce voluntary desegregation of downtown facilities.

During the early days of the campaign, the movement's
greatest need was for more participants. Only sixty-five people had turned out for the first "mass meeting," and many
times that number would be necessary to mount a successful
direct-action campaign. As Father Foley had said in his talk,
Birmingham's black leadership was far from being in full
agreement on the desirability of the demonstrations, despite
the unity efforts which had been made by King, Shuttlesworth, and the other SCLC leaders during February and
March. Accordingly, King spent most of his time during the
first week of the campaign meeting with groups of businessmen, professional men, and ministers, trying to convert them
to the cause or at least quiet their outright opposition. At
night he and his aides conducted meetings in the city's black
churches to build community support of the campaign and to
recruit new volunteers.

Over the weekend of April 6–7 the first protest marches
were held. One of these, on Saturday the 6th, was led by
Shuttlesworth to protest the city's refusal to issue a permit for
picketing of merchants who would not integrate their facilities. It was over this weekend that the first violence of the
campaign occurred. A police dog being used to "control"
the streets attacked a Negro bystander; whether the Negro
had first lunged at the dog with a knife was a matter of
dispute.

By this time it was clear that the movement was gaining
support—forty-two were arrested in the Saturday march and
twenty-six in the Sunday march, and large crowds of sympathetic black onlookers gathered to watch the demonstrations.
On the following Monday, Tuesday, and Wednesday the
demonstrations continued at the downtown stores on a some-

what larger scale. By the end of the first week more than 130 persons had been jailed, most of them on charges of parading without a permit or (in the case of persons sitting-in at lunch counters) trespass after warning. Most of those arrested had been released on three hundred dollars bail, provided from SCLC funds. At this stage the movement's strategy did not call for literally filling the city's jails; active supporters were needed back on the streets to help mobilize support within the black community.

So far, in arresting the demonstrators the Birmingham police had not used brutal methods. The strategy of the city authorities was to minimize the impact of the demonstrations and try to avoid attracting attention to the protest campaign. In the state capital, the Alabama legislature passed a resolution commending the city of Birmingham on the way it was handling the demonstrations and admonishing it to hold the line against further integration attempts. At the same time, a committee of the legislature approved a bill raising the maximum bond that a Birmingham city judge could set for persons appealing misdemeanor convictions to higher courts from $300 to $2,500.

The projected raising of the cost of bail bonds, a move that obviously could put the demonstration leaders in a severe financial bind if they wanted to continue to keep their supporters on the streets, reflected a general heightening of racial tension toward the end of the first week of the protests. Support for the demonstrations was increasing in Birmingham's black community as King and his aides began to reach both the leaders and the people. "The pace of the campaign increased today," *The New York Times* reported on April 10, "with the picketing of several downtown stores, a decoy march that lured police reserves to another area and a sit-in at the city library, on the edge of the business district."

The city authorities then moved to head off what they anticipated would be large-scale demonstrations on Good Friday and Easter Sunday, April 12 and 14. On the evening of

Wednesday, April 10, two attorneys for the city, John M. ("Matt") Breckenridge and Earl McBee, presented state circuit court judge William A. Jenkins, Jr., with an application for a temporary injunction directing the leaders of the demonstrations to cease their activities. The city's bill of complaint alleged that the respondents—Wyatt Tee Walker, Martin Luther King, Jr., Ralph Abernathy, Fred Shuttlesworth, A. D. King, some 133 other named individuals, and "Richard Roe and John Doe"—had during the April 3–10 period:

> Sponsored and/or participated in and/or conspired to commit and/or to encourage and/or to participate in certain movements, plans or projects commonly called "sit-in" demonstrations, "kneel-in" demonstrations, mass street parades, trespasses on private property after being warned to leave the premises by owners of said property, congregating in mobs upon the public streets and other public places, unlawfully picketing private places of business in the City of Birmingham, Alabama; violation of numerous ordinances and statutes of the City of Birmingham and the State of Alabama.

The bill went on to allege that the acts and conduct were "calculated to provoke breaches of peace in the city" and had in fact already done so; that the acts and conduct placed an undue burden on the Birmingham police force and were likely to cause injuries or loss of life to police officers; that the city's remedy at law was inadequate; and that an injunction was necessary "to prevent irreparable injury to persons and property in the city of Birmingham, Jefferson County."

Attached to the bill of complaint were affidavits of two captains in the Birmingham police department, setting forth their versions of events they had witnessed during the preceding week. The affidavit of Captain G. V. Evans stated:

> On Sunday afternoon, April 7, 1963, I was in the vicinity of St. Paul's Church, a Negro church at 6th Avenue and 15th Street, North, practically all afternoon. I observed a crowd of Negroes that grew larger and larger during the course of the

afternoon. These Negroes were not in the church but were in the vicinity thereof. About 5:30 in the afternoon a group of Negroes numbering approximately twenty came out of the church and began to march in a column Eastward on 6th Avenue. In the meantime the tremendous mob of Negroes numbering approximately 700 to 1000 began to move Eastward also. This mob of people began to yell and shout. In the 1700 Block of 6th Avenue North the column of marchers was stopped and placed under arrest for engaging in a parade or procession without having procured a permit as required by City Ordinance. In all other instances in which gatherings had occurred on previous days, the crowd had melted and dispersed. In this instance, however, the mob continued to stand upon and to block the public streets and to impede traffic thereupon. I had some other members of the Police Department working with me and we undertook to clear the streets, but were unable to do so. The mob continued to shout and to refuse to move. We had placed the Canine Corps on call. When we found that we could not control the mob without their assistance, we called them to the scene. The mob still refused to move until the police dogs came upon the scene. At that time some of them did move but others refused to move. One Negro attacked one of the dogs and was in turn thrown to the ground by the dog. In the mob of Negroes we heard voices indicating that the Police Department was at fault in the instance concerning the dog and obviously were attempting to work the Negroes up to the point that they would riot. We were compelled to place some of the Negroes under arrest for failing to obey the lawful order or command of a police officer in that they refused to move and to clear the sidewalk which was blocked by them, and eventually the mob did disperse. . . .

Captain Evans presented a similar account of the parading without permit on April 10, and then told the court:

Basing my opinion upon my experience for a period of twenty-five years in police work, if the activities and conduct of respondents in this case are not enjoined there is serious likelihood of bloodshed and violence resulting in possible death or serious injury to police officers of the City of Birmingham, members of the groups engaged in such conduct and other citizens and members of the public.

Such an application for an *ex parte* injunction does not require notification of or appearance by the parties against whom the injunction is sought. After examining the bill of complaint and the supporting affidavits and questioning the city attorneys about them, Judge Jenkins signed the injunction order about 9 P.M. It directed the named individuals and all other persons acting in concert with them to refrain from

engaging in, sponsoring, inciting or encouraging mass street parades or mass processions or like demonstrations without a permit, trespass on private property after being warned to leave the premises by the owner or person in possession of said private property, congregating on the street or public places into mobs, and unlawfully picketing business establishments or public buildings in the City of Birmingham, Jefferson County, State of Alabama or performing acts calculated to cause breaches of the peace in the City of Birmingham, Jefferson County, in the State of Alabama or from conspiring to engage in unlawful street parades, unlawful processions, unlawful demonstrations, unlawful boycotts, unlawful trespasses, and unlawful picketing or other like unlawful conduct or from violating the ordinances of the City of Birmingham and the Statutes of the State of Alabama or from doing any acts designed to consummate conspiracies to engage in said unlawful acts of parading, demonstrating, boycotting, trespassing and picketing or other unlawful acts, or from engaging in acts and conduct customarily known as "kneel-ins" in churches in violation of the wishes and desires of said churches.

After Judge Jenkins had signed the order, a "writ of injunction" had to be made up and copies prepared for serving on all one hundred and thirty-three people named in the bill of complaint. The writ incorporated the language of the order signed by Judge Jenkins, and directed the sheriff to serve it on the respondents. The paper work was finally finished about midnight. Shortly before 1 A.M. on April 11, Deputy Sheriff Raymond E. Belcher drove into Birmingham's Negro section to serve it on the Reverends King, Abernathy, Walker, and Shuttlesworth.

6

King Goes to Jail

ON WEDNESDAY EVENING, April 10, King and his associates were gathered in Room 30 of the Gaston Motel for a general strategy session. The Gaston Motel, owned by A. G. Gaston, the wealthiest local Negro property holder and a "moderate" SCLC supporter, was the best motel in the Negro section of Birmingham—a two-story brick building on Fifth Avenue North, between 15th and 16th Streets, near Kelly Ingraham Park. It was built in an L shape, with a large paved courtyard where King had been holding his press and TV conferences for the past week. The motel had a restaurant on the first floor, where middle-class blacks often went for Sunday dinner.

Room 30, on the second floor, was the only suite in the motel. It consisted of a large bedroom, used for staff meetings, a smaller bedroom, where King and his aide Bernard Lee slept, and a bathroom. Late in the day on Wednesday, word had reached King that the city attorneys would be going before Judge Jenkins seeking an injunction against all further demonstrations. There was little doubt that it would be granted.

To comply with the injunction, King and his colleagues readily agreed, would cripple the movement. King noted what had happened in Talladega, Alabama, where a broad injunction issued by a local court in April 1962 had spelled the end of a protest campaign mounted by students from Talladega College. Some of the Talladega students were in Birmingham, and the example of their defeat—reinforced by King's own experiences in Albany, Georgia—was fresh in the minds of the group meeting in Room 30.

The leaders decided that the circumstances surrounding this particular injunction were about as favorable as the movement could expect to get. The injunction had been sought by Bull Connor, a national symbol of diehard segregation. It was based on an ordinance vesting in the City Commission virtually unlimited power to issue parade permits, and two requests for a permit had already been denied by Connor. King's legal advisers had briefed him months earlier that this ordinance, and the way it was administered, was probably unconstitutional under U.S. Supreme Court decisions protecting First Amendment rights. And it was a state court, in an *ex parte* hearing, that was issuing the injunction, not a federal court, whose order would have created much more difficult problems of law and politics.

King described the way he saw the situation in his book on the Birmingham campaign:

> [W]e had decided that if an injunction was issued to thwart our demonstrators, it would be our duty to violate it. To some, this will sound contradictory and morally indefensible. We, who contend for justice, and who oppose those who will not honor the law of the Supreme Court and the rulings of federal agencies, were saying that we would overtly violate a court order. Yet we felt that there were persuasive reasons for our position.
>
> When the Supreme Court decision on school desegregation was handed down, leading segregationists vowed to thwart it by invoking "a century of litigation." There was more significance to this threat than many Americans imagined. The injunction method has now become the leading instrument of the

South to block the direct-action civil-rights drive and to prevent Negro citizens and their white allies from engaging in peaceable assembly, a right guaranteed by the First Amendment. You initiate a non-violent demonstration. The power structure secures an injunction against you. It can conceivably take two or three years before any disposition of the case is made. The Alabama courts are notorious for "sitting on" cases of this nature. This has been a maliciously effective, pseudo-legal way of breaking the back of legitimate moral protest.

One of the principal concerns of the leaders on this Wednesday evening was how the city attorneys and the court would make use of the contempt weapon. If they sought criminal contempt sentences, those defying the injunction would face jail for a maximum of five days and fines of up to fifty dollars for each offense. But if the lawyers pressed civil contempt charges as well, those marching in violation of the injunction could be locked away until they purged themselves of contempt, by apologizing for the violation and promising not to defy the injunction in the future. Wyatt Walker recalled later in an interview that King felt the city would not press civil contempt charges. "He thought the city would not risk putting the leaders in jail indefinitely. It would be sure to create sympathy for the movement and stir up the local Negro community behind us."

Even with that assumption, one problem remained: Should King personally march in defiance of the impending injunction or let others do the defying, at least at this stage in the campaign? So far, King had not led any of the sit-in or picketing demonstrations and had not been arrested; his role had been to meet with local Negro leaders to get their support, to coordinate overall strategy, and to speak at the evening church rallies. At some point, King was sure, he would lead a demonstration and go to jail himself, to show that he was a leader *with* his people, not over them.

The problem with King leading the Good Friday march was that the campaign's bail funds were rapidly running out, and there were rumors that the city was about to do several things that might worsen the situation dramatically, such as requiring larger real-property bonds or money deposits before releasing arrested demonstrators. While replacements had been arranged for all the other leaders in case they were jailed, King was irreplaceable if it should suddenly become necessary to raise large sums of bail money; his personal contacts with Northern supporters and his presence at fund-raising rallies around the country would be essential. So, on this matter, the Wednesday night meeting ended without a firm decision; whether King would personally defy the injunction would have to be decided as events unfolded.

Wyatt Walker recalls that there was no real disagreement on the question of putting off the march. "One option we eliminated was going to court to try to get the injunction dissolved. We knew this would tie us up in court at least ten days to two weeks, and even then we might not get it dissolved. We would have a lengthy lawsuit to appeal but no Birmingham campaign. All of our planning and organizing, a year's effort, would have been in vain, and that was exactly what the city was trying to accomplish by going to court."

Having made the decision to ignore the impending injunction, King instructed Walker to call the press and television people and have them on hand when the sheriff's deputy arrived. When Deputy Sheriff Belcher pulled up to the Gaston Motel at 1:15 A.M. and asked for King, he was directed to the restaurant, where he found King, Abernathy, and Shuttlesworth sitting at a table in their open-necked shirts, sipping coffee, with a full contingent of the press ready to record the event. The injunction papers were served, and pictures were taken of the three ministers reading the text of the order. Then, portions of it were read aloud for the TV cameras and the newspaper reporters. Fred Shuttlesworth commented that the injunction was "a flagrant denial of our constitutional rights," but that "in no way will it retard the thrust of this movement." Ralph Abernathy stated that neither "an injunction nor anything else will stop the Negro from obtaining citizenship in his march for freedom." King, not yet ready to make a public pronouncement in defiance of the order, said simply that "we'll have to show this to our lawyers, of course," and added that "regardless of what's in this injunction, we've got an injunction from heaven."

After the press conference broke up, at 1:30 A.M., King told Wyatt Walker to prepare a formal statement in reply to the injunction and to set up a press conference for noon on Thursday. With this, King went to bed.

Thursday morning at nine o'clock, Fred Shuttlesworth met with Norman Amaker, an attorney with the NAACP Legal Defense Fund. The previous afternoon, seeing that the problem of legal representation was becoming increasingly more important, Shuttlesworth had called Constance Motley, the assistant director of the Inc. Fund, asking that someone be sent from New York to Birmingham to coordinate the local legal efforts on behalf of the arrested demonstrators and to act as counsel for the campaign itself. Mrs. Motley had sent Amaker. Born and raised in New York City, a graduate of Amherst College and Columbia Law School, Amaker was one of the young Negro lawyers with the Inc. Fund who had been working with various movement groups in the South since the beginning of the 1960s.

Shuttlesworth showed the attorney a copy of the injunction, filled him in on the events of the preceding week, and told him about the press conference scheduled for noon. He did not consult Amaker about the press release (which had already been mimeographed), and he left the lawyer to study the legal documents while he helped with final arrangements for the noon meeting with reporters.

Shortly after twelve o'clock more than a hundred Negro

supporters crowded into the courtyard of the Gaston Motel and on to the balconies overlooking it. King, Abernathy, and Shuttlesworth were seated at a small round table set up in the middle of the courtyard, facing a battery of TV cameras, microphones jamming the table, and about twenty reporters with pencils poised in front of them. Two days earlier, seated at the same table to inform the press of the progress of the campaign, King, Abernathy, and Shuttlesworth had been dressed in conservative business suits and ties. Now, as the Birmingham campaign was moving into its critical phases, they wore faded blue denim overalls and open-necked white or blue shirts. Wyatt Walker noticed a lieutenant from the Brimingham police force, Maurice House, holding an open notepad, ready to take down what was said at the meeting.

King began by reading the text of the press release, issued in the name of the Alabama Christian Movement for Human Rights, which detailed the movement's reaction to the injunction. The statement opened by noting that American Negroes "have anchored our faith and hope in the rightness of the Constitution and the moral laws of the universe." The federal judiciary had vindicated those hopes by ruling "again and again" that First and Fourteenth Amendment privileges cannot be trampled upon "by the machinery of state government and police power." In the past, King said, "we have abided by Federal injunctions out of respect for the forthright and consistent leadership that the Federal judiciary has given in establishing the principle of integration as the law of the land." Now, however, "we are confronted with recalcitrant forces in the Deep South that will use the courts to perpetuate the unjust and illegal system of racial separation."

> Alabama has made clear its determination to defy the law of the land. Most of its public officials, its legislative body and many of its law enforcement agents have openly defied the desegregation decision of the Supreme Court. We would feel

morally and legally responsible to obey the injunction if the courts of Alabama applied equal justice to all of its citizens.

By contrast, King said, Southern law enforcement agencies have shown that they "will utilize the force of law to misuse the judicial process. This is raw tyranny under the guise of maintaining law and order.

> We cannot in all good conscience obey such an injunction which is an unjust, undemocratic and unconstitutional misuse of the legal process.
>
> We do this not out of any disrespect for the law but out of the highest respect for *the* law. This is not an attempt to evade or defy the law or engage in chaotic anarchy. Just as in all good conscience we cannot obey unjust laws, neither can we respect the unjust use of the courts.
>
> We believe in a system of law based on justice and morality. Out of our great love for the Constitution of the U.S. and our desire to purify the judicial system of the state of Alabama, we risk this critical move with an awareness of the possible consequences involved.

When King finished reading the statement, the Negro spectators cheered and applauded. After the tumult died down, King began to answer questions from the press. One newsman asked whether the statement meant that the demonstrations would continue. "Yes," King said, "the direct action will continue today, tomorrow, Saturday, Sunday, and on through." He also spoke of "kneel-ins" on Easter Sunday but refused to elaborate further on that effort. When asked specifically whether he and others named in the injunction would lead a march on Good Friday, King said yes, and added: "I am prepared to go to jail and stay as long as necessary." Fred Shuttlesworth read from a statement of his own, reaffirming what King had said, and commented that he too was fully aware of the injunction but that the movement would continue. Other questions were answered by Shuttlesworth and Abernathy, and the press conference closed after about thirty minutes.

After the press conference King, the other ministers, and Norman Amaker had lunch at the Gaston Motel. The injunction was discussed, and plans were made to hold a series of evening rallies at the local churches and at Kelly Ingraham Park in preparation for the Good Friday march. At three o'clock that afternoon half a dozen pickets appeared at Pizitz' department store. They were arrested and charged with parading without a permit and loitering. No charge of violating the injunction was lodged, since they had not been specifically named in that document.

During the afternoon Amaker met with the local attorneys, Orzell Billingsley and Arthur Shores, "trying to get a fix on the situation." He spoke by telephone with Jack Greenberg, the Inc. Fund's director in New York, and discussed strategies for dealing with the injunction. Greenberg felt that the Supreme Court's ruling in *NAACP v. Alabama* required them to try challenging the injunction in state court, rather than attempting to attack it in the federal courts. In any event, they anticipated losing at the initial stage, whether in state or federal court. Amaker recalls that there was never any serious discussion of counseling the leaders to go into court to seek relief prior to the Good Friday march. Going into court would have required forgoing the weekend marches, and that was unacceptable politically. "I knew that the movement had set its plans," Amaker recalls, "and I would never try to persuade the leaders to alter them. My job was to explain the law." He added: "I had been with Ralph Abernathy and Fred Shuttlesworth during the Freedom Rides. I knew how a lot of them viewed lawyers—as people who were very conservative, who generally tried to hold them back, who would say that they couldn't do something."

Early Thursday evening, meetings were held in several of

the churches. At the Zion Hill (Sixteenth Street) Baptist Church, King told a crowded audience that "injunction or no injunction, we're going to march. Here in Birmingham, we have reached the point of no return. Now they will know that an injunction can't stop us." Two outdoor rallies were also held in the Negro section.

But bad news also arrived Thursday evening, from two fronts. "Late Thursday night," King related in his book on Birmingham, "the bondsman who had been furnishing bail for the demonstrators notified us that he would be unable to continue. The city had notified him that his financial assets were insufficient. Obviously, this was another move on the part of the city to hurt our cause." Calls were placed to New York, but the word was not long in coming back, from Harry Belafonte and New York lawyer Clarence Jones, that no additional bail money could be provided immediately; the campaign coffers were bare.

It was on this issue that King, his associates, and the lawyers (twenty-five people in all) met in Room 30 at 8:30 Friday morning—Good Friday—the 12th of April.

Norman Amaker presented a briefing on the legal situation with regard to the injunction. "I tried to make clear to them what the situation was: if they did march, they would probably be in violation of the injunction. The injunction was probably unconstitutional, and would be attacked in the courts by the lawyers. Even though it might be unconstitutional, though, the leaders might be convicted for violating it, and they could get either criminal or civil contempt sentences. I said that whatever they decided to do—and that was their decision—we would try to find the best possible way of supporting their actions in the courts." Amaker reflected later that he and the local lawyers might have decided to file some kind of action in state or federal court that day if there had been enough time to prepare it, and if the movement leaders had approved, but everything was happening so quickly that they simply didn't consider that a practical possibility.

King responded to the briefing by remarking that he surely didn't want to spend the rest of his life in jail but that he would not repudiate what he had announced and call off the march. The real question was whether, in light of the bail-money crisis, he could personally lead fifty marchers in direct defiance of the injunction, as he had planned. King later recalled that "a sense of doom" and "hopelessness" hung over the gathering. Several of the leaders told King that he couldn't risk going to jail. If he did, his unique contacts and fund-raising talents would be lost, and with them, "the battle of Birmingham." Yet King was also aware that he had been urging hundreds of demonstrators to go to jail but had not seen the inside of a Birmingham cell himself. If he were to back down now from his pledge to submit to arrest, there could be an irretrievable loss of faith in him as a leader, especially among the dedicated young college students and SNCC workers who had been the jail victims time after time. Some of them already were bitterly saying that King would never break the law, even to save the movement.

King went into the small bedroom to think over his decision privately and to offer prayer. As he described the moment later, he thought of the twenty-four people in the next room, the three hundred demonstrators then in jail, the 100,000 Negroes in Birmingham whose future was in the balance. Beyond them, he thought of the twenty million black Americans "who dreamed that some day they might be able to cross the Red Sea of injustice and find their way to the promised land of integration and freedom.

"There was no more room for doubt. I pulled off my shirt and pants, got into work clothes and went back to the other room to tell them I had decided to go to jail." After stating his decision, King asked Ralph Abernathy to go with him, then "we all linked hands, and twenty-five voices in Room 30 of the Gaston Motel in Birmingham, Alabama, chanted the battle hymn of our movement: 'We Shall Overcome.' "

The participants in the meeting then left for the Sixteenth Street Baptist Church, from which the march was scheduled to leave at noon. It was already past noon when they arrived, and a large crowd had gathered outside the church. The police had been notified of the planned march and were there in force. King and his party went inside the church and sat down to go over their plans for the next few hours and days. King, Abernathy, and Shuttlesworth all expected to be in jail by mid-afternoon, and it would be up to their chief lieutenants to keep the campaign going. There were a good many details to be reviewed, and by the time they finished ironing them out it was after two o'clock. Outside the church the crowd had swelled to almost a thousand people.

The Sixteenth Street Baptist Church is a large, three-and-a-half-story brick building at the intersection of Sixteenth Street and Sixth Avenue. Two domed towers frame the central entrance, from which a wide set of stairs lead down toward a huge, forty-foot elm tree on the sidewalk. Martin Luther King, Jr., Ralph Abernathy, and Fred Shuttlesworth led their group of fifty volunteers down the steps shortly after 2:30 P.M. on Good Friday afternoon. Onlookers lined the streets outside the church, somewhere between five hundred and a thousand persons, and many of them fell into step behind the two-abreast marchers' file as it headed up Sixth Avenue. It was a warm, sunny spring day, the azaleas budding and yellow forsythia already in full bloom. Birmingham's police were also in full bloom, with a large part of the city's force stationed on foot, in patrol cars, in mobile communication centers, and on rooftops along the streets leading away from the church. Barricades had been set up to keep whites away and cordon off the march area.

The New York Times' correspondent, Foster Hailey, described what happened next:

> Instead of proceeding up Sixth Avenue toward City Hall, as the police had expected, the marchers turned south at the corner and marched on toward Fifth Avenue and the downtown business section.
>
> At Fifth Avenue they turned east again. The police, meanwhile, had re-deployed their forces and were waiting halfway down the block. As the head of the march passed behind some trucks at the entrance to a garage, Commissioner Connor told his forces "stop them there."
>
> Two motorcycle patrolmen and two detectives grabbed Dr. King and Dr. Abernathy and hustled them into a police van a few steps away. The order of the marchers, which had started out two abreast, had been disrupted as eager onlookers joined in behind them and on either side. Thus police had difficulty trying to sort the marchers from spectators. . . .
>
> There were shouts of anger from the several hundred Negroes who were in sight of the downtown arrests and who had been singing and clapping hands as they walked or ran alongside the marchers.
>
> When police moved toward them and ordered them back west down Fifth Avenue most of them gave way freely. Three who stopped to argue with policemen were arrested. . . .

In all, fifty-two demonstrators were arrested. Most were put into the regular cells, but King was given special treatment; he was lodged in solitary. He asked to make a phone call to his wife, who had just had their third child, but the request was refused. Norman Amaker showed up at the jail later in the afternoon, explaining that he was an attorney for King and asking to be permitted to consult with his client. The city hoped that King would be bailed out, but Amaker said that he was there only for consultations. The head jailer said Amaker could see King in a special room with guards present, an offer which Amaker refused, knowing that the

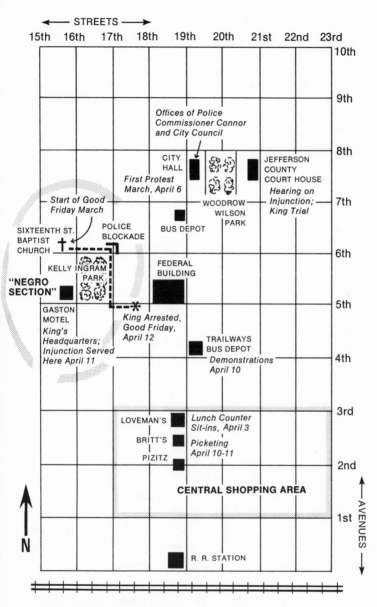

DOWNTOWN BIRMINGHAM, APRIL 1963

conversation should be confidential. Amaker spent most of the evening at the jail, and finally went back to Wyatt Walker about eleven o'clock and reported on King's situation in solitary and the refusal to allow a private meeting with counsel.

During the early morning hours of Saturday the 13th, Wyatt Walker called Burke Marshall, the chief of the Justice Department's Civil Rights Division, to inform him that King was being held incommunicado and to ask for federal help. Later on Saturday morning Mrs. King tried to reach President John Kennedy in Palm Beach, Florida. Before long, she was telephoned by Attorney General Robert Kennedy, who listened to her concern over the conditions of King's jailing and promised to see what he could do.

Meanwhile, Arthur Shores, Orzell Billingsley, and Norman Amaker went to see Bull Connor at his office in City Hall. They asked whether Connor wanted to be in the position of denying Dr. King the right to counsel. "I'm not denying that," Connor replied. "But if we can't see him alone," they answered, "there's no confidentiality with counsel." Connor finally agreed to let one lawyer see King alone for one or two short visits a day. Amaker went to the jail at once. The jailer, informed by telephone of Connor's decision, turned to a guard and said, "Bring that nigger King down here. Then open the door and let this nigger in." Amaker spoke with King, assured himself that he was well, and returned to report this to the leaders at the Gaston Motel.

As one journalist observed shrewdly, King's danger at that moment was not so much personal as political. Burke Marshall was disturbed that King was forcing the White House's hand, after having rejected advice from Robert Kennedy to postpone the Birmingham protest until after the Boutwell slate took office officially. Marshall called in reporters to announce that, while President Kennedy was personally concerned over events in Birmingham and had asked to be kept informed about Dr. King's jailing, "the Federal Government has no authority to take legal action to intervene in Birmingham as the situation now stands." He explained that the dispute so far "centered on a question of private rights" involving claims of free speech and assembly. There had been no "state action" that gave federal officials warrant to act. The *Times* story quoted Justice Department aides as saying that "Dr. King's refusal to abide by the injunction against demonstrations . . . had further complicated the Federal Government's position. . . . We believe in the right to free speech, but we also believe in the necessity of obeying court orders." It also mentioned that the Justice Department was pressing a case currently in the U.S. Supreme Court involving the refusal of Governor Ross Barnett of Mississippi to obey a federal appeals court ruling that he considered unconstitutional.

The *Times* account showed the Justice Department as concerned for King's safety but critical of his impetuosity. The same view was echoed in that week's *Time* magazine, which headed its story on King's arrest "Poorly Timed Protest." The *Newsweek* account was even stronger, portraying King and Bull Connor as equally doctrinaire protagonists, pressing for a confrontation.

In Birmingham the protest demonstrations continued over the weekend. On Easter Sunday morning groups of Negroes sought to gain admission to several white churches; they were turned away at all but two. On Sunday afternoon another march was held, at which thirty more protestors were arrested. The march attracted over a thousand black onlookers. Many of them surged into the streets following the procession, which was being led along the sidewalks by Rev. A. D. King and Rev. Wyatt Tee Walker. When the arrests were made, two or three people in the crowd started throwing rocks at the police; one of the rocks broke the windshield on a police motor scooter and another hit Birmingham *Post-Herald* photographer James Ware in the head. Three arrests were made immediately by the police. It was a brief episode, and the police had no further difficulty on the scene.

7

The Trial

THE JEFFERSON COUNTY COURTHOUSE, an impos-
ing nine-story building located across a small park from the
Birmingham City Hall, features a quotation from Thomas
Jefferson above its entrance: "Equal and exact justice to all
men, of whatever state or persuasion." The irony of that declaration was not lost upon the black people of Birmingham.
For years Birmingham's real concept of equal justice had
been symbolized by the signs saying "White" and "Colored" that set off separate drinking fountains and rest rooms
for the two races inside the court building. The courtrooms,
of course, were presided over by white judges, with white
clerks handling the administrative matters.

After King and the other protest leaders were arrested, the
movement's lawyers settled down to prepare for the legal
battles that would take place in this court building. The team
included two Birmingham attorneys who had been involved
since Project C was in its initial planning stages, Arthur
Shores and Orzell Billingsley, as well as several lawyers
from the NAACP Legal Defense Fund's New York office.
Norman Amaker was the only Inc. Fund lawyer who had actually witnessed the Good Friday march. He would be joined
the following week by staff attorney Leroy Clark, and later

by Jack Greenberg and Constance Motley, the Inc. Fund's two top lawyers.

Late in the afternoon on Good Friday, after King and the other demonstrators had been carried off to jail, Amaker and Shores went to the latter's office across the street from the Gaston Motel and began to prepare their case. They anticipated that some or all of the demonstrators arrested on Good Friday and Easter Sunday would be charged with contempt of court for violation of the injunction. Moreover, they feared the city might press civil as well as criminal charges. Working on the theory that the best defense is a good offense, they immediately set to work preparing papers in support of a motion to dissolve the injunction. Amaker, whose work on other Inc. Fund cases had given him a broad knowledge of constitutional law, concentrated on developing arguments about the invalidity of the injunction under the First and Fourteenth Amendments. Shores, who for years had been the leading black lawyer in Birmingham, focused his attention on problems of Alabama procedure.

Early Monday morning Shores and Amaker filed their application to dissolve the injunction. In all, eleven grounds of invalidity were alleged. These included arguments that the injunction order violated the ministers' right to due process of law because it was issued without notice to them and without any opportunity for them to be heard prior to its issuance; that its language was so broad and vague that it was impossible to know what specific conduct was prohibited; that it constituted an unlawful "prior restraint" on the exercise of the respondents' rights of free speech and expression; that its issuance was designed to enforce Birmingham's unconstitutional racial segregation policies; and that the parade-permit ordinance which was incorporated by the injunction was itself unconstitutionally vague.

As supporting documents, Shores and Amaker attached copies of city ordinances prohibiting restaurants to serve whites and Negroes on the same premises, forbidding members of the two races from playing cards or checkers together, and requiring separate toilet facilities for whites and Negroes. They also submitted affidavits from several members of the ACMHR attesting to recent instances where the Birmingham police had enforced segregation ordinances by arresting black citizens seeking restaurant service. Other legal papers would follow, but these provided the foundation on which later briefs and arguments would be built.

The papers filed by Shores and Amaker were referred to Judge Jenkins, who had issued the injunction. He ordered a hearing for 9:30 A.M. the following Monday, April 22. A few hours later, the attorneys for the city filed the expected contempt charges, naming fifteen ministers as defendants—SCLC leaders King, Walker, Abernathy, Shuttlesworth, Andrew Young, and James Bevels, and nine local clergymen and other civil rights activists. As anticipated, the city attorneys charged that participation in the Good Friday and Easter Sunday marches constituted criminal contempt of court. Walker, Young, and several of the other ministers had not actually participated in either march (King had insisted that some of the key SCLC leaders not get themselves arrested), but the city attorneys, Earl McBee and J. M. Breckenridge, sought to reach them too, alleging that their attempts to solicit volunteers for the two marches were violations of the injunction.

The city also charged that the statements made by King, Walker, Abernathy, and Shuttlesworth at the April 11 press conference constituted both criminal and civil contempt. The city's prayer for relief asked not only that all the defendants be ordered to show cause why they should not be punished for contempt but also that King, Walker, Abernathy, and Shuttlesworth show cause why they "shall not continue to be adjudged in [civil] contempt of this court and from time to time punished therefor unless they shall publicly retract or recant the statements made publicly at press conferences and mass meeting on April 11th, of their intention to violate the injunction.''

Judge Jenkins signed the show-cause order requested by the city attorneys and set it down for a hearing on the following Monday, April 22, when he also would hear the motion to dissolve the injunction. At the same time, he told reporters that the hearing on the city's contempt charges would take precedence over the motion seeking dissolution of the injunction. The lawyers for the movement thus approached the coming courtroom confrontation knowing that their faint hope of getting the injunction declared invalid prior to a contempt trial had proved illusory.

During the week of April 15–22 lawyers for both sides interviewed potential witnesses, reviewed legal precedents, and organized the presentation of their evidence. King's lawyers also started a legal counteroffensive on another front, seeking the aid of the federal courts. In midweek New York attorney William Kunstler filed papers in federal district court in Birmingham seeking to get the prosecutions for misdemeanors, such as unlawful picketing and parading without a permit, removed from the city recorder's court to federal court. He invoked an old federal statute that permitted such removal where state prosecutions had been instituted solely for the purpose of preventing persons from exercising their constitutional rights.

On Friday morning, April 19, Arthur Shores and the Inc. Fund lawyers also filed a suit in federal district court seeking to enjoin city officials from "pursuing and continuing to pursue a policy" of "denying to Negro citizens the right to peacefully protest state-enforced racial segregation in the City of Birmingham." The federal court was asked specifically to restrain the city from "continuing to hinder peaceful protests against discriminatory racial practices by arrests or threats of arrests" or by "abuse of state court process." Federal court officials said, however, that the earliest time any of the three judges in the district court could consider the case would be about two weeks away.

Late Friday afternoon Arthur Shores and Norman Amaker went to the Jefferson County Courthouse to file a list of the witnesses they planned to call in the contempt trial. The list included the names of Governor George Wallace; former governor John Patterson; a host of other state, county, and local officials; and the managers of a number of Birmingham stores and restaurants. Publication of the witness list led some to believe that perhaps the Inc. Fund lawyers would try to make the contempt trial a major political event at which prominent politicians would be subjected to hostile questioning about the legal structure of segregation. But although that possibility was fleetingly entertained by the Inc. Fund lawyers, it was not adopted. Instead, at a series of strategy sessions held over the weekend of April 20–21, the decision was made to stick to relatively traditional defense tactics. The views of three people—Jack Greenberg, Constance Motley, and Martin Luther King—were mainly responsible for the decision.

Greenberg was a long-time veteran of civil rights litigation. He had joined the Inc. Fund shortly after graduating from Columbia Law School in 1948, and had worked closely with Thurgood Marshall in *Brown v. Board of Education* and other desegregation cases decided by the Supreme Court and other federal courts during the 1950s. During the early 1960s he had been principally responsible for formulating the legal strategy employed by the attorneys who represented sit-in demonstrators in prosecutions for offenses such as trespass and breach of the peace. That strategy was oriented basically toward the appellate courts, particularly the U.S. Supreme Court. It called for the defense lawyers to raise a variety of defenses at the trial level, ranging from broad claims of constitutional protection for the particular form of demonstration to narrow and carefully presented arguments that a state statute or city ordinance did not apply in the circumstances of a particular case. Above all, it was a strategy that recognized the crucial importance of the courts to the success of the movement. Greenberg's style was that of a low-keyed, scholarly appellate lawyer; unlike William Kunstler, he would not be tempted to try to turn the trial of his clients into a media-oriented indictment of the prevailing system of justice.

Constance Baker Motley was the number-two person in the Legal Defense Fund. A tall, stately woman, the ninth of twelve children born to emigrants from the British West Indies, she had grown up in New Haven, where her father was a chef at Yale University. Like Jack Greenberg, she had attended Columbia Law School and had spent most of her professional career working for the Inc. Fund. Her particular specialty was attacking discrimination in education, and it was she who had guided James Meredith through the courts and into the University of Mississippi less than a year earlier. Mild in manner but firm and forceful in her arguments, Mrs. Motley had earned a reputation as a formidable advocate of civil rights causes. She shared the view that the courts were crucial to the success of the civil rights movement and that an attempt to put the Alabama courts themselves "on trial" could only be counterproductive.

Martin Luther King was also opposed to any such strategy. To him, it was not completely unthinkable that he and the other leaders might be treated fairly even at the hands of an Alabama court. Furthermore, he had no doubt that the principal thrust of the protest campaign should continue to be in the streets of Birmingham. To mount a major attack on Alabama justice at this point would only divert attention from the central objective of breaking the segregation barriers in Birmingham.

King and Ralph Abernathy, both sporting eight-day beards, were released from Birmingham City Jail on April 20 after posting $300 cash bonds. King said that he had been persuaded to post bail so that he could consult over the weekend with his lawyers and with the other SCLC and ACMHR leaders. He emphasized that the protest campaign would continue until four basic goals had been won: desegregation of lunch counters and other public facilities in downtown stores; adoption of fair employment practices (including the hiring of qualified Negroes for white-collar jobs) by the stores; withdrawal of charges by merchants against those arrested during sit-ins inside the stores; and appointment of a biracial commission to work out other desegregation steps.

The contempt trial began as scheduled on the morning of Monday, April 22, in Judge William A. Jenkins' courtroom on the third floor of the Jefferson County Courthouse. Completed in 1931, the building contained courtrooms for each of the thirteen judges of Alabama's Tenth Judicial Circuit (which encompassed all of Jefferson County) plus the judges of several other courts. Judge Jenkins' courtroom, about average in size, held 150–200 people. It was wood-paneled, warm in tone, and—unlike many courtrooms—not decorated with sculpture or paintings.

By 9:30 A.M., when the proceedings were scheduled to begin, the courtroom was packed with spectators, most of them either white reporters or black supporters of the protest leaders. There was also a sprinkling of white lawyers, some of whom had Birmingham business leaders as clients, and therefore had more than a passing interest in the outcome of the contempt trial. Interestingly, court attendants made no attempt to enforce segregated seating in the courtroom. At 9:35 the bailiff of the court called for everyone in the courtroom to rise, and Judge Jenkins, dressed in the traditional black robes, entered from a doorway at the front of the courtroom and walked briskly to the raised dais from which he would preside over the trial.

A native of Birmingham, Judge Jenkins was a World War II veteran who had returned to his hometown after the war, gone through Birmingham School of Law, and started a private law practice in Birmingham in 1950, at the age of thirty. His father had been a civil court judge in Birmingham, and when the elder Judge Jenkins died in 1954, the son was named to the vacancy. Three years later when a vacancy opened up in the Equity Division of the state's Tenth Judicial Circuit, Governor James E. ("Big Jim") Folsom named Jenkins to that post. The following year Judge Jenkins was elected to the circuit court for a full six-year term by the voters of Jefferson County, defeating two opponents in the Democratic primary. By 1963 he had accumulated a considerable amount of experience handling injunction cases and other equity matters. A husky, well-dressed man with a relaxed and easygoing manner, Judge Jenkins had a reputation for fairness in dealing with lawyers. He was not a strident segregationist; his political views were thought to be those of "an Albert Boutwell moderate." One Inc. Fund lawyer later said he seemed to be "a very decent guy, particularly as Southern state court judges go."

Judge Jenkins began the court session by turning immediately to the two applications that had been filed the preceding week—the defendants' motion to dissolve the injunction and the city's petition for a contempt citation. The contempt citation would be considered first, he stated, since even if the injunction order were invalid it was still "subject to the authority which the Court has." Arthur Shores objected, arguing that the motion to dissolve had been filed before the contempt petition and that the court did not have "jurisdiction" to issue an invalid order. Judge Jenkins ruled otherwise; the only questions he could see about jurisdiction, he said, were whether the court that issued the injunction was empowered to issue such an order and whether the parties named in it were properly notified of the injunction and were within the territorial jurisdiction of the court.

The issues for decision at the trial-court level were thus

sharply limited at the outset of the proceedings. "Jurisdiction" is one of those elusive legal concepts frequently defined in different ways. Some legal scholars (and a few judges) have maintained that a court does not have any "jurisdiction"—legitimate power—to issue an order that is unconstitutional and that any such order is void from its inception. Most courts have rejected this notion, however, preferring the limited meaning given to the term by Judge Jenkins. Under his definition there could be no real dispute over the court's jurisdiction: as a judge of the circuit court for Jefferson County, he clearly had the statutory authority to issue injunctions, and most of the principal defendants had undeniably been served with copies of the injunction shortly after it had been issued. Under Judge Jenkins' ruling, the only substantial issues to be decided at the trial would be whether the defendants had in fact violated the court order and had done so "knowingly."

From this point on, much of the trial consisted of an elaborate sparring match between the lawyers, with the attorneys for the city attempting to keep the testimony confined to the two narrow issues delineated by Judge Jenkins and the lawyers for the defendants seeking to bring out the realities of official policy in segregationist Birmingham. The defense lawyers had expected Judge Jenkins' ruling, of course; but even if the judge would not permit testimony on such matters to be introduced, at least they could raise the issues and try to make a record which might be helpful on appeal. The city's attorneys were fully prepared for such maneuvers. And in this case, they felt, they had not only state law on their side but also federal law, as embodied in the Supreme Court's decisions in the *Howat* and *Mine Workers* cases.

Matt Breckenridge and Earl McBee, the same two attorneys who had initially obtained the injunction from Judge Jenkins, handled the city's case. Like Greenberg, Motley, and Shores, they were veterans of the struggle over deseg-

regation in the South—but always on the side of segregationist Birmingham. One or the other of them, and sometimes
both, had represented the city of Birmingham in the succession of suits initiated by Fred Shuttlesworth and the Alabama
Christian Movement for Human Rights challenging various
aspects of racial discrimination in Birmingham: segregated
seating on the city's buses, segregated facilities at the bus terminal, segregated swimming pools and golf courses, and so
on. They had also been the lawyers for the city in many of
the prosecutions of Shuttlesworth and other local civil rights
activists who had been arrested for "breach of the peace"
and similar alleged offenses during past protest demonstrations. Just a few months earlier, Breckenridge had argued
against Constance Motley in the U.S. Supreme Court, seeking to uphold the convictions of Shuttlesworth and several
college students who had been arrested during sit-in demonstrations at dime-store lunch counters in Birmingham.

The two city attorneys were remarkably similar in several
other respects. Both had gone to college at Birmingham
Southern, had received their legal educations at Birmingham School of Law, and had practiced law in Birmingham
throughout their professional careers. Both were of medium
height and build, and a little on the paunchy side. McBee, at
sixty-one, was the older by five years. Between them, Breckenridge and McBee had a combined total of seventy years'
experience practicing law in Alabama courts, and they could
call upon their extensive knowledge of Alabama practice in
order to resist attempts by the defense attorneys to inject "ex-
traneous" issues of racial discrimination into the proceedings. As Jack Greenberg later recalled, "This was their home
ground, and they knew their way around it very well."

McBee, the more flamboyant of the two, was responsible
for presenting the city's case against the fifteen ministers.
Under Judge Jenkins' ruling at the outset of the trial, the elements of that case were really rather simple: all that McBee

had to show was that the defendants had received notice of the terms of the injunction and had violated those terms with full knowledge that they were disobeying a court order.

The problem of proving notice was easy in the case of nine of the defendants, including all of the key leaders. Papers filed with the court by the sheriff showed the date and the time that copies of the injunction had been served on each of the nine, and the defense attorneys made no attempt to challenge the accuracy of the notations. It was somewhat more difficult to prove that the other six—SCLC lieutenants Andrew Young and James Bevels, and Birmingham ministers Ed Gardner, Nelson Smith, Joshua Hayes, and Theodis Fisher —had known about the court order and what its commands were. Here McBee had to rely mainly on circumstantial evidence, such as the statements made about the injunction by King and the other leaders and the calls for volunteers at the mass meetings held following the issuance of the injunction. He also introduced the testimony of police officers who had interviewed Hayes, Smith, and several of the other Birmingham ministers following their arrests. These officers said that the arrested ministers had acknowledged "knowing about" the injunction.

The heart of the city's case lay in the testimony of the witnesses McBee put on the stand to describe the activities of the defendants between the time they were served with the injunction and the time of the Easter Sunday march. His two principal witnesses were W. J. Haley, chief inspector of the Birmingham police department, and Lieutenant Willie B. Painter, an investigator for the Alabama Department of Public Safety. Both Haley and Painter had been present at the Good Friday and Easter Sunday marches, and they described them in considerable detail. Painter also added some testimony about Wyatt Walker's role, a facet of the case that McBee went to particular pains to bring out.

Painter testified to having seen Walker giving directions to members of the crowd on both Good Friday and Easter Sunday, and told about a conversation he had had with Walker at the mass meeting on Friday night. At that time, Painter said, he and Walker had discussed the potential strength of SCLC's following in Alabama. According to Painter, Walker had calculated that approximately 2 percent of the people in Alabama, or about 25,000 persons, were active in or affiliated with the SCLC and that "this figure of two percent of the population was sufficient to create a revolution." In the same conversation, Painter added, Walker had described Martin Luther King as "a philosopher and a thinker" and himself as "a strategist and decision-maker."

To supplement the testimony of Haley and Painter about the actions of the defendants, McBee called three newsmen and four additional policemen to the stand. One of the newsmen, Associated Press reporter J. Walter Johnson, had been present at the Gaston Motel at the time the injunction was served early Thursday morning, April 11, and at the church meetings on Thursday and Friday evenings. He testified about some of the comments made about the injunction by the protest leaders on these occasions, such as Walker's remark that Negro students "can get a better education in five days in this jail than five months in those segregated schools." Another newsman, photographer James Ware, told of having been hit on the head by a rock while covering the Easter Sunday demonstration. He also identified Walker and A. D. King as two of the participants in the Easter Sunday march. The third witness, Elvin Stanton, news director of a Birmingham radio station, testified about various statements made by movement leaders at the church meetings he had attended on the evenings of April 11 and 12. He particularly recalled Martin Luther King saying at the meeting on April 11 that "injunction or no injunction, we are going to march tomorrow. In our movement here in Birmingham we have reached the point of no return. We have gone too far to turn back now.''

The testimony of the four police officers completed the presentation of the city's case. Lieutenant Maurice House, who had been present at the April 11 press conference at the Gaston Motel, identified the press release that King had read there, and it was introduced into evidence. House also recalled Shuttlesworth saying "that they had respect for the Federal Courts, or Federal injunctions, but in the past the State Courts had favored local law enforcement, and if the police couldn't handle it, the mob would.'' The other police officers testified briefly about the Good Friday and Easter Sunday marches. They brought out a few details about the marches not covered in the testimony of Haley and Painter, and also testified about post-arrest statements made by several of the Birmingham ministers to the effect that they had known about the injunction but marched anyway.

The city's case took a day and a half to present. The only surprise was the prosecution's failure to introduce any evidence at all against four of the Birmingham ministers and local activists who had been named as defendants—Ed Gardner, Abraham Woods, Calvin Woods, and Johnny Louis Palmer. These men were not the main targets, however. It had been plain from the outset that Breckenridge and McBee were chiefly interested in proving their case against the key leaders: "outsiders" Martin Luther King, Ralph Abernathy, and Wyatt Walker, and the long-time "local agitator" Fred Shuttlesworth. Their strategy had been to show not only that the leaders had committed technical violations of the injunction, but also that, in deliberately "taking the law into their own hands," they had sought to stir up violence.

One of the few sharp clashes during the first day and a half of testimony came during McBee's questioning of Inspector Haley. Defense counsel Arthur Shores objected to a question about the conduct of the crowd watching the Good Friday march, observing that "a crowd isn't on trial for contempt." McBee replied, "Your Honor, we expect to show from the evidence that this whole business is a planned business, and the crowd was gathered intentionally and purposely. The injunction is against the gathering of mobs, and we say this was a mob, and we are going to show before we get through that these defendants engaged in the gathering of those mobs. . . . He who gathers the mob together is responsible for what the mob does, in our theory." Judge Jenkins allowed this line of inquiry to continue.

Under McBee's questioning, Inspector Haley testified about bystanders at the march "clapping, and hollering, and hooping [sic] on the sidelines," about bystanders surging into the streets to follow the marchers, and about several rocks being thrown on Easter Sunday. On his cross-examination of Haley, Arthur Shores sought to bring out a very different picture of the actions of the ministers—to fix the responsibility for the gathering of crowds on the police, and to portray the marches as peaceful walks that did not obstruct traffic or interfere with pedestrians. Thus, for example, he elicited Haley's acknowledgment that the police had blocked off traffic in the area for several hours before the Good Friday march, that people normally congregate when they see police officers in an area, and that to the best of his knowledge the marchers themselves had been orderly and had not violated any traffic regulations.

Shores then tried to use his cross-examination of Haley to lay the groundwork for an argument that the marches were not "parades" within the meaning of the Birmingham parade-permit ordinance and to show that the ordinance should not apply to the protest marches at all. A series of heated exchanges took place as McBee resisted the attempt to inquire into Haley's understanding of how the permit ordinance was administered:

SHORES: Just what type of parade or procession may one obtain a permit for?

McBEE: I object. That is not his responsibility. The law sets out when and how to get a permit.

THE COURT: Sustained. . . .

SHORES: He said he was familiar with the ordinances and we are trying to bring out what, in his years of experience, just what a parade is . . .

THE COURT: I think the only question was did they or did they not have a permit. . . .

SHORES: Have you ever arrested a group of school children walking toward the Museum or Auditorium and being led by a teacher or some other student, probably a hundred or more, have you ever arrested any such group for walking down the street?

McBEE: May it please the Court, that is not and could not be a parade or procession under any circumstances, and I think the question answers itself that it's not customary to arrest a group of school children unless they are engaged in committing acts along with some agitators that constitute a violation of the law.

THE COURT: I will overrule the objection and allow him to answer.

HALEY: I have seen various parades, and I do not recall having made arrests for any parade that had a permit.

SHORES: Do you regularly require all groups that you see marching to have permits?

HALEY: We get notice of it in the Chief's office through regular channels because parades do constitute a traffic problem and we have to make preparations for it.

SHORES: That is for any sort of parade?

HALEY: That is for any legal parade.

SHORES: You say any legal parade; that is the question we are trying here. What is a legal parade?

McBEE: I object to it.

SHORES: He made the statement whether or not it was a legal parade. For these children, two or three hundred of them, to be marching in twos to go to the Auditorium for a symphony program, do they have to get a permit to march to the Auditorium?

BRECKENRIDGE: Your Honor, for ought that appears there has never been such a procession. It is incompetent, irrelevant and immaterial.

THE COURT: I will sustain the objection . . .

Shore's duel with McBee and Breckenridge over the question of what constituted a parade—and, more particularly, over who was to determine what constituted a parade requiring a permit, and how that determination was to be made— was an example of what would happen whenever the lawyers for the defendants attempted to get the slightest bit outside the narrow issues delineated by Judge Jenkins' ruling at the start of the trial. Breckenridge or McBee would object, and Judge Jenkins would sustain the objection. It was immensely frustrating to the defense lawyers, and the frustration was not eased by the knowledge that the rulings were consistent with the thrust of the generally prevailing doctrine of the *Mine Workers* case, that the validity of an injunction cannot be challenged in a contempt proceeding.

When the city rested its case shortly before noon on the second day of the trial, Arthur Shores made a *pro forma* motion for judgment for the defendants, arguing that the evidence showed that they had been engaged in conduct protected by the First and Fourteenth Amendments. Not unexpectedly, the motion was overruled. Shores then sought dismissal of the charges against Ed Gardner, Abraham Woods, Calvin Woods, Johnny Louis Palmer, Andrew Young, and James Bevels on the ground that there had been no testimony at all linking them with violation of the injunction. City attorney McBee agreed that there was no testimony with regard to the first four, but argued that testimony identifying Young and Bevels as being at church meetings where they were recruiting volunteers for the marches was sufficient to establish a prima facie case against them. Judge Jenkins overruled Shores's motion with respect to Young and Bevels, but granted it with respect to the other four, and the court then adjourned for lunch.

During the luncheon recess the defense lawyers reviewed their plans for presenting further testimony. They had several lines of attack in mind, and were thinking about what kind of evidence (or what attempts to introduce evidence) might be helpful in a subsequent appeal, not just at the trial level. Judge Jenkins' rulings prior to trial and during the presentation of the city's case had confirmed their belief that there was little hope of avoiding contempt convictions of at least some of the defendants. They did want, however, to avert a finding that King and the other leaders were guilty of civil as well as criminal contempt, and to build a record for a later appeal. They decided that the two lawyers most familiar with constitutional litigation, Jack Greenberg and Constance Motley, would handle this part of the case.

The principal constitutional position that the Inc. Fund lawyers sought to develop was based on a line of Supreme Court decisions holding that proof of discriminatory administration of a licensing law is a valid defense to a prosecution for acting without such a license. Judge Jenkins had already indicated that he would not hear evidence addressed to this point. The defense lawyers decided, nevertheless, to continue trying to bring out evidence that the city's parade-permit ordinance was administered in an arbitrary and discriminatory fashion.

When the trial resumed, Jack Greenberg called the city clerk, Judson Hodges, to the stand and started to ask him questions about how parade permits were granted by the city. McBee immediately objected, arguing that testimony about the city's procedures for granting permits would be irrelevant unless the defense could show that the protest leaders had made a request for a permit to the City Commission. Judge Jenkins sustained McBee's objections, and Greenberg then attempted to get his position on record:

> GREENBERG: Perhaps I can explain our position in briefer fashion. These respondents are in part being charged with not having applied to the City Commission for a permit. It is our position, among other things, that the City Commission does not grant permits and never has; that these are granted by the City Clerk at the request of the traffic division according to no published rule or regulation. We can establish it very easily because that is in fact the practice. . . .
>
> THE COURT: I will let you ask the question and then I will rule upon the objection.
>
> GREENBERG: Will you describe the practice in accordance with which permits are granted, Mr. Hodges?
>
> McBEE: We object to that, may it please the Court, unless they are talking about the particular incidents involved in any of the parades that were conducted related to the issues in this case. . . .

Again, Judge Jenkins sustained the objection, ruling that questions about the general practice regarding the issuance of parade permits could not be allowed because "the ordinance itself" was "governing in this situation." Greenberg pointed out that the procedure set forth in the ordinance had, "as far as we have been able to ascertain, never been followed." It would be a denial of the defendants' Fourteenth Amendment right to equal protection of the law, he argued, to require them to follow the procedure of applying to the full City Commission when the full commission had never acted before on an application for a permit. His argument was to no avail. Judge Jenkins observed simply that "The law requires it. Whether or not the Commission has done that is not any concern of this Court at this time."

Although Greenberg had been rebuffed in his attempt to obtain testimony about the actual administration of the

The first week of demonstrations began in Birmingham, Alabama, April 3–10, 1963. *Above,* pickets outside downtown department store, included blind singer, Al Hibbler (at right). *Below,* Rev. Fred Shuttlesworth led a prayer march to city hall. Both groups were arrested for parading without a permit.

Public Safety Commissioner Eugene ''Bull'' Connor led officers into the downtown area of Birmingham to make a series of arrests.

A state court order forbidding further marches and demonstrations was served about 1 A.M. on April 11. *Above,* Dr. Martin Luther King Jr. (center), Rev. Ralph Abernathy (left), and Rev. Fred Shuttlesworth read the injunction in the restaurant of the Gaston Motel, shortly after it was served.

The Good Friday march took place in defiance of the injunction. *Below,* King and Abernathy are shown leading marchers from the Sixteenth Street Baptist Church toward City Hall.

Police stopped the Good Friday marchers as they moved toward the downtown area. King and Abernathy were arrested, put into a waiting police van, and jailed.

Left, State Court Judge William A. Jenkins, Jr., who issued the April 10 injunction, presided over the contempt trial on April 22–24, and found King and his colleagues guilty, on April 26, 1963.

With King in jail, his brother, Rev. A. D. King, led more than 1,500 Negroes in an Easter Sunday protest march. *Below,* A. D. King being taken to jail.

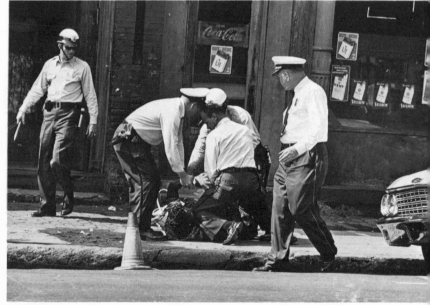

After the contempt verdict and the ministers' release on bail pending their
appeal, the demonstrations continued, reaching their high point in early
May. As the number of demonstrators swelled, the Birmingham police
used "crowd control" tactics that put these pictures in newspapers and TV
programs around the world. *Top left,* police dogs used against one
demonstrator. *Bottom left,* three policemen "subdue" a woman marcher.
Above, a fire hose is turned full force on a group of young Negroes.

On May 10, local business leaders announced an agreement with the Birmingham Protest Movement. *Top Right,* Attorney General Robert F. Kennedy congratulates Assistant Attorney General Burke Marshall, just back from six days in Birmingham assisting the negotiations.

During the spring and summer of 1963, civil rights demonstrations took place in hundreds of cities throughout the nation, and in August over 20,000 persons went to Washington for the "March for Jobs and Freedom." Then, on September 15, a bomb planted at the Sixteenth Street Baptist Church in Birmingham exploded during Sunday School services, killing four young black girls. *Bottom Right*, an empty stretcher waits to take the body of one of the victims.

The fruits of the Birmingham campaign. On July 2, 1964, President Lyndon
B. Johnson signed the Civil Rights Act of 1964, guaranteeing equal access to
public accommodations to all persons, regardless of race or color. Here,
President Johnson hands a souvenir pen to Dr. King, at the White House.

King found himself confronted by court orders forbidding demonstrations in several of his major campaigns during 1964–1968. *Above*, a federal marshal reads an injunction banning a proposed march from Selma to Montgomery on March 9, 1965. In front row are Andrew Young, Martin Luther King Jr., Bernard Lee, and A. D. King.

King's antiwar activities increased sharply in 1967. *Below,* he and Dr. Benjamin Spock lead 5,000 antiwar marchers through the Chicago Loop, on March 25, 1967.

During late 1966 and the first half of 1967, lawyers for Dr. King and the City of Birmingham briefed and argued the contempt appeal in *Walker v. Birmingham* before the United States Supreme Court. *Above*, Legal Defense Fund lawyers in the Fund's New York offices. From left, Jack Greenberg, Norman Amaker, and James Nabrit III.

On June 12, 1967, the Supreme Court upheld King's conviction for
contempt in violating the state court order against protest marches. *Above,*
Justice Potter Stewart, who wrote the opinion for the five-man majority.
Right, two of the four dissenters: at *top,* Chief Justice Earl Warren, and
bottom, Justice William J. Brennan, Jr.

Martin Luther King, Jr., in Birmingham jail, November 3, 1967, serving five-day contempt sentence affirmed by the U.S. Supreme Court in the *Walker* case. This photo was taken by his cellmate, Rev. Wyatt Tee Walker.

parade-permit ordinance, his carefully formulated statements of what he would prove if given an opportunity to do so had established a record that might be useful in a subsequent appeal. Co-counsel Constance Baker Motley followed essentially the same strategy in questioning Birmingham's public safety commissioner, Bull Connor. McBee, as expected, objected to questions designed to show that the full City Commission (of which Connor was, of course, a member) had never actually issued a parade permit. Judge Jenkins sustained the objections. But, simply by putting him in the position of refusing to consider evidence that the permit ordinance was administered in an arbitrary fashion, the defense had accomplished its basic objective.

On the same rationale the defense lawyers embarked upon several additional lines of proof. First, in order to support their contention that the demonstrations were orderly and peaceful, they called Birmingham police chief Jamie Moore to the stand. Arthur Shores drew from him an acknowledgment that the Birmingham police had been able to maintain law and order during the demonstrations without having to call upon the sheriff's office or the state police. Second, in an attempt to portray the patterns of officially sanctioned segregation in Birmingham, they started to call a series of witnesses through whom they hoped to show that city officials were requiring business enterprises to comply with unconstitutional segregation ordinances. Judge Jenkins squelched this attempt immediately, ruling that such matters were irrelevant to the question of whether the injunction had been knowingly violated. Third, they attempted to show that four of the remaining eleven defendants—Fisher, Smith, Bevels, and Hayes—had not received notice of the injunction, and thus could not be held in contempt for having encouraged people to march or for having marched themselves. On direct examination each of the four testified that he had not been served with a copy of the injunction prior to being arrested.

Under cross-examination by McBee, however, each admitted that he had "heard about" the injunction before coming to church meetings at which the marchers were organized.

Finally, on the morning of the third day of the trial, the defense called Mrs. Lola Hendricks, the ACMHR member whom Fred Shuttlesworth had dispatched to City Hall on the morning of March 30. Mrs. Hendricks told what happened when she and her companion went to Connor's office to try to get a permit in compliance with the ordinance:

> Commissioner Connor met us at the door. He asked, "May I help you?" I told him, "Yes, sir, we came up to apply or see about getting a permit for picketing, parading, demon- strating . . ." I asked Commissioner Connor for the permit and asked if he could issue the permit, or . . . refer me to persons who would issue a permit. He said, "No, you will not get a permit in Birmingham, Alabama, to picket. I will picket you over to the City Jail," and he repeated that twice.

Breckenridge was immediately on his feet, asking to have the testimony excluded from the record on the ground that it was irrelevant to the case, since Connor's statement could not bind the full commission. Again, Judge Jenkins agreed. For purposes of Judge Jenkins' consideration of the case, Mrs. Hendricks' statement was technically not before him. But it remained a part of the stenographic transcript of the trial, and the Inc. Fund lawyers would make good use of it later.

Before resting their case, the defense attorneys made a novel attempt to deal with the civil contempt. They gave Judge Jenkins a carefully worded "Statement of Counsel," authorized (but not signed) by King, Abernathy, Walker, and Shuttlesworth. This two-page document, though not quite an apology for the statements contained in the press release, stated that the four ministers desired "to clarify their position and publicly state to the Court that they have had no intention of violating the law." They intended, the statement went on, to do only "acts secured to them by the Fourteenth Amendment to the Constitution of the United States," such as urging citizens of Birmingham to protest peacefully against segregation, to exercise their right to vote, to attend church without regard to race, and to exercise their right to equal protection of the laws by remaining seated and seeking service at lunch counters in the city. According to the statement, the leaders agreed not to urge their followers to "engage in mass picketing" or "congregate into mobs," and they did "not intend to perform acts calculated to cause breaches of the peace."

The decision to submit this document was made only after a considerable amount of discussion among the movement leaders over whether to make any sort of gesture of respect at all to Judge Jenkins' court. Walker and Shuttlesworth were later to insist that they were prepared to go to jail for months, if necessary. But King was clearly anxious to avoid a judgment of civil contempt if this could be done without appearing to retract his earlier statements. The "Statement of Counsel"—which still avoided saying that the ministers had not intended to violate the injunction—was a compromise product of these discussions.

Judge Jenkins did not permit the document to be introduced as evidence. But, even though he ruled that the defendants would have to speak for themselves, the document may have served the purpose of indicating to Jenkins that the ministers retained some respect for the court. Judge Jenkins was known to be skeptical about the idea of imposing civil contempt judgments anyway, and the gesture of respect helped to ease the pressure on him.

At this point the defense lawyers rested their case, and the city presented a brief rebuttal. This consisted principally of recalling photographer James Ware and introducing into evidence his pictures of the Easter Sunday march that showed a crowd of black people (but not the marchers themselves) occupying the full width of the street on which the march was taking place.

The trial proceedings ended on the afternoon of Wednesday, April 24, with the presentation of closing factual and legal arguments by attorneys for both sides. On behalf of the eleven ministers who remained as defendants in the case, Constance Baker Motley stressed that in order to find the defendants guilty of criminal contempt, the city was required to prove "beyond a reasonable doubt" that they had violated the injunction. But, she pointed out, they actually had tried on at least two occasions to get a parade permit and had been rebuffed by Bull Connor. As for the statements made by the defendants, she said, "what they really meant by these statements was that they would not be stopped in their lawful protests against segregation." Discussing the Good Friday and Easter Sunday marches, she argued that the city had wholly failed to prove that the crowds had been gathered by the defendants, noted that the marchers themselves were orderly, and maintained that there was no evidence the defendants had done anything illegal. "I am sure," Mrs. Motley observed, "that this Court does not believe that walking down a public street on the sidewalk is an unlawful activity which a court of equity might enjoin."

Jack Greenberg shared the closing argument with Mrs. Motley, concentrating mainly on Supreme Court cases dealing with First Amendment rights. He compared the actions of the Good Friday and Easter Sunday marchers with the similar conduct of a group of 187 demonstrators who had been convicted of breach of the peace after marching peacefully on the grounds of the South Carolina statehouse to protest racial discrimination. Those convictions had been reversed by the Supreme Court in an 8–1 decision, *Edwards v. South Carolina,* which had been handed down only a few weeks earlier. Justice Potter Stewart's opinion in that case, Greenberg noted, had characterized the actions of the protesters as the exercise of free speech rights in their "most pristine form." It was true, Greenberg agreed, that there was no permit ordinance or injunction involved in the South Carolina case, but the principle was the same: the peaceful exercise of the right to protest was protected by the First Amendment. Such First Amendment rights, he insisted, cannot be restrained in advance of their exercise, and Judge Jenkins' injunction was therefore an invalid attempt to restrain those rights. Citing the Supreme Court's 1962 decision in *In re Green,* Greenberg argued that if the injunction was void to start with, it would not be contempt to violate it, just as it would not be unlawful to violate an invalid statute.

Earl McBee, making the closing argument for the city, relied heavily on the Supreme Court's opinion in *United States v. United Mine Workers* in responding to Greenberg's arguments on the law. The *Mine Workers* case, he said, had not been overruled by *Green* or any other decisions of the high court. Its principle was fundamental: an injunction must be obeyed until revoked by orderly proceedings, unless there had been a total usurpation of authority by the issuing court. "After all, this is a government of law, it is a government of order, and if we ever get away from that, we are in chaos."

Discussing the facts of the case, McBee warmed to his task. He ridiculed the defense contention that there was no proof of intent to violate the law, dwelling particularly on the statements of the leaders pledging to violate the injunction and on Painter's testimony about Walker organizing the crowds of onlookers at the marches. He barely mentioned Martin Luther King at all, focusing instead on the statements and actions of Wyatt Walker. It was Walker, McBee charged, who was "the strategist, the decision-maker . . . he was the man behind the scenes in all of this thing."

McBee's accusations against Walker, presented in his florid style, provided perhaps the most dramatic moment of the trial. Later, in the hallway outside the courtroom, someone asked him, "Where was your jury?" and McBee replied, "Out there" with a grand wave of his arm. As one Inc. Fund lawyer later recalled, "He really put on a show for the home folks."

Once McBee had finished his summation, Judge Jenkins swiftly brought the proceedings to a close. Stating that he didn't think it was necessary for the lawyers to file any further briefs discussing the law, he adjourned the case until 9:30 Friday morning. He would have his decision then.

8

The Larger Defense

IN JUDGE JENKINS' COURTROOM in Birmingham, neither King nor his lawyers were able to make a broad political defense. Limited to the question of the court's jurisdiction to issue an injunction, the lawyers could not mount the sustained challenge to segregation in Birmingham that would have brought the courtroom alive with social and political realities. Any effort to put Dr. King on the witness stand to indict Birmingham's racism would also have been squelched by the judge. So it was that the famous defense statement in the King trial of 1963 was made not in the courtroom but from the jail cell in which King had been locked up for eight days, following the Good Friday march.

"No one likes to go to jail, of course," Andrew Young reminisced, "but to Dr. King, it was a rare opportunity for reflection, to recharge his batteries and think through the basic problems of the campaign in which he was engaged. There were no rallies to organize, speeches to give, telephones to answer, or conflicting advisers to listen to. He always spoke of jail as a time for purification, prayer, and thought."

When King entered jail on April 12, his mind was on two advertisements that had appeared that day in the Birmingham *News*. One was a statement from more than sixty local Negro leaders (including A. G. Gaston, John Drew, and most of the local ministers) supporting the "current struggle" of King's movement. It specifically answered the charge that the demonstrations were rash and untimely:

> For two years or more, we have tried to say to the leaders of this community that the pressure of the discrimination and inequalities have been too hard to bear. We have had many conferences with city officials, Chamber of Commerce members, Senior Citizens and individual business and industrial leaders. We have waited with patience and restraint hoping for a change in attitude and climate in our community. As a result of conferences with leaders in this community, we waited past the gubernatorial election last year. We waited in September. We waited in March through the first election. We waited in April through the runoff. We feel compelled at this time to lay our case before the general public. We feel that under the Constitution of the United States of America the rights granted to every citizen are justly ours as contributing and law-abiding citizens in this community. We have never asked for any special privileges because of our racial or religious identity. We are not asking for any now. We are appealing to the people of goodwill in this community, people who believe in human rights and dignity to hear our case and permit us to help make a greater Birmingham. We call upon the City Officials to appoint immediately a bi-racial committee which will be charged with the responsibility of looking objectively at the problems in this community where race is involved. It is our general conviction that only in this manner with official sanction can Birmingham become truly the "Magic City."
>
> The current struggle in our community is an expression of the uttered or unexpressed deep yearnings of the heart of every Negro in this community. This struggle is not one of strife, but of striving to say to our friends and neighbors of whatever race and creed, "Let us live together in human dignity as American citizens and sons of God."

The other statement published on April 12 was quite different. Eight of the leading white clergymen in Birmingham, representing the major Catholic, Protestant, and Jewish congregations in the city, joined in a public call for an end to the demonstrations. In the past these clergymen had been a voice for "moderation"; they had issued a statement earlier in 1963 advocating "law and order and common sense" in dealing with racial problems. They had urged "honest convictions" to be presented to the courts and said that the resulting court rulings should be "peacefully obeyed." Their April 12 statement recited this history, and added their belief that the recent municipal election promised the "opportunity for a new constructive and realistic approach . . ."

Then the clergymen lowered their moral boom on Dr. King and the Birmingham movement:

> However, we are now confronted by a series of demonstrations by some of our Negro citizens, directed and led in part by outsiders. We recognize the natural impatience of people who feel that their hopes are slow in being realized. But we are convinced that these demonstrations are unwise and untimely.
>
> We agree rather with certain local Negro leadership which has called for honest and open negotiation of racial issues in our area. And we believe this kind of facing of issues can best be accomplished by citizens of our own metropolitan area, white and Negro, meeting with their knowledge and experience of the local situation. All of us need to face that responsibility and find proper channels for its accomplishment.
>
> Just as we formerly pointed out that "hatred and violence have no sanction in our religious and political traditions," we also point out that such actions as incite to hatred and violence, however technically peaceful those actions may be, have not contributed to the resolution of our local problems. We do not believe that these days of new hope are days when extreme measures are justified in Birmingham.
>
> We commend the community as a whole, and the local news media and law enforcement officials in particular, on the calm manner in which these demonstrations have been handled. We urge the public to continue to show restraint should

the demonstrations continue, and the law enforcement officials to remain calm and continue to protect our city from violence.

We further strongly urge our own Negro community to withdraw support from these demonstrations, and to unite locally in working peacefully for a better Birmingham. When rights are consistently denied, a cause should be pressed in the courts and in negotiations among local leaders, and not in the streets. We appeal to both our white and Negro citizenry to observe the principles of law and order and common sense.

The white clergymen's appeal distressed King sorely. Not only might this statement exert a strong influence among white and Negro moderates locally, but it was sure to be picked up by the national news media and read by Northern liberals and the Kennedy Administration. Already, the theme that Project C was "ill-timed" had been voiced by Attorney General Robert Kennedy and by some national civil rights leaders. King decided that he could not let the appeal go unanswered.

On Saturday morning King began composing his reply. As he related later, it was "begun on the margins of the newspaper in which the statement appeared," then "continued on scraps of writing paper supplied by a friendly Negro trusty, and concluded on a pad my attorneys were eventually permitted to leave me." It took four days to compose and was dated "April 16, 1963" when it was issued as *A Letter from Birmingham Jail.* Soon it was being read throughout the United States and the world.*

> *My dear Fellow Clergymen,*
>
> While confined here in the Birmingham City Jail, I came across your recent statement calling our present activities "unwise and untimely." . . .

* Copies of the full 8,000 word text are available from the American Friends Service Committee, the *New Leader* magazine, and the Southern Christian Leadership Conference. Our edited version uses about half of this, omitting primarily the theological discussions.

[S]ince I feel that you are men of genuine goodwill and your criticisms are sincerely set forth, I would like to answer your statement in what I hope will be patient and reasonable terms.

I think I should give the reason for my being in Birmingham, since you have been influenced by the argument of "outsiders coming in." . . .

Several months ago our local affiliate here in Birmingham invited us to be on call to engage in a nonviolent direct action program if such were deemed necessary. We readily consented and when the hour came we lived up to our promises. So I am here, along with several members of my staff, because we were invited here. I am here because I have basic organizational ties here. Beyond this, I am in Birmingham because injustice is here. . . .

Moreover, I am cognizant of the interrelatedness of all communities and states. I cannot sit idly by in Atlanta and not be concerned about what happens in Birmingham. Injustice anywhere is a threat to justice everywhere. . . . Never again can we afford to live with the narrow, provincial "outside agitator" idea. Anyone who lives inside the United States can never be considered an outsider anywhere in this country.

You deplore the demonstrations that are presently taking place in Birmingham. . . .

I would not hesitate to say that it is unfortunate that so-called demonstrations are taking place in Birmingham at this time, but I would say in more emphatic terms that it is even more unfortunate that the white power structure of this city left the Negro community with no other alternative. . . .

There can be no gainsaying of the fact that racial injustice engulfs this community. Birmingham is probably the most thoroughly segregated city in the United States. Its ugly record of police brutality is known in every section of this country. Its unjust treatment of Negroes in the courts is a notorious reality. There have been more unsolved bombings of Negro homes and churches in Birmingham than any city in this nation. These are the hard, brutal, and unbelievable facts. On the basis of these conditions Negro leaders sought to negotiate with the city fathers. But the political leaders consistently refused to engage in good faith negotiation. . . .

You may well ask, "Why direct action? Why sit-ins, marches, etc.? Isn't negotiation a better path?" You are exactly right in your call for negotiation. Indeed, this is the purpose of direct action. Nonviolent direct action seeks to create such a crisis and establish such creative tension that a community that has constantly refused to negotiate is forced to confront the issue. It seeks so to dramatize the issue that it can no longer be ignored. . . . We, therefore, concur with you in your call for negotiation. Too long has our beloved Southland been bogged down in the tragic attempt to live in monologue rather than dialogue.

One of the basic points in your statement is that our acts are untimely. Some have asked, "Why didn't you give the new administration time to act?" The only answer that I can give to this inquiry is that the new administration must be prodded about as much as the outgoing one before it acts. . . .

While Mr. Boutwell is much more articulate and gentle than Mr. Connor, they are both segregationists dedicated to the task of maintaining the status quo. The hope I see in Mr. Boutwell is that he will be reasonable enough to see the futility of massive resistance to desegregation. But he will not see this without pressure from the devotees of civil rights. My friends, I must say to you that we have not made a single gain in civil rights without determined legal and nonviolent pressure. History is the long and tragic story of the fact that privileged groups seldom give up their privileges voluntarily. Individuals may see the moral light and voluntarily give up their unjust posture; but as Reinhold Niebuhr has reminded us, groups are more immoral than individuals.

We know through painful experience that freedom is never voluntarily given by the oppressor; it must be demanded by the oppressed. Frankly I have never yet engaged in a direct action movement that was "well timed," according to the timetable of those who have not suffered unduly from the disease of segregation. For years now I have heard the word "Wait!" It rings in the ear of every Negro with a piercing familiarity. This "wait" has almost always meant "never." . . .

We have waited for more than three hundred and forty years for our constitutional and God-given rights. The nations of Asia and Africa are moving with jet-like speed toward the goal of political independence, and we still creep at horse and buggy pace toward the gaining of a cup of coffee at a lunch counter.

I guess it is easy for those who have never felt the stinging darts of segregation to say wait. But when you have seen vicious mobs lynch your mothers and fathers at will and drown your sisters and brothers at whim; when you have seen hate filled policemen curse, kick, brutalize, and even kill your black brothers and sisters with impunity; when you see the vast majority of your twenty million Negro brothers smothering in an air-tight cage of poverty in the midst of an affluent society; when you suddenly find your tongue twisted and your speech stammering as you seek to explain to your six-year-old daughter why she can't go to the public amusement park that has just been advertised on television, and see tears welling up in her little eyes when she is told that Funtown is closed to colored children, and see the depressing clouds of inferiority begin to form in her little mental sky, and see her begin to distort her little personality by unconsciously developing a bitterness toward white people; when you have to concoct an answer for a five-year-old son asking in agonizing pathos: "Daddy, why do white people treat colored people so mean?"; when you take a cross country drive and find it necessary to sleep night after night in the uncomfortable corners of your automobile because no motel will accept you; when you are humiliated day in and day out by nagging signs reading "white" men and "colored"; when your first name becomes "nigger" and your middle name becomes "boy" (however old you are) and your last name becomes "John," and when your wife and mother are never given the respected title "Mrs."; when you are harried by day and haunted by night by the fact that you are a Negro, living constantly at tiptoe stance never quite knowing what to expect next, and plagued with inner fears and outer resentments; when you are forever fighting a degenerating sense of "nobodiness";—then you will understand why we find it difficult to wait. There comes a time when the cup of endurance runs over . . .

You express a great deal of anxiety over our willingness to break laws. This is certainly a legitimate concern. Since we so diligently urge people to obey the Supreme Court's decision of 1954 outlawing segregation in the public schools, it is rather strange and paradoxical to find us consciously breaking laws. One may well ask, "How can you advocate breaking some laws and obeying others?" The answer is found in the fact that there are two types of laws: There are *just* laws and there are *unjust* laws. I would be the first to advocate obeying just laws. One has not only a legal but moral responsibility to obey just laws. Conversely, one has a moral responsibility to disobey unjust laws. I would agree with Saint Augustine that "An unjust law is no law at all."

Now what is the difference between the two? How does one determine when a law is just or unjust? A just law is a man-made code that squares with the moral law or the law of God. An unjust law is a code that is out of harmony with the moral law. To put it in the terms of Saint Thomas Aquinas, an unjust law is a human law that is not rooted in eternal and natural law. Any law that uplifts human personality is just. Any law that degrades human personality is unjust. All segregation statutes are unjust because segregation distorts the soul and damages the personality. It gives the segregator a false sense of superiority and the segregated a false sense of inferiority. . . .

I can urge men to obey the 1954 decision of the Supreme Court because it is morally right, and I can urge them to disobey segregation ordinances because they are morally wrong. . . .

Let me give another explanation. An unjust law is a code inflicted upon a minority which that minority had no part in enacting or creating because they did not have the unhampered right to vote. Who can say the legislature of Alabama which set up the segregation laws was democratically elected? Throughout the state of Alabama all types of conniving methods are used to prevent Negroes from becoming registered voters and there are some counties without a single Negro registered to vote despite the fact that the Negro constitutes a majority of the population. Can any law set up in such a state be considered democratically structured?

These are just a few examples of unjust and just laws. There are some instances when a law is just on its face but unjust in its application. For instance, I was arrested Friday on a charge of parading without a permit. Now there is nothing wrong with an ordinance which requires a permit for a parade, but when the ordinance is used to preserve segregation and to deny citizens the First Amendment privilege of peaceful assembly and peaceful protest, then it becomes unjust.

I hope you can see the distinction I am trying to point out. In no sense do I advocate evading or defying the law as the rabid segregationist would do. This would lead to anarchy. One who breaks an unjust law must do it *openly, lovingly* (not hatefully as the white mothers did in New Orleans when they were seen on television screaming "nigger, nigger, nigger") and with a willingness to accept the penalty. I submit that an individual who breaks a law that conscience tells him is unjust, and willingly accepts the penalty by staying in jail to arouse the conscience of the community over its injustice, is in reality expressing the very highest respect for law. . . .

We can never forget that everything Hitler did in Germany was "legal" and everything the Hungarian freedom fighters did in Hungary was "illegal." It was "illegal" to aid and comfort a Jew in Hitler's Germany. But I am sure that, if I had lived in Germany during that time, I would have aided and comforted my Jewish brothers even though it was illegal. If I lived in a communist country today where certain principles dear to the Christian faith are suppressed, I believe I would openly advocate disobeying these anti-religious laws.

I must make two honest confessions to you, my Christian and Jewish brothers. First I must confess that over the last few years I have been gravely disappointed with the white moderate. I have almost reached the regrettable conclusion that the Negroes' great stumbling block in the stride toward freedom is not the White Citizens' "Counciler" or the Ku Klux Klanner, but the white moderate who is more devoted to "order" than to justice; who prefers a negative peace which is the absence of tension to a positive peace which is the presence of justice; who constantly says "I agree with you in the goal you seek, but I can't agree with your methods of direct action"; who paternalistically feels that he can set the time-table for another man's freedom; who lives by the myth of time and who constantly advises the Negro to wait until a "more convenient season." . . . Actually, we who engage in nonviolent direct action are not the creators of tension. We merely bring to the surface the hidden tension that is already alive. We bring it out in the open where it can be seen and dealt with. . . .

You spoke of our activity in Birmingham as extreme. At first I was rather disappointed that fellow clergymen would see my nonviolent efforts as those of the extremist. I started thinking about the fact that I stand in the middle of two opposing forces in the Negro community. One is a force of complacency made up of Negroes who, as a result of long years of oppression, have been so completely drained of self-respect and a sense of "somebodiness" that they have adjusted to segregation, and of a few Negroes in the middle class who, because of a degree of academic and economic security, and because at points they profit by segregation, have unconsciously become insensitive to the problems of the masses. The other force is one of bitterness and hatred and comes perilously close to advocating violence. It is expressed in the various black nationalist groups that are springing up over the nation, the largest and best known being Elijah Muhammad's Muslim movement. This movement is nourished by the contemporary frustration over the continued existence of racial discrimination. It is made up of people who have lost faith in America, who have absolutely repudiated Christianity, and who have concluded that the white man is an incurable "devil." I have tried to stand between these two forces saying that we need not follow the "do-nothingism" of the complacent or the hatred and despair of the black nationalist. There is the more excellent way of love and nonviolent protest. . . . If this philosophy had not emerged I am convinced that by now many streets of the South would be flowing with floods of blood. . . .

Oppressed people cannot remain oppressed forever. The urge for freedom will eventually come. This is what has happened to the American Negro. . . . Recognizing this vital urge that has engulfed the Negro community, one should readily understand public demonstrations. The Negro has many pent-up resentments and latent frustrations. He has to get them out. So let him march sometime; let him have his prayer pilgrimages to the city hall; understand why he must have sit-ins and freedom rides. If his repressed emotions do not come out in these nonviolent ways, they will come out in ominous expressions of violence. This is not a threat; it is a fact of history. . . .

I am thankful, however, that some of our white brothers have grasped the meaning of this social revolution and committed themselves to it. They . . . have written about our struggle in eloquent, prophetic, and understanding terms. Others have marched with us down nameless streets of the South. They have languished in filthy, roach-infested jails, suffering the abuse and brutality of angry policemen who see them as "dirty nigger lovers." . . .

Let me rush on to mention my other disappointment. I have been so greatly disappointed with the white Church and its leadership. . . . [W]hen I was suddenly catapulted into the leadership of the bus protest in Montgomery several years ago [I felt] that we would have the support of the white Church. I felt that the white ministers, priests, and rabbis of the South would be some of our strongest allies. Instead, some have been outright opponents, refusing to understand the freedom movement and misrepresenting its leaders; all too many others have been more cautious than courageous and have remained silent behind the anesthetizing security of stained glass windows. . . .

Far from being disturbed by the presence of the Church, the power structure of the average community is consoled by the Church's silent and often vocal sanction of things as they are. . . .

I hope the Church as a whole will meet the challenge of this decisive hour. But even if the Church does not come to the aid of justice, I have no despair about the future. I have no fear about the outcome of our struggle in Birmingham, even if our motives are presently misunderstood. We will reach the goal of freedom in Birmingham and all over the nation, because the goal of America is freedom. Abused and scorned though we may be, our destiny is tied up with the destiny of America. Before the pilgrims landed at Plymouth, we were here. Before the pen of Jefferson etched across the pages of history the majestic words of the Declaration of Independence, we were here. For more than two centuries our foreparents labored in this country without wages; they made cotton "king"; and they built the homes of their masters in the midst of brutal injustice and shameful humiliation—and yet out of a bottomless vitality they continued to thrive and develop. If the inexpressible cruelties of slavery could not stop us, the opposition we now face will surely fail. We will win our freedom because the sacred heritage of our nation and the eternal will of God are embodied in our echoing demands.

I must close now. But before closing I am impelled to mention one other point in your statement that troubled me profoundly. You warmly commended the Birmingham police force for keeping "order" and "preventing violence." I don't believe you would have so warmly commended the police force if you had seen its angry violent dogs literally biting six unarmed, nonviolent Negroes. I don't believe you would so quickly commend the policemen if you would observe their ugly and inhuman treatment of Negroes here in the city jail; if you would watch them push and curse old Negro women and young Negro girls; if you would see them slap and kick old Negro men and young Negro boys; if you will observe them, as they did on two occasions, refuse to give us food because we wanted to sing our grace together. I'm sorry that I can't join you in your praise for the police department.

It is true that they have been rather disciplined in their public handling of the demonstrators. In this sense they have been rather publicly "nonviolent." But for what purpose? To preserve the evil system of segregation. . . . Mr. Connor and his policemen have been rather publicly nonviolent, as Chief Prichett was in Albany, Georgia, but they have used the moral means of nonviolence to maintain the immoral end of flagrant racial injustice. . . .

I wish you had commended the Negro sit-inners and demonstrators of Birmingham for their sublime courage, their willingness to suffer, and their amazing discipline in the midst of the most inhuman provocation. One day the South will recognize its real heroes. They will be the James Merediths, courageously and with a majestic sense of purpose, facing jeering and hostile mobs and the agonizing loneliness that characterizes the life of the pioneer. They will be old, oppressed, battered Negro women, symbolized in a seventy-two-year-old woman of Montgomery, Alabama, who rose up with a sense of dignity and with her people decided not to ride the segregated buses, and responded to one who inquired about her tiredness with ungrammatical profundity: "My feets is tired, but my soul is rested." They will be young high school and college students, young ministers of the gospel and a host of the elders, courageously and nonviolently sitting in at lunch counters and willingly going to jail for conscience sake. One day the South will know that when these disinherited children of God sat down at lunch counters they were in reality standing up for the best in the American dream and the most sacred values in our Judeo-Christian heritage, and thus carrying our whole nation back to great wells of democracy which were dug deep by the founding fathers in the formulation of the Constitution and the Declaration of Independence. . . .

If I have said anything in this letter that is an overstatement of the truth and is indicative of an unreasonable impatience, I beg you to forgive me. If I have said anything in this letter that is an understatement of the truth and is indicative of my having a patience that makes me patient with anything less than brotherhood, I beg God to forgive me. . . .

Yours for the cause of
Peace and Brotherhood,
MARTIN LUTHER KING, JR.

"As soon as the *Letter* was completed," Andy Young related, "the American Friends Service Committee printed and distributed fifty thousand copies. It was reprinted everywhere, and it pulled supporters together . . ."

9

Verdict in Birmingham— and in Washington

WHEN COURT RECONVENED on Friday morning, April 26, Judge Jenkins read his opinion in *City of Birmingham v. Wyatt Tee Walker et al.* After reviewing the procedural history of the case and summarizing the basic positions of both sides, he held that the conduct of the defendants had represented acts of disobedience and disrespect punishable as criminal contempt. (Judge Jenkins never did state his reasons for dismissing the civil contempt charge. If the legal reasoning behind this omission was unclear, the practical reason was not: none of the business leaders relished the idea of Martin Luther King languishing indefinitely in a Birmingham jail, while a national campaign to free him created terrible publicity for the city.)

The judge then went on to hold that the city's parade-permit ordinance was "not invalid upon its face," in the "absence of a showing of arbitrary and capricious action" by the City Commission in denying defendants a parade permit. "The legal and orderly processes of the Court," he said, require that the defendants attack any unreasonable denial of a permit by a motion to dissolve the injunction, "at which time this Court would have the opportunity to pass upon the question of whether or not a compliance with the ordinance was attempted and whether or not an arbitrary and capricious denial was made . . ." Since such a motion was not made, he continued, the validity of the injunction order rested upon the court's "prima facie authority to execute the same."

Judge Jenkins found that all eleven of the defendants had actual notice of the injunction; that their violation of the order constituted "deliberate and blatant denials" of the court's authority; and that there had been "no apology" or indication that those defendants intended to comply with the order in the future. The decision quoted extensively from Justice Felix Frankfurter's concurring opinion in the *Mine Workers* case, saying that it "should be a guide to us all when considering the jurisdictional authority of a Court of law." He sentenced each of the defendants to a fine of fifty dollars and a jail term of five days in the custody of the sheriff of Jefferson County, beginning at 10 A.M. on May 16. They were allowed to go free on bond in the meantime.

Although the sentences were the maximum permitted under Alabama law for criminal contempt, King and his followers viewed them (and especially the failure to hold the defendants in civil contempt until they complied with the injunction) as a light punishment. It was a sign, King announced, that the bastions of segregation in Birmingham were weakening. King's lawyers gave notice that they were appealing the verdict, and the *Walker* case dropped from public view temporarily as the attention of the movement and the nation shifted to what was happening in the streets.

Throughout the period between the Good Friday march and the end of the contempt trial, the picketing and sit-ins had continued in the downtown business district. This was a small-scale operation, however, involving only about a dozen or so people each day. In the meantime the protest leaders sought to bring other pressures to bear upon the white business and political leaders. Northern-based civil rights groups used the jailing of King as a basis for initiating nationwide boycotts of chain stores that had branches in Birmingham and for stepped-up appeals to the Kennedy Administration to intervene in the Birmingham situation. While the appeals were not heeded at this point, both the white elites in Birmingham and the Administration officials in Washington were made aware that a further heightening of racial tension would bring still stronger pressure for federal intervention.

In Birmingham itself, informal negotiations between ad hoc groups of blacks and whites had been going on privately since mid-April. The discussions involved a number of Birmingham clergymen, a few members of King's staff, and some businessmen and professional men (including, significantly, several whites who had been active in the drive to change the city's form of government and in Boutwell's mayoralty campaign). However, the black leadership held little hope that these talks would produce an acceptable settlement without further pressure. For one thing, few of the city's true power holders were involved in these early discussions. For another, although Mayor-elect Boutwell made several vague public statements indicating his readiness to work to improve the city's race relations, he was reluctant to say anything more specific, and possibly affect adversely the outcome of the litigation initiated by the old City Commission. What the April negotiations seem to have done, more than anything else, was to make clear to the protest leaders that their demands would not be met unless they could bring still greater pressure to bear on those who held real power in the city.

While the court proceedings and the negotiations went forward, a group of SCLC aides led by James Bevels and Andrew Young continued with the organizational work. The nightly mass meetings in the churches continued, now supplemented by recruiting efforts in the city's black colleges, high schools, and elementary schools.

About a third of the active participants in the first three

weeks of the campaign had been high school and college students. By the end of April several thousand students of all ages had attended the SCLC's church-based meetings and workshops on nonviolence, had seen films of earlier successful direct-action movements, and had pledged to participate in the campaign. On the evening of Wednesday, May 1, with no visible progress being made in the negotiations, King and his fellow leaders decided to use the young people in demonstrations the following day. They did so realizing that proof of their continued role in planning or participating in mass demonstrations without permits would constitute a fresh offense of contempt of the Jenkins injunction order of April 10, for which they could be prosecuted anew.

In retrospect, this decision was probably the most crucial one of the entire campaign. In making it, the leaders risked severe censure on the ground that they were exploiting immature youngsters and greatly increasing the risk of violence. But there were also obvious advantages to the move. Large numbers of black students milling around the small downtown area could produce considerable disruption of ordinary business activity. Since the students did not hold jobs, economic sanctions could not be used against them as they could against adults. Although some might be arrested, even a large number, any attempt to arrest and detain many thousands would produce a terrific overload on the juvenile detention and court facilities. And if the city were to use undue force against the students, public opinion would be likely to go against the Birmingham authorities.

On Thursday, May 2, literally thousands of black elementary and secondary school students participated in the demonstrations. Approximately one thousand were arrested, but there were no reports of violence. The next day even more volunteers turned out, and it was then that Bull Connor made a fateful choice: he decided to use police dogs and fire hoses to keep the demonstrators from reaching the downtown area.

This resulted in dramatic scenes—recorded for the nation by newspaper photographers and TV cameramen—of police dogs lunging at young children and fire hoses pinning others against brick walls. And it resulted in more violence as a few adult black onlookers retaliated by throwing bricks and bottles at the police and firemen. Hundreds of demonstrators were arrested. That night, with the campaign clearly approaching a crisis point, King addressed a mass meeting at the Sixteenth Street Baptist Church. He spoke of his reaction to the day's events and of the objectives of the demonstrations:

> Birmingham was a mean city today. But . . . we must confront her with our kindness and our goodness and our determination to be nonviolent. As difficult as it is, we must meet hate with love. As hard as it is, we must meet physical force with Soul Force. . . .

He went on to say that "the great glory of democracy is the right to protest for rights.

> Embedded deep down in the Constitution of our nation is the First Amendment—freedom of speech, freedom of press, freedom of assembly. If we lived in Russia, we would understand all this mess they're carrying on down in Birmingham, Alabama. But we live in the United States. . . . Organized labor has demonstrated over and over again our right to picket and yet in Birmingham, Alabama, we can't picket. We can't engage in an orderly nonviolent protest. . . . [But] we love America, and we love democracy. . . . We're struggling not to save ourselves alone, but we're struggling to save the soul of this nation.

The demonstrations continued over the weekend, with Bull Connor again directing his men to use fire hoses and police dogs to control the crowds. Hundreds more were arrested,

and although most of the children actually seemed to be en-
joying themselves, rocks were again thrown by some of the
adult bystanders. The protests continued into the next week,
reaching a peak of intensity on Tuesday, May 7, when thousands of black schoolchildren thronged the downtown business district. By that time more than three thousand had been
arrested, and Jefferson County sheriff Melvin Bailey told a
Tuesday meeting of Birmingham business leaders that if the
police continued to arrest the demonstrators, the only facility
large enough to hold them all would be the city's football sta-
dium.

The very fact that the city's leading businessmen had at
last come together to consider the problem of Birmingham's
race relations indicated that a turning point had been reached
in the struggle. Vincent Harding, a black minister and writer
who was present at the May 7 meeting of the businessmen,
later described it:

> Among the whites were men of high influence in Bir-
> mingham, and as a group they came as close to representing
> the economic power structure as any group could. Included
> were merchants, industrialists,, corporation and bank presi-
> dents, prominent insurance and real-estate men. Also present
> was Mayor-elect Boutwell and several persons high in his ad-
> ministration.
>
> While there was a sense of urgency about the session, there
> was also a certain sense of self-satisfaction, for these men had
> finally decided to stand together in defiance of the racist sen-
> timent that had so long ruled the city. Together they repre-
> sented—by their own estimate—more than eighty percent of
> the hiring power of the Birmingham area. They proceeded to
> offer a timetable for store desegregation and a plan for exten-
> sive upgrading and reform in hiring practices. Just as impor-
> tant, they decided to name a committee headed by a real-estate
> man, Sidney Smyer, that would take public responsibility for
> any agreement reached. When a standing vote on this action

was called for, there was a unanimous favorable response.
. . . Late that afternoon they made contact with the chairman
of the Negro negotiating team and asked for a meeting that
night.

The direct pressure of the demonstrations on the business
life of the city was obviously a primary force behind the
businessmen's decision to open top-level negotiations with
the black leaders. But there were also important indirect pressures. Indeed, one might say that the real turning point in the
campaign had come the preceding Friday. On that day the
Kennedy Administration, responding to the publicity over
Bull Connor's use of fire hoses and police dogs, finally began
taking action of the kind the protest leaders had long hoped
for. Attorney General Robert Kennedy, although publicly
deploring the timing of the demonstrations and the use of the
children, took the lead in organizing a concerted Administration effort to bring about a settlement that would go at least
part way toward meeting the Negro leaders' demands.

James Reston related in *The New York Times* on May 9
how the Administration's appeal to the moderates was being
carried out.

Very quietly in the last few days literally hundreds of tele-
phone calls have been made from here and elsewhere in the
North and South to responsible private citizens and officials in
Birmingham.

Officials here, beginning with Attorney General Robert
Kennedy, have been on the phone to officials in the South who
might have some influence in producing a truce. Secretary of
the Treasury [Douglas] Dillon has been talking to bankers
and other friends in Alabama. Leaders of large national businesses, with branch stores in Birmingham, have been talking
to their branch managers there . . .

Burke Marshall, the quiet head of the Justice Department's

Civil Rights Division, and Assistant Attorney General Louis F. Oberdorfer, an Alabaman, were sent to Birmingham to try to mediate the dispute.

Telephones started ringing. Chain store executives were urged to agree to desegregate their branches in Birmingham when it was legal under local law to do so. Moderate ministers in the North and South called the Birmingham ministers to urge that the efforts at mediation be given time to work. Lawyers called on former classmates in Birmingham to speak out for moderation, and apparently all this has had some effect.

Nobody here is prepared to predict what will happen from hour to hour, but at least moderation is being given a chance.

With the entry of the Justice Department officials and the top-echelon Birmingham businessmen into the negotiations, it became apparent that some kind of agreement could be reached. On the morning of May 8 King announced that a settlement appeared at hand and that demonstrations would be suspended while the final details were worked out.

The final agreement, made public on Friday morning, May 10, was, of course, a compromise. It called for desegregation of lunch counters, rest rooms, fitting rooms, and drinking fountains within ninety days; the hiring of Negroes in job categories previously denied to them, including employment as clerks and salesmen, within sixty days (by firms not publicly identified and in numbers not publicly specified); persuading city officials to release jailed demonstrators on bond or on their own recognizance; and the establishment within two weeks of a biracial committee that would have the function of improving communications between whites and Negroes. No mention was made of the problem of school integration.

On the issues of segregated public facilities and job discrimination, the protest leaders had settled for promises of future action rather than immediate concessions. Nevertheless, the agreement did represent a commitment to change on the part of Birmingham's white business leaders—an acceptance of the legitimacy of the protest leaders' demands and a public pledge to support revision of the city's previously existing racial policies. Not surprisingly, King, Abernathy, and Shuttlesworth hailed the agreement as a victory:

> The City of Birmingham has reached an accord with its conscience. The acceptance of responsibility by local white and Negro leadership offers an example of a free people uniting to meet and solve their problems. Birmingham may well offer for Twentieth Century America an example of progressive racial relations; and for all mankind a dawn of a new day, a promise for all men, a day of opportunity, and a new sense of freedom for all America. Thusly, Birmingham may again become a Magic City.

Announcement of the agreement provoked a wide range of reactions. Many Birmingham blacks thought it gave them too little. One was quoted as saying, "I think the same thing about that agreement as I do of the one that the white man made with the Indians." New York Black Muslim leader Malcolm X criticized the whole Birmingham campaign harshly, characterizing it as "an exercise in futility." He stated that "real men don't put their children on the firing line" and noted that the Birmingham situation had changed radically when black bystanders who did not subscribe to Dr. King's nonviolent philosophy had lost their tempers.

The response of Birmingham's white extremists was predictable: on the night after the agreement was announced, the Gaston Motel and the home of Rev. A. D. King were shattered by bomb blasts. Miraculously, no one was killed, but angry blacks reacted by setting fire to two white-owned stores in a Negro neighborhood and stoning firemen who attempted to reach the scene. Rioting continued throughout the night, with fifty people injured seriously enough to require hospitalization. Order was finally restored with the aid of a somewhat unlikely coalition of peacekeepers: the city's own black leaders, Martin Luther King and other SCLC leaders, the city police, and the white business community.

During the next two weeks tensions gradually eased. A series of judicial decisions helped to clarify the situation. First, on May 15, the Alabama supreme court agreed to review the convictions of King and the other ten ministers who had been found guilty of contempt for violating the injunction, and granted a further stay of the sentences pending the outcome of the appellate proceedings. Then, on May 20, the U.S. Supreme Court handed down a series of decisions in the sit-in cases that had been argued six months earlier. In each case—including the two from Birmingham—the convictions of the demonstrators were reversed on the ground that the prosecutions had been devices for enforcing clearly unconstitutional segregation laws and policies.

On the same day that the rulings in the sit-in cases were announced in Washington, the Birmingham Board of Education (composed mainly of allies of the old City Commission) declared that the students arrested during the demonstrations—more than one thousand—were being expelled from school. However, this time the protest movement was able to turn a court's injunctive power to its own advantage. Two days later, on May 22, Elbert Tuttle, chief judge of the U.S. Court of Appeals for the Fifth Circuit, issued a temporary injunction restraining the board from taking any disciplinary action against the students until a full hearing could be held.

Finally, on May 23, the Alabama supreme court resolved the dispute over occupancy of Birmingham's City Hall by ruling that Boutwell and the nine City Council members elected with him constituted the proper city government. One of the Boutwell government's first acts upon taking office was to announce an end to the city's segregation ordinances.

Meanwhile, the example of successful protest in Birmingham was leading to a wave of similar demonstrations against discrimination in other cities around the country. The Southern Regional Council identified more than nine hundred Birmingham-style direct actions during the summer and early fall of 1963, not just in the South (where more than a hundred communities were involved) but across the country from Boston to San Francisco. More than twenty thousand persons were arrested by the police. While the demonstrations were generally peaceful, there were enough incidents of violence—rocks thrown, store windows smashed, fistfights at demonstration sites, and terrorist acts against civil rights leaders—to provide an edge of fear around any large-scale protest campaign.

During this period a variety of more aggressive direct-action tactics were added to local campaigns, especially in the CORE-led protests in the North. In support of demands for more jobs for blacks, school integration, fair housing, and similar goals, demonstrators chained themselves to the doors of school buildings to prevent access; blocked construction sites by lying down in roadways and in excavations; conducted large-scale sit-ins in the lobbies of hotels and banks, in restaurants, and in business offices; tied up traffic on bridges and tunnels; and sat in the hallways leading to state legislative chambers.

In both North and South, law enforcement officials frequently sought court injunctions to ban disruptive demonstrations, citing interference with traffic, business, and public functions, and fears over outbreaks of violence. While requests for injunctions were occasionally denied and the right to demonstrate upheld by some local or federal courts, more often the injunctions were granted. For SNCC leaders in the South and CORE chapters in the North, defying injunctions became standard operating procedure. When arrested, the demonstrators would either serve their sentences immediately or post bond pending trials (some of which were delayed or dropped as agreements were negotiated to resolve the disputes). Thus, injunctions against demonstrations in 1963 were defied by CORE groups in Tallahassee, Florida; San Diego, California; Plaquemine, Louisiana; and Belair, Maryland. Sometimes, defying the court order helped to sustain and unify the equality campaign, but at other times enforcement of the injunction by local officials was effective in defusing the protest. As Augustus Meier and Elliott Rudwick have written in their history of CORE, "In situations such as Seattle's fair-housing campaign, and the Cleveland school site lie-in, court injunctions were enough to discourage continuation of disruptive tactics."

Whenever the question of defying injunctions arose in 1963, the "glorious example of Birmingham" was cited as the model for appropriate response. By refusing to call off the Good Friday march, King had turned the entire nation around on civil rights. The fact that a five-day jail sentence and a fifty-dollar fine hung over his head (and the heads of the other ministers) was almost too trivial to consider. The basic approach, as King had announced, was that imprisoned civil rights demonstrators were "political prisoners," and that going to jail for disobeying an unjust law was the highest form of fidelity to the Constitution.

But, as always, what might be simple questions for other civil rights activists were not always that easy for King himself. In the South, which was still King's main theater of operations, the help of the courts (especially federal courts) was badly needed to spur compliance with desegregation, and King could not afford to lay himself open repeatedly to charges of violating a court order. It was one thing to proclaim defiance of a state court injunction in Birmingham, where the SCLC itself had made a major commitment of time, resources, and prestige. When local civil rights leaders sought his aid in battles of their own, and it was not a major

SCLC effort, King walked a very careful line on the injunction issue.

For example, in June 1963, a state court injunction obtained by local officials in Gadsden, Alabama, resulted in the arrest of over 450 persons for demonstrating in violation of the injunction. King came to Gadsden for a week, at the invitation of local leaders. At church meetings he urged the black community to press forward despite the injunction, but he never violated it himself. A month later officials in Danville, Virginia, obtained a federal court injunction specifically restraining him (as well as the SCLC, CORE, SNCC, and individual black activists in Danville) from engaging in peaceful demonstrations. The day before he was scheduled to address a rally in Danville, he canceled his appearance until the lawyers had had a chance to contest the injunction in the federal courts. On July 10 the injunction was lifted, and King spoke the following day to a large audience.

While the civil rights struggle continued in the streets and the courts, Justice Department lawyers in Washington were drafting new civil rights legislation that included provisions requiring the desegregation of public accommodation facilities. Work on the new legislative proposals began in May, and early in June, President John F. Kennedy went on nationwide television and radio to seek support for them. His address reflected a greater concern about racial inequalities than any President had ever publicly manifested. He stressed the futility of counseling victims of racial discrimination to have patience and accept delay, one hundred years after Emancipation, and then continued:

> We preach freedom around the world, and we mean it. And we cherish our freedom here at home. But are we to say to the world—and much more importantly, to each other—that this is the land of the free except for Negroes; that we have no second-class citizens, except Negroes; that we have no class or

caste system, no ghettos, no master race, except with respect to Negroes.

Now the time has come for this nation to fulfill its promise. The events in Birmingham and elsewhere have so increased the cries for equality that no city or state or legislative body can prudently choose to ignore them. The fires of frustration and discord are burning in every city, North and South. Where legal remedies are not at hand, redress is sought in the streets, in demonstrations, parades and protests which create tensions and threaten violence—and threaten lives.

We face, therefore, a moral crisis, as a country and a people. It cannot be met by repressive police action. It cannot be left to increased demonstrations in the streets. It cannot be quieted by token moves or talk. It is a time to act in the Congress, in your state and local legislative body, and, above all, in all of our daily lives. . . .

In a sense, this address justified the Birmingham campaign. Substantial gains—or at least the promises of gains—had been made in the city of Birmingham itself, national consciousness of the race problem had been aroused, and now the President of the United States had committed himself to the enactment of sweeping new civil rights legislation. The Birmingham campaign was a major success.

Of course, there were some internal disagreements among civil rights leaders. But they all had a strong interest in seeing major civil rights legislation enacted by Congress, and they worked together in pressing for passage of the legislation proposed by the President. At the same time, they tried to keep enough of a rein on Negro demonstrations so that they did not erupt into large-scale violence. The summer's activities culminated in the famous March on Washington, on August 28, 1963, when over 200,000 people gathered on the mall to demonstrate support for new civil rights laws. It was on this occasion that King delivered his famous "I Have a Dream" speech, rousing the crowd—and millions more watching on television—with an intensely moving vision of a future America that would be truly free.

In Birmingham, meanwhile, racial discord had been simmering all summer. As city officials began to take the first halting steps toward implementing the May 10 agreement, incidents of Klan-type violence erupted, including the bombing of attorney Arthur Shore's home. Then, on Sunday morning, September 15, came the most shocking episode of all—the explosion of a bomb in the basement of the Sixteenth Street Baptist Church. Four Negro girls attending Sunday school inside the church were killed. Once again the destructive fury of lawless white extremists in Birmingham had been manifested to the nation. The church bombing could easily have set off a new round of violent racial conflict in Birmingham, but an uneasy peace was somehow preserved. Later, some were to observe that it was the church bombing that really caused the Birmingham power structure to bring white extremists under control and live up to the commitments it had made to King and the other protest leaders in the spring of 1963.

A little over two months later, on November 22, 1963, President John F. Kennedy was assassinated in Dallas, Texas. On November 27, Lyndon Johnson made his first address to Congress as President of the United States, and invoked his predecessor's memory in urging enactment of the legislation Kennedy had called for in his June 11 speech. "No memorial oration or eulogy could more eloquently honor President Kennedy's memory," Johnson said, "than the earliest possible passage of the civil rights bill for which he fought so long." Despite this plea, the Administration's civil rights proposals were adamantly opposed by virtually all the Southerners in Congress as well as by some of the more conservative legislators from other parts of the country.

But the momentum built up by the civil rights forces during 1963 was too much for the South and its allies to stop. In February 1964 the House of Representatives passed a civil rights bill which was stronger in some respects than the one drafted by the Justice Department the preceding spring. In June, after taking the virtually unprecedented step of invoking cloture to shut off a filibuster by Southern senators, the Senate passed a bill which differed only slightly from the House bill. The House quickly accepted the Senate version, and on July 2 President Johnson signed it into law as the Civil Rights Act of 1964.

The act, in many ways a direct response to the demands enunciated during the Birmingham campaign, was the most comprehensive civil rights law passed by Congress since the Reconstruction era. Among other things, it outlawed racial discrimination in hotels, restaurants, theaters, gas stations, and other public accommodations affecting interstate commerce; forbade racial discrimination by either employers or labor unions having more than a hundred employees or members; created the Federal Equal Employment Opportunity Commission to administer the employment discrimination provisions; established the Community Relations Service to help conciliate racial disputes; and gave the Attorney General the power to bring enforcement suits against public accommodation owners who discriminated and on behalf of persons whose constitutional rights had been violated in segregation cases.

This, at last, was the sweeping federal legislation that civil rights leaders had been seeking for decades. The democratic political process had finally been unfrozen, and the Good Friday march in Birmingham had played a major role in that development.

The exact price of the Good Friday march had not yet been paid, however. The reckoning would come in the courts, beginning first in the Alabama supreme court. During the month of June 1963, Inc. Fund attorneys Norman Amaker and Leroy Clark spent much of their time drafting a brief to that court on behalf of the convicted ministers.

Although Alabama, like most states, has two levels of appellate court review, a peculiarity of state law allows persons convicted of contempt of court to skip the intermediate stage and petition the state's highest court to exercise its discretion to review the trial court proceedings. This was what the Alabama supreme court had agreed to do when, on May 15, 1963, it granted the petition of the eleven ministers for a writ of certiorari asking for review of their convictions. Consenting to review the convictions was, of course, an entirely different matter from reversing them, and the Inc. Fund lawyers had few illusions about their chances for success. Their general view of Southern state appellate courts—and of the problems faced there by civil rights activists—was reflected in an essay written in 1965 by a former Inc. Fund staff attorney, Michael Meltsner. Meltsner observed that although state judges had a duty to follow the decisions of the U.S. Supreme Court, in practice they often did not do so:

> Negroes cannot rely on southern state courts to uphold the supremacy of Federal law. In order to maintain the status quo, state judges have not hesitated to evade or ignore Federal law and to exploit a deeply rooted national tradition of deference to local authority. . . . Occasionally, there are shows of prudence and duty from state appellate courts, but they are not frequent enough to rely upon and usually flow from a recognition that a Federal court will ultimately reverse the conviction. Generally, the higher state courts rubber-stamp the outrages of their inferiors. At the worst, state appellate courts throw up obstacles to review of their decisions by the U.S. Supreme Court.

One of the devices used by Southern appellate courts to defeat constitutional claims raised by civil rights activists, Meltsner noted, was to avoid deciding questions involving those rights. If, for example, the highest court of a state refused to decide a freedom-of-speech question (an issue of federal law), and instead based its decision on state rules of procedure, the U.S. Supreme Court would ordinarily not review the case out of deference to the principle of state autonomy in our federal system. This was known as the "adequate state ground" doctrine. As Meltsner noted, this doctrine did have some limitations; the Supreme Court could, if it chose, examine "whether the principle of state law is substantial and has been applied fairly." In recent years it had on several occasions decided that state procedural grounds were not substantial enough to prevent it from exercising review. Nevertheless, lawyers for civil rights litigants had to be constantly alert to avoid even a minor procedural misstep in the state courts, for fear that the court would seize upon it as a basis for deciding the case.

From the point of view of the Inc. Fund lawyers, the record of Alabama's highest court in civil rights cases was about the worst of any Southern appellate court. One study of the disposition of civil rights cases in Southern supreme courts, done by political scientist Kenneth Vines, showed that between 1954 and 1963 Negro litigants before the Alabama supreme court won only 7.7 percent of the cases which involved any kind of civil rights issue. For the South as a whole the figure was 29.2 percent. Vines, like Meltsner, observed that many of the decisions unfavorable to black litigants were couched in terms of state procedural requirements. *Walker v. City of Birmingham* (as the case was now titled on the appeal) was, of course, a case in which the Alabama supreme court could readily invoke a state procedural rule—that the validity of an injunction can be tested only by a motion to dissolve the injunction.

Working on the brief for King and the other ministers, Amaker and Clark took care to include all the constitutional points they had previously raised in Judge Jenkins' court.

They particularly stressed the argument that the injunction was an invalid order—an unconstitutional restraint on First Amendment rights. Since it was void to start with, they argued, it was not unlawful for the ministers to participate in the marches; the injunction was "a nullity." Jack Greenberg and Constance Motley reviewed the brief and made some relatively minor revisions in it, and copies were then sent to the Alabama supreme court and the city's attorneys.

Less than a month after the Inc. Fund's brief had been filed, Matt Breckenridge and Earl McBee submitted the city's brief. They responded to all of the arguments made by the Inc. Fund attorneys, attempting, for example, to show that the permit ordinance and the injunction were reasonable measures designed to protect the safety of Birmingham's citizenry. But their primary point was that Alabama law did not allow questions about the validity of the injunction to be raised in a contempt proceeding or on review of a contempt conviction. It was an argument clearly calculated to appeal to the Alabama supreme court's penchant for avoiding constitutional questions and resting decisions in civil rights cases on state procedural law.

Since the Inc. Fund attorneys had made no request for oral argument, feeling that it would be futile, Breckenridge and McBee felt no need to do so either. On August 22, 1963, the case was officially accepted on the briefs and trial transcript alone. By long tradition, the seven-man Alabama high court was divided into two "divisions." Each consisted of three justices plus the chief justice. The *Walker* appeal was assigned to the division sitting that day, made up of chief justice J. Edwin Livingston, and associate justices Thomas Lawson, John Goodwyn, and James S. Coleman, Jr. One of these four men would have primary responsibility for studying the case and preparing an opinion for the court, to be reviewed by the other three. Only if there were a dissent within the four-member panel would the full seven-member court become involved in the review process. It was not known by anyone outside the court at the time, but the case was assigned (on the basis of the court's regular random assignment procedure) to Justice Coleman, a jurist who was famous for his long delays in getting opinions written.

10

From Birmingham to Selma

IF THE BIRMINGHAM contempt case had reached the U.S. Supreme Court in 1964 or 1965, when memories of Bull Connor's police dogs were still fresh and national support for civil rights groups was at an all-time high, it is hard to resist the conclusion that the justices would have found a way to void the convictions of the Birmingham leaders. But *Walker v. Birmingham* was not to arrive in 1964 or 1965. It was being aged slowly in the cask of the Alabama supreme court, and while it was, King moved into a series of new protest campaigns.

One of the recurring problems for King that carried over from Birmingham was how he should respond to court orders banning his demonstrations. Two of King's next campaigns—St. Augustine in 1964 and Selma in 1965—illustrate how critical the courts were, for good or ill, in his struggles against racial injustice.

St. Augustine, Florida, reputedly the oldest city in the United States, is a small town of fifteen thousand (one-quarter black) on the eastern coast of central Florida. During the early 1960s it was one of the most thoroughly segregationist communities in Florida, with a large Klan membership in the town and region, a far-right-wing political leadership, and a local court system that provided little justice for its Negro residents. In 1961, when the student sit-in movement reached St. Augustine, it was typical of the town's style that students from the local Negro college sitting-in at a variety store were locked inside and then severely beaten by Klansmen without hindrance by the police or later action by prosecutors. The local sheriff, L. O. Davis, maintained an auxiliary force of about a hundred special deputies, among them many well-known Klansmen or Klan sympathizers.

In May 1964 King came to St. Augustine to help lead what would become the last major campaign against segregation in public accommodation facilities. Since St. Augustine's economy was heavily dependent on the tourist industry, it seemed a particularly appropriate place to dramatize the need for the public accommodations legislation that was then pending in Congress. The tactics used in the campaign were similar to those used at the start of the Birmingham campaign a year earlier—mass meetings in Negro churches to rouse the support of the black community, requests by interracial groups for service in St. Augustine's restaurants and motel coffee shops, wade-ins at segregationist beaches, and protest marches through the center of the town.

The reaction of the white townspeople was significantly different from the responses of whites in Birmingham a year earlier. In Birmingham whites had largely ignored the protesters, the police had been relatively restrained in their handling of the demonstrations (at least until these reached a peak in early May), and some whites had been willing to participate in negotiations. In St. Augustine, though, there were no negotiations, and groups of white toughs repeatedly attacked the demonstrators, undisturbed by the police. On May 28, for example, after black demonstrators had marched to the center of town and were kneeling in prayer, local police and sheriff's deputies looked on passively while club-wielding white men attacked the demonstrators and beat newsmen covering the vigil. No arrests were made. The response of Sheriff Davis was to ban all further night marches; efforts to hold a march the next night were forcibly blocked by local police and state troopers.

With the danger of violence rapidly escalating, King decided to avoid a confrontation on the streets, and turned to the courts—this time seeking to use the judiciary's injunctive powers to aid the civil rights forces. He went to Jacksonville with William Kunstler and other SCLC lawyers to ask federal judge Bryan Simpson to issue an order that would permit the night marches to be held. Judge Simpson held a hearing at which evidence of Sheriff Davis' racist law enforcement practices was brought out in considerable detail. On June 9 he issued an injunction which directed the sheriff and other St. Augustine officials to stop banning the night marches, cease imposing excessive bail for arrested civil rights demonstrators, and provide humane living conditions in the jail.

Judge Simpson's order allowed the night marches to resume, but his admonitions to St. Augustine's officials did not result in an end to white violence. White toughs carrying bicycle chains and iron pipes still assaulted Negroes when they marched through town or tried to swim at "white" beaches. Throughout the month of June there were repeated instances of blacks being attacked and beaten without any police action being taken—and, incredibly, without violent reprisals by St. Augustine's blacks. Martin Luther King called the town the "most lawless" community the SCLC had ever worked in.

Even after July 2, when the Civil Rights Act was signed into law, many businesses in St. Augustine still failed to comply with it, and Klansmen continued to attack Negroes who tried to use public accommodation facilities. However, a new weapon had been added to the legal arsenal by the Civil Rights Act: SCLC lawyers went to federal court and secured an order requiring St. Augustine hotels, motels, and restaurants to serve Negroes—an order that would not have been granted prior to passage of the act. The order also enjoined any individual from interfering with Negroes exercising their rights under federal law. Faced with contempt charges themselves if they did not obey the injunction, local businessmen and politicians announced that "everybody must abide by the law, whether we like it or not." It was clear that the injunction issued by a federal judge had been critical in the "success" that Dr. King declared the St. Augustine campaign to be.

Other racial events in mid-1964 suddenly drew attention away from the SCLC's campaigns. On July 18 riots broke out in Harlem, beginning the first "long hot summer" of urban racial violence. Rochester, Jersey City, Philadelphia, and other cities exploded in rioting (generally within the black communities), set off by seemingly minor events. The ghetto tensions produced widespread shootings, looting, burning of cars and stores, and police pacification campaigns. It was, to some commentators, the summer that civil rights leaders lost control of the black revolt. The leaders were still generally able to call the shots in their own protest efforts. But their authority did not run into the depths of the ghettos, where achieving the right to eat in restaurants alongside whites did not help with the problems of unemployment, drugs, and despair.

The second half of 1964 was also the period when civil rights workers Andrew Goodman, Michael Schwerner, and James Cheney were killed in Mississippi; when the black-led Mississippi Freedom Democratic Party walked out of the Democratic national convention; when Martin Luther King, Jr., received the Nobel Peace Prize; and when J. Edgar Hoover called King the "most notorious liar in the country," in response to King's complaint that FBI agents in the South were not vigilant in protecting civil rights.

As 1965 began, the top political priority of the civil rights leaders was to get federal legislation to protect Negro voting rights. Before the year was half over, one community—Selma, Alabama—would prove the key through which King mobilized national opinion on the voting rights issue. And it was in Selma that King would be put to his most painful personal test on the issue of how to respond to a court injunction.

Selma, the county seat of Dallas County, was a town of 13,000 whites and 14,500 blacks, located in the heart of Alabama's "black belt." The town had been occupied by a black regiment at the close of the Civil War, but ever since the end of Reconstruction, whites had been firmly in control of its political, economic, and social life. The franchise was one important instrument of control. In January 1965, fewer than 2 percent of Selma's black residents were registered to vote. Local officials used a variety of devices, including manipulation of the times of voter registration and arbitrary administration of literacy tests, to forestall black voter registration. It would take massive pressure locally, or a new federal law, to open up the ballot box.

SNCC and SCLC organizers had tried several times to get civil rights campaigns started in Selma during the early 1960s, but had consistently been met with determined white resistance. Federal courts had been no help either, mainly because Dallas County was in the territorial jurisdiction of the federal district court presided over by an old-line Southern conservative named Daniel A. Thomas. Like many Southern federal judges, Judge Thomas was not a blatant segregationist, but he interpreted the Supreme Court's equality rulings as narrowly as possible. When civil rights lawyers brought a suit challenging the Dallas County voting registrars' discriminatory practices, he was characteristically reluctant to intervene.

Martin Luther King arrived in Selma on January 2, 1965, while a black voter registration drive was already under way. He told an audience of seven hundred blacks that the drive had to be stepped up dramatically, since only with the vote could the Negroes who made up the majority of Selma's population (and of the Alabama black belt as a whole) win the rights to which they were entitled. He called for willingness to ''go to jail by the thousands.''

During the rest of January, SCLC staff aides repeatedly led Selma Negroes on marches to the county courthouse to appear before voting registrars. On the afternoon of January 18 King himself led a group of five hundred marchers to the courthouse. After standing in line for a long time, they were told by Dallas County sheriff Jim Clark that they should go home because no registrars were working that day. At a church rally the same evening, King warned that if local or state officials did not act promptly to reform the registration system, thousands would march and fill the jails ''to arouse the federal government.''

Demonstrations were stepped up during the last two weeks of January, and they increasingly began to evoke harsher responses. Sheriff Clark and his deputies started arresting the marchers on charges such as unlawful assembly—and handling them roughly in doing so. Clark, like Bull Connor, was precisely the type of adversary the nonviolent movement needed: a symbol of the white South's rawest kind of resistance to black equality demands.

On the morning of Monday, February 1, King, Abernathy, and the local Selma leaders set off at the head of 750 marchers, many of them students, to demonstrate in the downtown area. The marchers were all arrested and jailed, and another five hundred were jailed the next day. While King was in jail, Inc. Fund lawyers went before Judge Thomas seeking an order to forbid Sheriff Clark from interfering with blacks who were attempting to register. Judge Thomas announced that "unnecessary arrests have been made" but said they were "provoked by unnecessary assemblage by people at improper places." He ordered the sheriff to issue numbers 1 to 100 to those appearing on regularly scheduled days, and directed the registrars to meet "more often" than once every two weeks to handle the numbered registrants. The registrars did, but they also adopted the practice of asking such detailed and complex questions of each applicant that, after three full days of registration proceedings and with hundreds of Negroes waiting in line, only seventy persons had been processed. Judge Thomas subsequently amended his order to forbid such questioning at length, directed the work to be speeded up, and ruled that no one could be arrested for "peacefully" encouraging Negroes to secure their voting rights.

After remaining in jail for four days, King was released. He announced immediately that he was going to Washington to urge President Johnson's support for strong new federal voting rights legislation. Harry Wachtel, one of King's lawyers, was delegated to call the White House and try to arrange for a meeting between King and LBJ. The initial response was distinctly negative: the President's reaction was that "nobody—not even a Nobel Prize winner—had the right to invite himself to the White House." Moreover, White House advisers were preoccupied with a sudden new problem. A crisis was developing in Southeast Asia, which by the following Tuesday would lead to the first U.S. bombing of North Vietnam. Wachtel persisted, however, and ultimately a compromise was arranged under which King would meet on Tuesday, February 9, with Vice-President Hubert Humphrey and Attorney General Nicholas Katzenbach.

At the meeting Humphrey expressed doubts about Congress passing another civil rights bill so soon after the 1964 act. But he acknowledged that it might do so "if the pressure was unrelenting." King also met briefly with the President on the same day; he stated afterward that the meeting had been "very successful," with the President assuring him of the Administration's commitment to the removal of all barriers to voting.

King's talks in Washington had reinforced his conviction that only an expansion of the Selma conflict could provide the necessary heat to produce federal voting rights legislation. During February the size and tempo of the demonstrations increased. Sheriff Clark and his forces responded by adopting even more aggressive tactics than before, including the use of electric cattle prods. Now the voting drive and Selma's reaction to it had become front-page and prime-time news, and whites, especially Northern clergymen, were coming to join the marchers. By mid-February, Sheriff Clark had arrested more than three thousand persons, the jails were filled, law enforcement resources were strained, the local courts were overflowing with trials, and world attention was riveted on the events.

On Friday, March 5, King announced that a fifty-five-mile march from Selma to Montgomery would begin that Sunday, to call on Governor George C. Wallace and the state legislature to enforce voting rights for Negroes. SCLC minister Hosea Williams and SNCC leader John Lewis would lead the march, since King had to be back in Atlanta for Palm Sunday services. The following day, Governor Wallace issued an order forbidding the march and directed Colonel Al Lingo, head of the state troopers, to stop the blacks in any way necessary.

On Sunday, March 7, with large press and TV contingents on hand, five hundred people marched to Edmund Pettus Bridge. The bridge crossed the Alabama River; on the other side was the four-lane highway leading to Montgomery. On the Selma side of the bridge, Sheriff Clark was waiting with his armed deputies; on the far side of the bridge were state highway troopers with gas masks in place and mounted troopers carrying clubs and bullwhips. Sheriff Clark's men stepped aside to let the marchers onto the bridge. When they were halfway over, trooper Major John Cloud shouted through his bullhorn that the marchers had "two minutes" to turn about.

Even before the two minutes had expired, the troopers were ordered forward. Those on foot rushed onto the bridge, clubs flailing, followed by mounted troopers who lashed the marchers with bullwhips. Canisters of tear gas and nausea gas were thrown, and the marchers were caught in clouds of choking fumes. Bloody, limping, and gasping for breath, they were driven back across the bridge to the Selma side. There, Sheriff Clark's men pushed and clubbed them on to "Colored Town." Sixteen blacks had been seriously injured, and forty more were given hospital treatment. John Lewis had a fractured skull.

By nightfall Selma was the object of national and international rage. In Montgomery, Governor Wallace stated that the action of the troopers saved many lives since, had the blacks crossed the bridge, they could not have been protected against angry whites along the march route. In Atlanta, a shocked Martin Luther King announced that he would personally lead a Selma-to-Montgomery march within forty-eight hours.

The next day, Monday, March 8, SCLC lawyers went to federal district court in Montgomery seeking an injunction to restrain Governor Wallace, Colonel Lingo, and Sheriff Clark from interfering with the protesters' right to assemble and demonstrate to redress their grievances over deprivation of the right to vote. The lawyers specifically asked the court to protect their right to walk peaceably along the public highway between Selma and Montgomery.

By naming Wallace as a defendant and filing the suit in Montgomery, the SCLC lawyers were able to keep the case out of Judge Thomas' court and have it heard instead by Judge Frank Johnson, who presided over the district in which

Montgomery was located. Johnson had been one of the judges on the three-judge court that had declared Montgomery's bus segregation unconstitutional in 1956. He had also issued the broad injunction restraining the Klan from interfering with the Freedom Riders in 1961. Getting the case before Judge Johnson seemed like a shrewd tactical move from the standpoint of the lawyers seeking a favorable ruling on the injunction application, but it quickly had the effect of placing King in an acute dilemma. Judge Johnson, noting that some of the defendants (Wallace *et al.*) had not been notified of the application, denied the request for an immediate restraining order and set down the matter for a full hearing on Thursday, March 11. Knowing that a march was planned for the following day, Tuesday, March 9, he also enjoined any further demonstrations until the Thursday hearing could be held.

This brought King face to face again with the "obedience to court orders" issue. After his experiences in Albany, Birmingham, Gadsden, and Danville, he found himself facing a federal injunction against a march that he had pledged he would lead, at a time when a tremendous emotional response was building up in Selma and throughout the country. One thing he was certain of—there had to be a response to the outrageous brutality on the bridge on Sunday. As Andy Young recalled the mood in King's headquarters, "There just had to be a march, some kind of nonviolent demonstration to get the expression out. If there wasn't, you would have had real violence. You just can't turn off the spiggot, not in a religious movement where confronting wrong is absolutely fundamental. This was not the NAACP, and as we looked around the room at the bandages and bruises, we knew we had to do something." Furthermore, Young recalls, "King was not in the position of a general giving orders to obedient officers and disciplined troops. He was trying to guide people already moving under their own power, in an open leadership format. We knew that whatever we did, the SNCC people—

like John Lewis—were going to be on that bridge, and the real question was, 'Who would lead the people, and in what?' "

It was not only the emotional needs of the local people and the pressure from the militants, though. King himself was highly sensitive to the charge that he had abandoned the battlefield just before the big attack, leaving others to face danger and punishment. Writing later in 1965, King said, "I shall never forget my agony of conscience for not being there, when I heard of the dastardly acts perpetrated against nonviolent demonstrators that Sunday. As a result, I felt I had to lead a march." This was always the dilemma for King—to show by his own willingness to march up to the assembled police and troopers, to be arrested, to go to jail, and to endure mistreatment that he was not asking his followers to do anything that he himself would not do. Moreover, whites and blacks were already streaming into Selma from all over the country, and to call off the march now might produce a collapse like the one in Albany three years earlier.

Yet there were powerful considerations on the other side of the ledger too. King remained keenly aware of the important role that the federal courts in general continued to play in helping the Negro's cause. Just a year earlier, for example, the U.S. Supreme Court had overturned the $500,000 libel judgment against four black Alabama ministers and *The New York Times* that had been awarded to Montgomery city commissioner L. B. Sullivan back in 1960. This had been a critical decision for the SCLC; an adverse ruling could have bankrupted King's organization. And in a myriad of other situations where the civil rights forces were attacking inequality, the federal courts were counted on for assistance. Furthermore, Judge Johnson was one of the strongest protectors of civil rights in the federal judiciary, South or North.

There was also President Johnson and the Justice Department. The President had contacted King on Monday, even before the federal injunction had been issued, asking him not to respond to the Sunday attack with a march that might lead to large-scale bloodshed. King had replied that he had to march. When Judge Johnson signed the injunction on Monday, he handed it to John Doar, the Justice Department aide who had been active in getting federal court injunctions against Southern registrars, sheriffs, and other local officials who were denying Negroes constitutional rights, and who had gotten to know King and the SCLC people fairly well during the previous four years. Doar spoke personally with King by telephone. "This is a *federal* order," he stressed, "issued by a strong and solid judge who has enforced Negro rights time after time. The Department of Justice will have no choice but to protect the integrity of the federal courts. We'll have to support Judge Johnson." Doar expressed his confidence that at the Thursday hearing King's right to demonstrate would be protected. He urged King to wait and let the court formulate some rules for holding the march. Finally, from Washington came the report of a public statement from President Johnson asking Dr. King to postpone his march. The message was clear: to march in violation of the injunction would severely strain, perhaps rupture, the existing helpful relations between King and the Johnson Administration.

As Monday afternoon and evening wore on, King and his advisers sat in their hotel room balancing the pros and cons. King's lawyers talked by phone at length with Attorney General Katzenbach, who consistently urged that the march be postponed. At 4 A.M. King told his aides he had made a decision: "It's better to die on the highway than make a butchery of my conscience," he declared, then went to bed. An hour later the telephone rang; Katzenbach was making a direct appeal to King to hold off the march until the court hearing. Katzenbach went over the salient points, while King stressed the police brutality, the voting rights to which Negroes were entitled, and the justice of their demonstration. Finally, King made the ultimate argument: "Mr. Attorney General, you have not been a black man in America for three hundred years." The conversation ended with no promises given. Katzenbach recalls feeling that King probably would not violate the injunction, and was trying to find some way not to, but that the issue was still in doubt.

Then King had another telephone call, from former Florida governor Leroy Collins, the head of the Federal Community Relations Service. He too tried to persuade King to cancel the march—now only hours away—but King said he couldn't do that. Collins went next to the Pettus Bridge to talk to Lingo and Clark. The two agreed that there would be no trouble if the marchers simply crossed the bridge and stopped short of Route 80, where the troopers would be stationed. Collins then explained the situation to King, and asked him to "stop your people on the far side until we can get this thing straightened out in court." According to one account of that meeting, "The pastor began to smile. Incredibly, there was a way out of this mess. Incredibly . . ."

Before the march was scheduled to begin, King's lawyers had a final conference via telephone. As Harry Wachtel remembers it, nobody discussed the possibility that there might not be a march; the lawyers were concerned with what the probable consequences would be and what legal steps the attorneys should be prepared to take. Jack Greenberg and Wachtel differed on what to expect, with Greenberg taking the view that application of the *Mine Workers* doctrine would result in contempt convictions that would be very difficult to overturn. Wachtel, who had always believed that the *Mine Workers* doctrine was bad law, was more optimistic about ultimate vindication. When the lawyers concluded their conversation, King instructed Wachtel to call Katzenbach and tell the Attorney General that he was "starting out, injunction or not."

On Tuesday, a lovely early-spring day, the marchers set out from Brown's Chapel, their ranks swelled by blacks and whites from all over the country. After joining in a prayer led by Dr. King, the marchers—fifteen hundred strong—reached the bridge. A hundred yards ahead of them, on Route 80, were the wooden police barricades, with a small army of deputies and troopers behind them. Word had been passed to them that King would turn back, and their weapons remained sheathed. The marchers reached the barricades. Dr. King stopped, then began a prayer. When that was done, he called out, "Turn back, turn around." Somewhat confused but following King's directions, the marchers strode back to the church, where King declared to his audience and the world's press, "We have had the greatest demonstration for freedom today that we have ever had in the South." He emphasized that the marchers—as he had promised—had crossed the bridge.

In Washington, Attorney General Katzenbach sighed in relief. President Johnson realized that he had gained some time, but he read the voting rights situation as still highly volatile, and was at work on a civil rights address to a joint session of Congress. In Selma that night, four white men spotted Rev. James Reeb, a white minister who had been in the march, coming out of a restaurant. They beat him with a two-by-four, crushing his skull, and he died later that night.

In Selma and elsewhere in the nation, some civil rights leaders condemned King for his actions at the Pettus Bridge; they felt he had engaged in a charade, promising to defy a court order but finding a way not to do so. In Washington, however, King's action was regarded by Johnson Administration officials as a measure of high statesmanship and responsibility. "It took tremendous courage for King to do what he did," Burke Marshall stated, "to walk the line between the two contending forces, making his protest without having defied the federal courts."

At a press conference on March 13, President Johnson announced that he was sending to Congress a new voting rights bill, which *The New York Times* called "a sweeping, bipartisan bill to erase all discrimination against citizens seeking to register and vote." Later, appearing before a joint session of Congress to outline the bill and ask for its speedy passage, the President closed his speech with a line from the marching song of the nonviolent protest movement, delivered in his deep southern-Texas accent: "And . . . we . . . shall . . . overcome!"

President Johnson had also announced at his March 13 press conference that he was alerting federal troops near Selma to do whatever was necessary to protect the rights of civil rights demonstrators once these had been clarified by a federal court order. After a meeting with the President, Governor George Wallace said that he would withdraw his order against the Route 80 march if the courts so directed him.

For four and a half days, concluding on March 17, witnesses were heard in Judge Frank Johnson's courtroom in Montgomery on the injunction suit of *Hosea Williams et al. v. Honorable George C. Wallace, et al.* The basic question was whether the First Amendment rights of the marchers would be given preference over the usual limits on interference with vehicle traffic on highways. Beyond that, there was the question of whether threats to the safety of civil rights marchers from white vigilantes gave the state of Alabama reason to ban the march or whether that situation required the state to provide affirmative protection to the marchers. And beyond that was the question whether King had committed contempt by leading the Wednesday march, even though it had stopped short of entering on Route 80. Judge Johnson ordered King, Sheriff Clark, and Colonel Lingo to appear, and subjected them all—especially King—to close questioning.

"Is it correct to say," the judge pressed Dr. King, "that when you started across the bridge, you knew at the time that you did not intend to march to Montgomery?'' ''Yes, it is,'' King answered. ''There was a tacit agreement at the bridge that we would go no further.'' With this statement King was off the hook in terms of contempt, though he paid a price: some civil rights activists charged him with ''betraying'' the cause by engaging in ''behind-the-scenes bargaining.''

Judge Johnson also examined the state troopers, hearing them say that they could not effectively protect the marchers along the fifty-five miles from Selma to Montgomery. But the lawyers for the Selma movement were ready. They presented a detailed ''Plan for March,'' which set out elaborate arrangements for a five-day, peaceful march, moving along the apron of the road so as not to impede traffic, providing mobile kitchen and toilet facilities, and furnishing clean-up squads.

On March 19 Judge Johnson issued his order. He authorized the march, directed the governor and other officials of Alabama to give affirmative protection to the marchers, and recognized the power of the President to use federal troops to augment such protection. Replying to the contention that the march would intrude upon the interests of other citizens using the highway and that it would place a heavy burden on public officials, Judge Johnson spoke of the need to protect Negro rights of demonstration in terms broader than any American court had used before:

> The extent of a group's constitutional right to protest peaceably and petition one's government for redress of grievance must be . . . commensurate with the enormity of the wrongs being protested and petitioned against. This is particularly true when the usual, basic and constitutionally-provided means of protesting in our American way—voting—have been deprived.

Reviewing the continued blockage of Negro voting registration and the police brutality used against demonstrators,

Judge Johnson observed that "in this case, the wrongs are enormous."

On Sunday, March 21, 3,000 marchers set off from Selma under the protective mantle of Judge Johnson's order, 1,800 U.S. Army military policemen, and two U.S. Army helicopters. Once on the highway, the marchers were reduced to 300, as specified by Judge Johnson, and the next four days proved exciting but uneventful. On Thursday morning 20,000 marchers assembled outside Montgomery for the final triumphant entry into the city.

Almost before the success of the march could be celebrated, the press reported the fatal shooting of Mrs. Viola Liuzzo, a white mother who had come to Selma from Detroit to work in the campaign. Again, the nation was confronted with the murder of civil rights workers in the South.

But the renewed violence of the white extremists strengthened the civil rights position in Congress, and the Administration's proposed legislation was passed less than four months later. On August 6 President Johnson signed the Voting Rights Act of 1965, guaranteeing the right to vote, creating federal authority to register voters in cases of obstruction by local officials, restricting the use of discriminatory questioning of potential voters, and starting a process of extending the franchise that promised, in the end, to transform the face of Southern politics. Signing day was a glorious occasion, with civil rights leaders arrayed around the President as he signed the historic act. Every editor and political analyst agreed that passage of the Voting Rights Act had been the result of the Selma crisis and that it might otherwise have taken years for such legislation to emerge from Congress.

Then, on August 11, less than a week after President Johnson signed the Voting Rights Act into law, a five-day riot erupted in the predominantly black Watts district of Los Angeles. It resulted in thirty-four deaths, over eight hundred injuries, more than three thousand arrests, and property damage in the millions of dollars. President Johnson issued a statement on August 15 condemning the violence. "Those who strike at the fabric of ordered liberty," he said, "also erode the foundations on which the house of justice stands. The enforcement of this truth is the responsibility of all Americans, and is a special challenge to the Negro community and those who are its leaders." Former Attorney General Ramsey Clark recalls that "when word of the Watts riot came in, everything seemed to collapse. The days of 'We Shall Overcome' were over."

While all the momentous events of 1964 and 1965 were going on, the Alabama supreme court was saying absolutely nothing about the contempt case submitted back in the summer of 1963. Delays in deciding cases were not unusual in the Alabama supreme court during this period. The court invariably had a huge backlog of undecided cases, and its slowness in rendering opinions was a chronic source of complaints by lawyers. But even by the court's own standards two years was an unusually long period to hold a case. Since all of the ministers were free on bond, however, and since the Inc. Fund lawyers had a myriad of other cases to worry about—many of them regarded, at the time, as far more serious than *Walker v. City of Birmingham*—no one involved in the case was particularly concerned about the delay.

Justice James S. Coleman, Jr., who had been assigned primary responsibility for drafting the court's opinion in the case, was a native Alabaman, as were the other three justices on the "division" of the court in which he was sitting during this period. Born in Mobile, Coleman had been raised in Eutaw, Alabama, in the heart of the "black belt," where his father had been a public figure of some prominence as the editor for thirty-seven years of the *Greene County Democrat*. After graduating from the University of Alabama Law School in 1934, Coleman practiced law for several years in Eutaw, then joined the Navy at the outbreak of World War II. After the war he turned to politics, and served for eight years in the Alabama state senate before being elected to the state's supreme court in 1956. In 1963, when he was assigned to the case of *Walker v. Birmingham,* Justice Coleman was fifty-seven years old. Balding, with a fringe of white hair, and wearing wire-rimmed glasses, he had a somewhat scholarly appearance.

Coleman was a strong segregationist, and so too were the other three justices who would decide the case. Chief justice J. Edwin Livingston, a former University of Alabama law professor who knew most of the members of the Alabama bar on a first-name basis, was particularly outspoken on the issue. "I'm for segregation in every phase of life and I don't care who knows it," he had said a few years earlier, adding that "I would rather close every school from the highest to the lowest before I would go to school with colored people." The other two justices on the panel, Thomas ("Buster") Lawson and John Goodwyn, were less vociferous about their views, but no less consistent in their handling of cases involving civil rights issues.

Alabama's "Judicial Building," where the state's supreme court is located, fronts on Dexter Avenue in Montgomery, not far from the church where Martin Luther King began his career as a minister and civil rights leader. A former Scottish Rite temple which had been remodeled in 1940 for use by the judiciary, the building in 1965 housed not only the supreme court, but also the Alabama court of appeals, the state's intermediate appellate court. It was to the latter court that appeals would ordinarily be taken in criminal cases (contempt cases were a special exception), and in due course some of the cases involving misdemeanor convictions arising out of the 1963 Birmingham demonstrations found their way to it. One of the first cases involved the recorder's court conviction of

Fred Shuttlesworth, who, like King and Abernathy, had been arrested on Good Friday for violation of the parade-permit ordinance (a misdemeanor) as well as for violation of the injunction. In a 2–1 decision which surprised almost everyone, the court of appeals ruled in November 1965, in *Shuttlesworth v. Birmingham,* that the misdemeanor conviction should be reversed because the parade-permit ordinance was unconstitutional. Agreeing with arguments advanced by the Inc. Fund lawyers, Judge Aubrey Cates wrote a forceful opinion for the majority that held the ordinance invalid on two grounds: it left city officials unfettered discretion to regulate peaceful expressions of views on the streets, and it had been administered in a racially discriminatory manner.

The chagrined city attorneys, Matt Breckenridge and Earl McBee, announced immediately that they would seek to have the decision reviewed by the Alabama supreme court. The Inc. Fund lawyers were delighted as well as surprised; their belief that the ordinance was invalid had now been vindicated by Alabama judges. Both sides knew, however, that the Alabama supreme court could easily reverse the court of appeals. Moreover, the court of appeals' decision reversing the misdemeanor conviction would not control the disposition of the contempt case; as McBee and Breckenridge were quick to point out, different evidence had been introduced in the contempt trial, and other issues were involved. Because of the crucial role that injunctions could play in combating protest movements, it was the contempt case which was by far the more important of the two.

On December 9, 1965, a month after the court of appeals' decision had been announced (though more than twenty-seven months after the briefs of the parties had been submitted to it), the Alabama supreme court rendered its opinion in *Walker v. City of Birmingham.* Written by Justice Coleman, it had the concurrence of all the justices on the panel.

Justice Coleman began his opinion with a lengthy review of the testimony dealing with the press conference and the two protest marches. This evidence, he found, clearly established that the protest leaders had violated the terms of the injunction: "Petitioners did engage in and incite others to engage in mass street parades and neither petitioners nor anyone else had obtained a permit to parade on the streets of Birmingham." From there, Coleman went on to deal adroitly with the Inc. Fund's basic contention that the conviction could not stand because the injunction itself was void. He did not respond directly to the argument that the injunction was invalid because it abridged the defendants' First Amendment rights, nor did he discuss any of the earlier Alabama cases which had indicated that a contempt conviction could be upset if an injunction was "void on its face." Instead, he simply cited Alabama statutes which provided that circuit courts had the power to issue injunctions, noted that the defendants had made no motion to dissolve the injunction until after the Good Friday and Easter marches, and then quoted at length from U.S. Chief Justice Fred Vinson's 1946 opinion in the *United Mine Workers* case. The quotation included a portion of Vinson's opinion which cited the high court's 1920 decision in *Howat v. Kansas* as "impressive authority for the proposition that an order issued by the court with jurisdiction over the subject matter and person must be obeyed by the parties until it is reversed by orderly and proper proceedings." "This is true," Vinson's opinion had said, referring specifically to the *Howat* case, "without regard even for the constitutionality of the Act under which the order is issued."

For Justice Coleman, the extensive quotation from Vinson's opinion was a sufficient treatment of the law on the question of whether the injunction had to be obeyed. "No useful purpose would be served," he said, "by further discussion of this point.'' Relying explicitly on the case of *Howat v. Kansas* as support for the constitutionality of his position, he framed the court's ground for deciding the case in terms of a state rule of procedural law:

> We hold that the circuit court had the duty and authority, in the first instance, to determine the validity of the ordinance, and, until the decision of the circuit court is reversed for error by orderly review, either by the circuit court or a higher court, the orders of the circuit court based on its decision are to be respected and disobedience of them is contempt of its lawful authority, to be punished.

Having thus stated the governing rule of law, Justice Coleman went on to review briefly the evidence related to the only questions left to decide: whether there was proof that each of the petitioners had (1) received notice of the injunction, and (2) violated it ''knowingly.'' Petitioners King, Abernathy, Walker, Shuttlesworth, and A. D. King, he noted, had been personally served with copies of the injunction on April 11 and were shown by uncontradicted testimony to have been ''active in inciting others to parade'' and to have ''actively participated in the parades or marches'' themselves.

As to the other six ministers, the case was less clear. Justice Coleman held that the judgments against Porter, Hayes, and Fisher should be affirmed because there was sufficient evidence that they had participated in the parades after having had adequate notice of the injunction. Finding that it was not clear whether Smith had had actual knowledge about the injunction, and that there was no evidence that Young and Bevels had participated in either of the two marches, he concluded that the conviction of these three should be quashed.

The affirmances of the convictions of Martin Luther King and the other key protest leaders came as no surprise. From the first stages of the case, the lawyers for both sides had felt that there was a good chance that the case would ultimately have to be decided by the U.S. Supreme Court. It was to that court that the lawyers would next turn their attention.

The setting for the Inc. Fund's appeal to the high court was somewhat bleaker than they would have wished. A week after the Watts riot was over in August, California governor Edmund Brown appointed an eight-member commission headed by former CIA chief John McCone to explore the underlying causes and suggest preventive measures for the future. The 101-page McCone Commission report, made public on December 6, 1965, just three days before the Alabama supreme court decision was rendered, cited a number of contributing causes, among them "the rising encouragement of civil disobedience by the civil rights movement." It stated that:

> The accusations of the leaders of the national movement have been picked up by many local voices and have been echoed throughout the Negro community here. As we have said in the opening chapter of this report, the angry exhortations and the resulting disobedience of the law in many parts of our nation appear to have contributed importantly to the feeling of rage which made the Los Angeles riots possible.

Martin Luther King had toured Watts after the riots, in the company of Bayard Rustin. King's message, delivered in the streets and at many meetings, was that rioting was not the way; that nonviolence was the only means of carrying forward the struggle of black Americans for jobs, rights, and justice. Rustin recalls that there was anger and doubt in the faces of the Watts residents. They were not kept from registering and voting; they could use any public accommodations that they had the money to pay for. But they had either low-paying jobs or no jobs, and their status as second-class citizens was even more complicated and difficult to work upon than the overt, unlawful racism that Negroes faced in the South, and that King had been able to confront head on. "The day of Birmingham was over," Rustin felt. Now that equal access to public accommodations and the right to vote had been guaranteed by federal law, it would take new strategies to develop an economic and political program for the civil rights struggle.

The summer of 1965 was also the time when King criticized President Lyndon Johnson's decision to order additional American troops into the Vietnam conflict. For many civil rights leaders and Negro-Americans, this was not an event directly related to the struggle for equality. But to Martin Luther King, Jr., winner of the Nobel Peace Prize in 1964, it was an issue on which he had to express himself. At a speech before SCLC affiliates in Virginia in early July, he began to speak out against escalating the war, warning that there must be a negotiated settlement with the Vietcong and the North Vietnamese. "The war in Vietnam must be stopped," he declared, threatening that if this was not done, he would call on his followers to organize peace rallies and teach-ins. This drew angry responses from Johnson Administration officials and civil rights leaders alike: stick to the struggle for equality, King was told, where he knew what was what and where his leadership was needed. King's answer was firm: "I'm not going to sit by and see the war escalated without saying anything about it. It is worthless to talk about integrating if there is no world to integrate in."

Even before the Watts riot, King had begun to think of a campaign aimed at the social and economic injustices suffered by Negroes outside the South. After witnessing the destruction wrought by the rioting and sensing the pervasive despair among blacks in Watts and other urban ghettos outside the South, his mind was made up. The next campaign would aim at discrimination in a Northern city. Chicago was chosen as the target; discrimination in housing would be the central issue.

11

Gaining Entry to the Supreme Court

DURING THE EARLY MONTHS of 1966, while King and his aides were making plans for their forthcoming Chicago campaign, the lawyers for the Inc. Fund went back to work on the contempt case. Their first task was to prepare a petition to the Supreme Court for a writ of certiorari, asking the nation's highest court to review the Alabama supreme court's decision.

As the Inc. Fund lawyers were aware, such review was by no means guaranteed. Even though a case may involve important questions of federal law, and thus be technically eligible for review by the Supreme Court, so many appeals are presented to the justices (almost three thousand in 1965–66) that, to be sure they have time for careful consideration of the most critical ones, the justices accept only about 250 cases each year for review on the merits.

As experienced court watchers know, however, some kinds of cases are virtually certain to be reviewed. In 1952, for example, when a federal court declared that President Truman's seizure of the nation's steel mills was unconstitutional, there was little doubt that the Supreme Court would review the decision. *Walker v. City of Birmingham* was not quite as sure a bet for review, but the Inc. Fund lawyers were fairly confident that the court would agree to hear it. For one thing, its First Amendment issues were important, the sort that the justices had been grappling with throughout the 1960s. For another, the case involved a jail sentence for the leading spokesman of the black protest movement in America; it seemed highly unlikely that the justices would decline to scrutinize an Alabama supreme court mandate jailing Martin Luther King.

Since only four "aye" votes are necessary for certiorari to be granted, the Inc. Fund lawyers had to convince any four justices that the case warranted in-depth consideration. But they were also concerned about the influence their presentation of facts and legal arguments would have on the ultimate disposition of their case. The justices would be getting their first view of the case through the petition.

One particularly thorny problem was how to deal with the "adequate state ground" doctrine. In affirming the contempt convictions of the eight ministers, the Alabama supreme court had stressed that Alabama law did not allow the constitutionality of an injunction to be challenged in a contempt proceeding. The attorneys for the city would be sure to claim that this Alabama procedural rule provided a constitutionally adequate basis for deciding the case, and that the U.S. Supreme Court was therefore precluded from considering the petitioners' arguments about the parade ordinance and First Amendment rights. The precedent of the Supreme Court's 1922 decision in *Howat v. Kansas* added force to this argument, since the court in that case had refused to review a Kansas state court decision holding that the constitutional validity of an injunction could not be attacked in a contempt proceeding. The court's ruling in *Howat* had been unanimous, with the opinion holding that the deference owed to state law in a federal system left the court "no choice" but to dismiss the appeal from the Kansas court, since the matter had been disposed of in the state courts on "principles of general, and not federal law."

Closely related to the problem of how to deal with the "adequate state ground" doctrine was the problem of how to handle the more recent (1947) precedent of the *Mine Workers* case. Although the *Mine Workers* decision did not establish a rule of constitutional law binding on both federal and state courts (rather, it set forth a rule of procedure governing injunctive proceedings only in federal courts), it raised two troublesome problems for the *Walker* case. First, the opinion of Chief Justice Vinson gave explicit endorsement to the *Howat* case, thus giving *Howat* renewed strength as a precedent applicable to proceedings originating in the state courts. Second, embodied in the opinions of both Vinson and Frankfurter were clear statements that, as a matter of general principles desirable for the federal courts, the validity of an injunction should not be decided in a contempt proceeding. Hence the Inc. Fund lawyers were not simply in the position of attacking a state rule of procedure; in challenging the adequacy of the Alabama rule, they would also be challenging a rule that the Supreme Court had thought sufficiently wise legal policy to establish for the federal courts.

This posed a difficult strategic dilemma. Should the Inc. Fund lawyers try to meet the anticipated "adequate state ground" and *Mine Workers* arguments head-on in their petition for certiorari? Or should they focus on other issues, and try to minimize the significance of those two doctrines? King's lawyers were divided on this issue, out of differing estimates of how closely the nine current justices were wedded to the *Mine Workers* principle. Harry Wachtel, citing the court's 1962 decision in *In re Green,* felt that a majority of the justices would welcome an opportunity to overrule *Mine Workers,* or at least limit its applicability. Jack Greenberg and others on the Inc. Fund staff were less sanguine about this possibility. They agreed that the *Mine Workers* doctrine had to be attacked, but they favored an approach which stressed other issues and sought to limit the doctrine rather than overturn it completely. They also wanted to avoid spotlighting the "adequate state ground" problem.

Greenberg's position was adopted and the drafting of the certiorari petition undertaken, mainly by Norman Amaker, Leroy Clark, and James Nabrit III. Amaker and Clark had been in Birmingham at the time of the trial, had worked on the appeal to the Alabama supreme court, and were intimately familiar with the facts of the case and the arguments developed in the lower courts. Nabrit was a long-time Inc. Fund lawyer who had replaced Constance Motley as associate director when in 1965 Mrs. Motley was elected as borough president of Manhattan. Though Nabrit had not been involved in the case previously, he had extensive experience in Supreme Court litigation.

As finally drafted, the Inc. Fund's petition for certiorari was forty-five printed pages in length, and consisted of two main parts. First, a fifteen-page introductory section set forth a detailed history of the case, beginning with an outline of segregation in Birmingham as it stood on the eve of the 1963 demonstrations. This section was designed to show the basic justice of the movement's campaign to hold peaceful demonstrations against racial segregation. It also detailed the efforts made to comply with the parade-permit requirements, and the arbitrary administration of the permit ordinance. Several paragraphs reviewed the attempts made by Lola Hendricks and Fred Shuttlesworth to obtain parade permits from Bull Connor and the trial court's exclusion of evidence showing how Birmingham administered the parade-permit statute.

Next came a twenty-five-page section entitled "Reasons for Granting the Writ." Here King's lawyers stressed that the case presented important questions of constitutional law arising under the First and Fourteenth Amendments, and that these questions had been wrongly decided by the Alabama courts. Their legal arguments were basically the same as those that had been laid out by Amaker and Clark in their initial motions to Judge Jenkins, that Arthur Shores and Jack Greenberg had offered during the trial, and that had been subsequently presented to the Alabama supreme court. They maintained the injunction was unconstitutionally broad and vague; it incorporated a parade-permit ordinance that was clearly unconstitutional because it vested in the licensing officials uncontrolled discretion over the use of the city's streets; evidence of arbitrary administration of the ordinance had been improperly excluded at the trial; and there had been no evidence that the petitioners had participated in an "unlawful" parade.

It was not until two-thirds of the way through the petition that the Inc. Fund lawyers began to discuss the *Mine Workers* rule. This was a deliberate tactic, reflecting the belief of Greenberg and Nabrit that their chances of success—with respect to both the granting of certiorari and the ultimate disposition of the case if certiorari were granted—would be increased if they could show the court that there were other grounds upon which the case could be decided in favor of the eight ministers. Once they reached the *Mine Workers* issue, however, they did not minimize its importance. "First Amendment freedoms may be destroyed," they cautioned, "if citizens may be punished for disobeying *ex parte* injunctive decrees which violate the First Amendment. . . . Plainly, some courts will use the injunctive power to suppress free expression of unpopular ideas. Plainly, the power to enforce unconstitutional law is the power to govern unconstitutionally." To prevent such harm, they maintained, the *Mine Workers* decision should either be distinguished (primarily on the ground that there had been no claim in the *Mine Workers* case that the injunctive order had been unconstitutional or had affected free speech rights) or flatly overruled, as inconsistent with First Amendment rights.

The "adequate state ground" problem was touched on only lightly in the petition. Discussing the *Mine Workers* rule, the lawyers for the Inc. Fund commented that the issue of its applicability in a First Amendment conflict was so vital it could not turn "solely on the basis of local practice or procedure." The *Howat* case was not mentioned at all.

The Inc. Fund's petition was filed with the clerk of the Supreme Court on June 18, 1966. It was a time of trial for King and the civil rights movement generally. Long-simmering factional disputes were breaking out into the open, and the strains of the movement's traditional marching song, "We Shall Overcome," were increasingly competing with shouts of "Black Power!" In Chicago, where the SCLC was centering its efforts during 1966, the problems of maintaining a successful campaign against discriminatory practices were very different from what they had been in Southern cities such as Birmingham and Selma. But on one matter—the issue of whether to obey a court-ordered injunction—Chicago was to pose problems similar to those of the Southern campaigns.

In such a huge city as Chicago, demonstrations involving a few hundred people or even several thousand did not attract the kind of attention they had in the smaller Southern cities. Racial discrimination, though pervasive in areas such as housing, employment, and education, was less blatantly obvious than in the South. The city's political leadership, far from being openly hostile, was publicly friendly, and mayor Richard J. Daley proved to be a far more formidable opponent than Bull Connor in Birmingham or sheriff Jim Clark in Selma. His well-oiled Democratic organization (regarded by professional politicians as the most effectively organized and broadly based urban machine in the country) included many Negroes in its leadership cadres and as recipients of city largesse, and the press spoke of further ties with ghetto criminal elements. When King had discussed his Chicago plans with Bayard Rustin, Rustin asked him: "Martin, are you prepared to go in and fight to topple Daley from power?'' When King said he was not going to do that, Rustin warned him to stay away from Chicago entirely. ''You won't beat Daley on his home ground,'' he said, ''and you'll come away with nothing meaningful for all your efforts.''

The summer of 1965 had seen one major racial flare-up in Chicago, a two-day battle between police and black residents of the West Side ghetto that resulted in over seventy-five people being injured. A year later the disturbances were much more serious. On July 12, 1966, after the police had turned off fire hydrants that black children were using to keep cool during a hundred-degree heat wave, gangs of Negro youths stoned police cars. The police began making arrests, and the rioting quickly spread, punctuated by sniper fire from windows and rooftops. By the time order was finally restored four days later, with the aid of four thousand armed National Guardsmen, two people had been killed, hundreds more had been injured, and estimates of property damage were in the millions. While Mayor Daley did not blame Martin Luther King personally, he did charge that some members of King's staff had been active in fomenting the disorder. King, who had worked to help end the rioting, publicly deplored the violence. He also commented that the conditions in the ghetto were a major cause of the riots, and sought an early meeting with Daley. A few days later the mayor met with King and other black leaders, and agreed to some mild demands such as turning the hydrants back on, putting spray nozzles on them, bringing portable swimming pools into ghetto neighborhoods, and appointing a citizens committee to make recommendations on improving police/community relations.

Once the rioting had died down, King and other black leaders started putting new pressure on the city. In late July they began holding marches through white neighborhoods in support of open housing, a major concern for Chicago Negroes long kept out of the white ethnic enclaves by a combination of discriminatory real estate practices and community violence against any Negro "intruders." The marches evoked violent reactions—cars burned by white counter-demonstrators and stone throwing by white residents, including one rock that hit Dr. King and sent him to his knees. Though the city had been furnishing as many as twelve hundred policemen to guard the marchers against white violence, by mid-August the frequency of the marches and the growing restiveness of many white residents led city officials to fear that a major riot might be forthcoming. Moving to negotiate, Mayor Daley offered promises of some housing aid, jobs for blacks, and general expansion of the city's urban renewal program during the next two years.

When several meetings between the Chicago campaign leaders and Mayor Daley and his aides failed to produce an accord, the city turned to the courts. Mayor Daley went on television on August 19 to announce that the city's legal officers were going to Cook County circuit court for a temporary restraining order against the marches. After an *ex parte* proceeding, Judge Cornelius J. Harrington ordered King, his principal aides, three protest organizations, and several local black leaders to observe a series of court-imposed limits on their demonstrations: only one demonstration could be held each day, no night marches, no marches between 7:30 and 9 A.M. and between 4:40 and 6 P.M., no more than five hundred marchers at a time, and twenty-four hours' notice in writing to the police on the time and place of each demonstration.

The circuit court order did not ban all demonstrations, as the Birmingham injunction had done, but it would have sharply reduced the pressure that the Chicago movement was generating against the city. In a press release King declared that the city's move was "unjust, illegal, and unconstitutional," and indicated that the movement was prepared to put thousands of supporters into the streets. When reporters asked whether he would defy the order, King replied that this was possible. He made no public commitment to do so, however, and conferred quickly with his legal advisers, among them Inc. Fund attorneys James Nabrit and Norman Amaker, both fresh from their work on the certiorari petition in *Walker v. City of Birmingham*. Their advice was that the injunction was not patently unconstitutional, so there would be less justification for disobeying it than there had been for disobeying Judge Jenkins' sweeping injunction in Birmingham. It would be better to contest it in court first, they felt, and try to get the most severe restrictions relaxed. King agreed, but at the same time he moved to keep the pressure on the city.

While Nabrit and the other lawyers were preparing a motion to dissolve or modify the injunction, King announced on August 21 that he would lead a massive march on Sunday, August 28, into the all-white town of Cicero, Illinois. Since Cicero was outside the territorial boundaries of the Cook County circuit court, it was not covered by the injunction. Cicero was a virulently anti-black suburb, and the prospect of violent confrontations on the borders of Chicago spurred the city administration to fresh negotiations. These culminated on August 26 when the black protest leaders met with Mayor Daley, other city officials, and representatives of Chicago's business community. They quickly concluded what became known as the "Summit Agreement," in which the businessmen and city officials promised to establish new, non-discriminatory housing policies. King hailed it as "one of the most significant programs ever conceived to make open housing a reality." He called off the march planned for Cicero and began to close up shop in Chicago. There would be no violation of an injunction in this campaign.

As in Birmingham and Selma, King was bitterly criticized by some of the more militant activists in the black community, who complained that the "Summit Agreement" contained nothing but empty rhetoric; they also expressed concern that King's acquiescence would break the back of the protest movement. But, as historian David Lewis has pointed out, the agreement was no less specific—and considerably more comprehensive—than the agreement that had been reached in Birmingham. The big difference was that the Birmingham movement had led to the Kennedy Administration's commitment to sweeping civil rights legislation, as well as to commitments by local leaders. The Chicago campaign of 1966 had no comparable national impact, and its local impact was short-lived.

While King was trying to mount his campaign in Chicago during 1966, his Birmingham allies of three years earlier were continuing the fight for racial equality in the "Magic City." A number of changes had been made in race relations in Birmingham since 1963, but the basic conflict was still present. For example, despite the passage of the Voting Rights Act of 1965, Jefferson County officials were continuing to use evasive tactics to prevent large-scale registration of Negro voters. In response, Fred Shuttlesworth and the Alabama Christian Movement for Human Rights opened a campaign for the appointment of federal voting registrars.

Demonstrations also were held to demand the employment of Negroes in various city and county civil service positions. In one incident during this period, Negro customers at a grocery store in a Negro section of town were manhandled by store employees. A picket line was set up outside the store for two months, with many of the Negro ministers in Birmingham joining the protest. City officials obtained an injunction to limit the size of the picketing, saying that the order was necessary to protect public safety. During the picketing, five unarmed and peaceful marchers were shot from a car by a white man, who said that he only shot in self-defense. He was not prosecuted.

In a booklet summing up the Birmingham situation in

1966, Fred Shuttlesworth noted with pride that the movement had won some significant advances through its struggles, but always over the bitter resistance of official Birmingham. "The buses are desegregated," he noted, "and so are the parks, with the shameful exception of the closed swimming pools. School segregation has been broken, even though integration is still token. Public eating places are integrated, if one can afford to eat in them; Negro police have been hired, although in token numbers. At least a few Negroes are working in jobs never open to them before; the bars to Negro voter registration have been torn down." Most important of all, Shuttlesworth added, "white police cannot with impunity terrorize and brutalize Negroes on the streets and in their homes, as they once could and did in Birmingham."

For Matt Breckenridge and Earl McBee, the challenge in mid-1966 was how to keep King and the other SCLC leaders from wriggling off the hook on which the contempt conviction of 1963 and the Alabama supreme court affirmance of 1965 had caught them. They felt that they had a good case, but they knew that the U.S. Supreme Court had consistently found ways to upset Southern state court convictions of civil rights protesters.

In drafting their response to the petition for certiorari, Breckenridge and McBee presented a very different account of the Good Friday and Easter Sunday marches than that by the Inc. Fund. Where the petition had described the marches as "peaceful protest demonstrations," the city's response spoke of "unruly mobs." The Easter Sunday demonstration was described as a "procession filling the entire street and overflowing the sidewalks on either side" that turned into "a howling, rock-throwing and violent mob injuring a news reporter."

This characterization of the demonstrations was important for one of the city's main legal arguments—its contention that First Amendment rights were not involved in this case at all. In the words of Breckenridge and McBee,

> . . . assembling of a violent unruly mob such as that of Sunday, April 15, 1963, commandeering the entire street from curb to curb and overflowing both sidewalks in a march, the route and destination of which were shrouded in secrecy, sponsored, fomented, incited and encouraged by petitioners, the leaders of whom had openly declared war upon city and state laws and the orders of state court judges in the south, can no more be entitled to such constitutional protection than would Ku Klux Klansmen be so entitled to commandeer the public streets to perpetrate a flogging or other unlawful activity in the name of freedom of speech or freedom of assembly.

The other key element of the city's response was a heavy reliance on the Supreme Court's prior opinions in the *Howat* and *Mine Workers* cases as support for the contention that the Alabama supreme court decision rested on an "adequate state ground" and should not be reviewed. Noting pointedly that the *Howat* case had "apparently either been overlooked or ignored" in the Inc. Fund's petition, the city's brief emphasized that the *Howat* rule had been given explicit endorsement in the *Mine Workers* decision, had been relied on by the Alabama supreme court in affirming the convictions of the petitioners, and was "obviously directly in point."

The city's thirty-seven-page brief in opposition to the certiorari petition was filed on July 18, 1966. The court had concluded its 1965–66 term a month earlier, and most of the justices were trying to enjoy some vacation time. They would not formally reconvene until early October, but during August and September most of them were busy working with their law clerks, reviewing the hundreds of applications for review that had been pouring into the court clerk's office. When the court's 1966–67 term began, the justices met in daily conferences to discuss the pending applications for review and decide which ones to grant. On October 10, 1966, the court clerk's office made public the results of their first week of conferences. More than six hundred applications had been denied, and only twenty-nine granted. One of the twenty-nine was *Walker v. City of Birmingham.*

12

Nine Men in Black

DURING 1966 AND 1967, while the *Walker* case was moving into the Supreme Court, observers of civil rights developments began to think about an unpleasant historical analogy. During the early part of Reconstruction following the Civil War, strong legislation to protect the legal and civil rights of former slaves had been enacted by the Republican Congress, and much interracial progress was made in the border states and even in the Deep South. Although the dominant white element in the South generally resisted the movement toward equality, the presence of federal troops supported Negroes who sought to exercise their rights. Between the late 1870s and early 1900s, however, a mood of white disengagement set in in the North. Federal troops were withdrawn from the South in 1877, in a Republican *quid pro quo* for Southern Democrats' acceptance of the Electoral Commission decision awarding the disputed election of 1876 to Republican Rutherford B. Hayes. Efforts to enforce compliance with federal civil rights laws also began to wane. In 1883 the U.S. Supreme Court, with only one dissent, reflected this climate of white opinion by striking down the federal Civil Rights Act of 1875, which forbade racial discrimination in public accommodation facilities. Such "social" discriminations, said the court, were private matters which could not be subjected to federal regulation.

John Marshall Harlan, a Kentuckian and former slaveholder, was the only justice to dissent from the ruling. He argued that the basic purpose of the Fourteenth Amendment had been to extend national citizenship to the Negro, that allowing public accommodation owners to deny service on the basis of race limited such citizenship rights, and that the final section of the Amendment gave Congress the power to pass appropriate legislation to prevent such actions. Harlan's voice was a lonely one, however. During the years that followed the 1883 decision, many states and localities took their cue from the majority opinion and enacted laws that required separation of Negroes and whites in places such as restaurants and railroad trains. In 1896, again over the lone dissent of Justice Harlan, the Supreme Court upheld such laws in the famous case of *Plessy v. Ferguson,* stating that "separate but equal" facilities required by law did not deny anyone equal protection.

Events in 1965–66 raised the specter of a similar withdrawal of protective law. The cries of "Black Power" and the increased popularity of Malcolm X among ghetto blacks sent currents of fear through many whites, especially when it became clear that "responsible" black leaders such as Martin Luther King could not exercise control over the new militants. The bloody riots in the Watts area of Los Angeles and on Chicago's West Side in August 1965 suggested that violence rather than civil disobedience might be the "new movement" among urban blacks. The "long hot summer" of 1966 continued the pattern: fresh riots in Chicago, with the National Guard called to patrol the streets; riots in Cleveland's Hough area, again with Guardsmen called in; and major street fighting and violence in September in as urbane a community as San Francisco.

Many white liberals and moderates, looking at the newly

enacted federal civil rights laws of 1964 and 1965, began to say that the time had come to consolidate the gains of the past decade, to let Negroes use their newly won voting rights to express their demands for political and legislative reforms, and to bring the use of legally sheltered confrontations and protests to a halt. What course the Supreme Court would take—either continue stretching constitutional rights to help blacks correct a century of legalized racism, or shift to an "even-handed" restoration of the "rule of law"—would be absolutely critical both to the leadership of the black struggle and to the climate of civil rights action as a whole.

Wyatt Tee Walker, reminiscing later about his feelings during this time, recalled thinking about some of the historical parallels:

> The Supreme Court's 1954 decision in the school desegregation cases was something like the Emancipation Proclamation—it lifted oppressive legal restraints from black people, but it didn't result in anything like full equality. Then, the period from 1954 to 1965 had been a lot like the early Reconstruction years—America was no Promised Land, but at least some good laws got passed and you could sense some progress being made. Of course, most of the progress was due to the pressures we generated ourselves. By 1966 you could see that a lot of white people in the North were beginning to get uptight. Some of us were starting to think that it might be only a question of time until the Supreme Court—which had been our strongest ally—began to turn away from us.

Walker had ample basis for his concern about the Supreme Court's future direction. Throughout most of its history, far from being a champion of oppressed minorities, the court had been primarily concerned with protecting property rights and laissez faire. Then, in 1937, with the major economic and social changes of the New Deal, came what T. R. Powell called "the shift in time that saved nine." In the wake of

President Franklin D. Roosevelt's landslide reelection in 1936 and faced with his threat to enlarge the court and appoint more liberal justices, the court majority in 1937 abandoned its intransigent opposition to New Deal social measures. From then on, welfare measures enacted by legislatures would generally be treated as constitutional if they were rationally directed to the problems involved, despite the fact that some justices might have different notions of good economics and social policy.

In place of a property-rights focus, the court of the 1940s and 1950s began to pay increasing attention to issues of personal liberty—freedom of expression, rights of racial and religious minorities, and procedural rights in the criminal process. There were some periods of advance and some of retreat in the flowering of civil liberties decisions in the Supreme Court—for example, the arrival of the cold war in the late 1940s brought a wave of rulings upholding loyalty oaths and other restrictive measures against "subversives"—but the overall trend (particularly after Earl Warren became Chief Justice in 1953) was for the court to expand the constitutional rights of minorities and to open official and unofficial political processes to greater participation by such groups. The trend was accelerated in 1962 when President Kennedy appointed Arthur Goldberg to fill the vacancy on the court created by the retirement of Felix Frankfurter. Goldberg joined with Chief Justice Warren and Justices Hugo Black, William O. Douglas, and William Brennan to form a five-man "liberal-activist" majority in most civil rights and civil liberties cases. Although Goldberg left the court in the summer of 1965 to become U.S. Ambassador to the United Nations, his replacement, Abe Fortas, adopted a similar voting pattern in such cases.

But although the general trend had been toward decisions favorable to minorities, many of the court's key "libertarian" decisions of the early and mid-1960s were made by narrow 5–4 or 6–3 margins. And, as close observers of the court were aware, sharp cleavages were developing among the justices over how the law should treat those who engaged in various kinds of protest demonstrations. One of the justices usually counted in the liberal majority—Hugo Black—expressed strong reservations about protest activity when it involved trespass or other physical acts, not "pure speech." The court as a whole, while it consistently decided cases in favor of civil rights demonstrators during the early 1960s, almost invariably rested its decisions on the narrowest possible grounds.

Most of the protest cases to reach the court during the early 1960s involved convictions for breach of the peace or trespass, generally arising out of lunch-counter sit-ins or similar demonstrations against segregation practices. Between 1960 and 1963 the court reversed convictions in all such cases in which it granted review, generally by unanimous vote. Sometimes the ground for reversal would be lack of evidence to support the conviction. Other times it would be that the statute under which the demonstrators were prosecuted was overly vague or that the convictions had the effect of enforcing segregation policies of state or local governments.

In none of these cases did the opinion of the court reach the two broad constitutional arguments advanced by the attorneys who represented the demonstrators: (1) that the demonstrators' nonverbal protests were the equivalent of speech and entitled to the same treatment as other forms of speech protected by the First Amendment; and (2) that even if a state did not itself have a policy of requiring segregation in public accommodations, the equal protection clause of the Fourteenth Amendment prohibited the use of state courts to enforce the segregationist policies of a property owner who operated a facility open to the public, such as a restaurant or motel. Justice Douglas had indicated in several concurring opinions that he agreed with the second theory, but none of the other justices had explicitly dealt with either of the arguments.

The court decided its first major street-demonstration case of the 1960s, *Cox v. Louisiana,* in January 1965. It was a complex case, arising out of a demonstration held by approximately two thousand black college students in Baton Rouge, Louisiana, to protest the arrest the day before of twenty-three fellow students who had been picketing stores that maintained segregated lunch counters. The demonstration leaders had been convicted of three different offenses under Louisiana law—disturbing the peace, obstructing public passages, and picketing before a courthouse. All three convictions were reversed by the court, by margins ranging from 9–0 to 5–4, but the rhetoric of the opinions reflected a concern on the part of all the justices about the need for municipalities to be able to maintain order. Justice Goldberg, speaking for a majority composed of himself, Warren, Douglas, Brennan, and Stewart, made a point of emphasizing that street demonstrations were not entitled to precisely the same degree of protection as other forms of speech:

> The rights of free speech and assembly, while fundamental in our democratic society, still do not mean that everyone with opinions or beliefs to express may address a group at any public place and at any time. The control of travel on the streets is a clear example of governmental responsibility to secure this necessary order. . . . We emphatically reject the notion urged by appellant that the First and Fourteenth Amendments afford the same kind of freedom to those who would communicate ideas by conduct such as patrolling, marching and picketing on streets and highways, as these amendments afford to those who communicate ideas by pure speech. . . .

Justice Black concurred with the majority in reversing the convictions for breach of the peace and obstructing public passageways, but dissented vigorously from the reversal of the conviction for picketing near a courthouse. For Black, who was born and raised in the rural South, mass demonstrations near a courthouse conjured up visions of Klan mobs and brutal lynchings. His dissent in *Cox,* joined by Clark, Harlan, and White, included some sharp criticism of the advocates of street demonstrations as a means for bringing about redress of grievances:

> The streets are not now and never have been the proper place to administer justice. Use of the streets for such purposes has always proved disastrous to individual liberties in the long run, whatever fleeting benefits may have appeared to have been achieved. And minority groups, I venture to suggest, are the ones who always have suffered and always will suffer most when street multitudes are allowed to substitute their pressures for the less glamorous but more dependable and temperate processes of the law. Experience demonstrates that it is not a far step from what to many seems the earnest, honest, patriotic, kind-spirited multitude of today, to the fanatical, threatening, lawless mob of tomorrow. And the crowds that press in the streets for noble goals today can be supplanted tomorrow by street mobs pressuring the courts for precisely opposite ends. Minority groups in particular need always to bear in mind that the Constitution, while it requires States to treat all citizens equally and protect them in the exercise of rights granted by the Federal Constitution and laws, does not take away the State's power, indeed its duty, to keep order and to do justice according to law. . . .

In November 1966 the court for the first time in the 1960s upheld convictions of nonviolent demonstrators. *Adderley v. Florida* involved trespass convictions of thirty-two black college students, part of a group of about two hundred who had gathered on the grounds of a county jail in Tallahassee, Florida, to protest earlier arrests of students who had attempted to integrate local theaters. The majority was composed of Justices Black, Clark, Harlan, White, and Stewart, with the opinion written by Black. After noting that jailhouse grounds were not generally regarded as open to the public because of security reasons and rejecting claims that the trespass statute was unduly vague, Black continued:

> The State, no less than a private owner of property, has power to preserve the property under its control for the use to which it is lawfully dedicated. For this reason, there is no merit to the petitioners' argument that they had a constitutional right to stay on the property, over the jail custodian's objections, because this "area chosen for the peaceful civil rights demonstration was not only 'reasonable' but also particularly appropriate. . . ." Such an argument has as its major unarticulated premise the assumption that people who want to propagandize protests or views have a constitutional right to do so whenever and however they please. That concept of constitutional law was vigorously and forthrightly rejected in *Cox v. Louisiana*. We reject it again. The United States Constitution does not forbid a State to control the use of its own property for its own lawful non-discriminatory purpose.

Justice Douglas, joined by Chief Justice Warren and Justices Fortas and Brennan, registered a concerned dissent:

> Conventional methods of petitioning may be, and often have been, shut off to large groups of our citizens. Legislators may turn deaf ears; formal complaints may be routed endlessly through a bureaucratic maze; courts may let the wheels of justice grind very slowly. Those who do not control television and radio, those who cannot afford to advertise in newspapers or circulate elaborate pamphlets may have only a more limited type of access to public officials. Their methods should not be condemned as tactics of obstruction and harassment as long as the assembly and petition are peaceful, as these were. . . .
>
> Today a trespass law is used to penalize people for exercising a constitutional right. Tomorrow a disorderly conduct stat-

ute, a breach of the peace statute, a vagrancy statute will be put to the same end.

The decision in *Adderley* was handed down on November 14, 1966, as the Inc. Fund lawyers were working on an early draft of the brief they would soon be submitting to the Supreme Court in *Walker*. The ruling came as a blow, but not a wholly unexpected one; it had been apparent to them for the past several years that demonstration cases would face difficult sledding in the court. What concerned them most was that Stewart, who up until then generally voted to uphold the demonstrators (though always on narrow grounds), had not only voted to affirm the convictions in *Adderley* but had joined in Black's strongly worded opinion rejecting the protesters' First Amendment arguments.

Their concern about Stewart's position reflected the Inc. Fund lawyers' keen appreciation of the fact that the court, far from being a monolithic entity, really consists of nine individuals who often have quite divergent views about specific issues. Although the court sometimes functions with unanimity, it has often been divided into two or three coherent voting "blocs" in specific subject areas. The make-up of the blocs will differ from one area to another, depending on the individual justice's views about the substantive problem and the kind of action that the court is asked to take in a given appeal; but the existence of such groupings is a consistent feature of constitutional policy making. For example, in most of the constitutionally critical cases that it decided, the Supreme Court during FDR's first term (1932–36) was divided into one bloc of four extremely conservative justices (McReynolds, Van Devanter, Butler, and Sutherland), who regarded almost all state or federal New Deal measures as clearly unconstitutional; three liberals (Stone, Brandeis, and Cardozo), who would have upheld most New Deal measures as constitutional; and two moderate-conservatives (Roberts and Chief

Justice Hughes), who generally voted with the extreme conservatives between 1932 and 1936. It was the shift of Roberts
and Hughes in 1937 to an alliance with the three liberals that
produced the majority for upholding key social legislation in
that year.

Such a "swing" by the moderate or middle-road justices
in a three-bloc divided court has been a frequent pattern in
major constitutional decisions. This explains why, among
students of American constitutional politics, a close study of
the court's blocs, and especially the values, approaches, and
behavior of the "swing" justices, is every bit as important
for understanding the Supreme Court as knowledge of the
court's past precedents or scrutiny of the great intellects,
writers, and jurists among the justices. Typically a swing justice is one not wedded to strict ideological positions. He is
more likely to be pragmatically oriented, attuned to major
changes in national opinion that bear upon the constitutionally sensitive issues of each era, concerned over the
court's need to preserve its prestige, and mindful of the necessity for the court to keep its options open. In 1937, for example, Hughes and Roberts clearly felt that FDR's court-
packing proposal would be approved by Congress if the court
continued to strike down New Deal social welfare legislation.
Their swing away from the conservative bloc was unques-
tionably influenced by a well-grounded fear that the court
would be grievously wounded as an institution if they did not
find a way to uphold the constitutionality of the New Deal's
key legislation.

During the Supreme Court's 1966–67 term, the most readily identifiable bloc in civil liberties cases was the four-
member group consisting of Warren, Douglas, Brennan, and
Fortas. Not only had all four of them voted together in the
demonstration cases of the 1960s, but they had also consistently taken a libertarian, activist position in other civil liber-

ties cases. In case after case, they had voted to strike down state or federal laws (as well as executive actions) which they saw as infringing on guarantees of the Bill of Rights, particularly in the First Amendment area.

In Warren's case, this tendency had come as a considerable surprise to President Eisenhower. He had named Warren as Chief Justice in 1953 knowing that he was a life-long Republican with experience as a district attorney, attorney general, and governor of California. (Eisenhower later termed the appointment "the worst darn mistake I ever made.") Before becoming Chief Justice, Warren had been a strong exponent of states' rights and an admirer of Justice Felix Frankfurter's philosophy of deference to principles of federalism and judicial self-restraint. But once on the bench Warren found the Frankfurter jurisprudence too sterile and confining. More than anything else, Warren was a man concerned with questions of elemental fairness in the treatment of people by the institutions of society, and he found himself more comfortable with a concept of constitutional law that gave primacy to principles of equality and the values embedded in the Bill of Rights. It was Warren, manifesting a characteristic willingness to take responsibility upon himself, who wrote the court's historic 1954 opinion in *Brown v. Board of Education* and who also authored the opinions for the court in many highly controversial legislative reapportionment and criminal due process cases of the 1960s.

Like Warren, Justice William J. Brennan had proven to be something of a surprise to Eisenhower, who had appointed him in 1956 from the New Jersey supreme court. Although a Democrat, Brennan had been highly recommended by New Jersey's chief judge, Arthur Vanderbilt, who had close ties to the Eisenhower Administration. Once on the court, Brennan quickly established himself as a liberal on questions involving the guarantees of the Bill of Rights. On several occasions, for example, he wrote opinions for the court that struck down state statutes as overly broad and stifling of First Amendment freedoms. These freedoms, he commented in one opinion, are "delicate and vulnerable, as well as supremely precious in our society"; they need "breathing space" in order to survive. Like Warren, Brennan joined in Douglas' opinion for the majority in *In re Green,* the 1962 decision which seemed to undercut the *Mine Workers* rule. And while he declined to join in some of the broad concurring opinions of Douglas and Warren in the sit-in cases, he consistently voted to reverse the convictions of the protesters, often finding narrow grounds on which one or two other justices would join.

Justice William O. Douglas, an ardent outdoorsman, prolific author, and outspoken liberal, had been appointed to the court by FDR in 1939, and for many years his voting record was remarkably similar to Justice Black's. Often, particularly during the late 1940s in cold-war loyalty/security cases, they registered the only dissents when the rest of the court rejected assertions of individual rights. In the mid-1960s, however, when questions about the limits of permissible protest activities came to the fore, Douglas took a far broader view than Black of the kinds of expression protected by the First and Fourteenth Amendments. Of all the justices, Douglas—the author of the majority opinion in *In re Green,* the dissent in *Adderley,* and several concurring opinions expressing agreement with the broad equal protection and First Amendment arguments advanced by lawyers for the civil rights protesters—was probably the one most sure to vote for reversal in *Walker.*

The fourth justice in this group, Abe Fortas, was the newest member of the court. Born in Memphis, Tennessee, Fortas had grown up and gone to college in his hometown, and then had gone on to graduate at the top of his class from Yale Law School in 1933. After teaching law at Yale for a few years, Fortas went to Washington, where he worked for a decade as a top-level lawyer and bureaucrat in a succession of government agencies. During the late 1940s he formed a partnership with two other well-known former New Deal lawyers, and the firm—Arnold, Fortas, and Porter—quickly became one of the most prosperous and prestigious in Washington. Although its clients were usually large corporations, the firm also took on a number of civil liberties cases, generally without fee. Fortas himself had handled one of the most famous of these cases, *Gideon v. Wainwright,* in which the Supreme Court ruled in 1963 that indigent defendants charged with felonies were constitutionally entitled to the assistance of counsel. He was appointed to the court in 1965 by Lyndon Johnson, a close friend and former client. According to some reports, he remained an informal confidant and adviser to the President even after going on the court. Although his voting record had been consistently liberal during his first year on the bench, Inc. Fund lawyers were a bit worried that his close association with Johnson might color his view of the *Walker* case at a time when demonstrations against the Vietnam War—joined by King—were growing larger and louder. Of the four "liberals," Fortas' vote was the least certain, but still probably safe.

The real challenge to the Inc. Fund lawyers was to obtain a fifth vote. All of the remaining justices had voted against the protesters in one or another demonstration case of the 1960s, and all had joined in Black's recent opinion in *Adderley v. Florida.* Of course, there were a number of ways in which the *Walker* case was different from earlier demonstration cases. A justice might, for example, look with great disfavor upon street demonstrations, yet have an even greater distaste for the practice of issuing sweeping injunctions abridging First Amendment rights—particularly where the injunction was issued without notice to the party enjoined, as had been the case in *Walker.* On the other hand, he might have a strong sympathy with the need for minority groups to have an opportunity for peaceful protest, yet feel an even stronger commitment to the concept of respect for court decrees and orderly judicial processes.

Of the five justices in the *Adderley* majority, two—Tom Clark and John Marshall Harlan—seemed particularly unlikely to vote for reversal in *Walker*. Harlan and Clark tended to take conservative positions on most issues that came before the court. They had voted to affirm state court convictions in a number of the demonstration cases of the mid-1960s, and had made it clear (in their *In re Green* dissent) that they favored the *Mine Workers* doctrine.

Clark, a Texan who was the only Truman appointee still left on the court, had been Attorney General of the United States between 1945 and 1949. During that time one of the cases he had successfully handled for the government (arguing it himself before the Supreme Court) was *United States v. United Mine Workers*. As a justice, Clark tended to uphold the government position in most civil liberties cases, especially those involving loyalty/security issues and criminal due process questions. Occasionally, however, he confounded his liberal critics, as in 1961 when he cast the deciding vote and wrote the court's opinion in *Mapp v. Ohio,* a landmark case holding that evidence which had been seized in violation of the constitutional prohibition against illegal searches could not be introduced at state criminal trials. In the sit-in cases of the early 1960s, he generally voted to reverse the convictions, but always on narrow grounds. In the demonstration cases which reached the court during 1965 and 1966, however, he had voted to affirm the convictions.

Harlan, grandson of the dissenter from the court's 1883 and 1896 rulings upholding segregation, had been a partner in an elite Wall Street law firm and served briefly as a federal appellate court judge before being appointed to the Supreme Court by President Eisenhower in 1954. Often described as a "lawyer's lawyer," Harlan had the high regard for precedent that most lawyers possess, and tended to deal with issues in a very orderly, logical fashion. After Felix Frankfurter's retirement in 1962, Harlan became the court's leading advocate of judicial self-restraint. During the mid-1960s, as the Kennedy and Johnson appointees to the court made their presence felt, he increasingly found himself writing dissents criticizing the majority's precedent-shattering decisions in fields such as reapportionment and criminal due process. He voted against the demonstrators more than any other justice during the 1960s, frequently writing opinions suggesting that established legal principles should not be stretched beyond recognition in order to reach a result that might be thought socially desirable.

Harlan was a strong believer in the virtues of federalism, but he could also be sensitive to claims that state actions had abridged fundamental rights protected by the First and Fourteenth Amendments. In the long series of cases arising out of Alabama's attempt to outlaw the NAACP, for example, he had written several opinions upholding the NAACP's position that the privacy of its membership records was entitled to First Amendment protection. This series of cases had also given Harlan (as well as the other justices) a good view of how manipulative the Alabama courts could be where racial issues were involved. In the course of the NAACP litigation, Harlan had rejected a number of procedural arguments made by Alabama officials, including some based on the "adequate state ground" doctrine, which he had often relied on in other cases involving federal/state relations. He could be expected to pay particular attention to this issue in the *Walker* case.

The remaining three members of the court—Justices Hugo Black, Potter Stewart, and Byron R. White—were the ones whose votes would be most difficult to predict. If the lawyers for the convicted ministers were to succeed in winning the *Walker* case, they would pretty surely have to convince one of these three. Although all three had joined in some opinions (generally written by Black) which vigorously condemned some of the "direct action" tactics of the civil rights demonstrators, each had also written or joined in other opinions which gave the Inc. Fund attorneys some ground for hoping that they could be persuaded to vote for reversal. Of the three, Stewart was probably the most likely to be open to persuasion, Black the least likely.

Black was the senior member of the court, and was more thoroughly acquainted with the context from which the *Walker* case arose than any of the other justices. Born and raised in rural Clay County, Alabama, Black had started a law practice in Birmingham in 1907, shortly after his graduation from the University of Alabama Law School. As a part-time Jefferson County solicitor from 1915 to 1917, Black received national notice when he prosecuted police authorities in nearby Bessemer for their use of third-degree practices upon Negro suspects. But his reputation in Alabama came mainly from his success as a lawyer winning personal injury cases brought against large corporations. In 1926 he was elected to the Senate, and during the ten years that followed he became known as a vigorous investigator of utility companies, a sponsor of minimum wage laws and other pro-labor legislation, and a leading critic of the old Supreme Court's favoritism to property rights and unconcern with "human rights." In 1937 when President Roosevelt appointed him to the Supreme Court, critics attacked the appointment on the grounds that Black had once been a member of the Ku Klux Klan. Black resisted pressure for his resignation, pointing out that he had resigned from the Klan many years earlier after a period of membership that lasted only a few months and denying that he was racially prejudiced. In fact, in the years that followed, he often became the subject of bitter attack by the Klan and its sympathizers because of his votes in civil rights cases.

During his thirty years on the court, Justice Black had, in

the words of one biographer, "preached the doctrine that the government should at the same time be both all-powerful and all-weak: that over the economy it should have all the power needed to cope with the problems of each day, and that over the thought, speech and spirit of the citizen it should have no power at all." This was a philosophy that gave primacy to the Bill of Rights, and particularly to the First Amendment. To Black, the First Amendment meant precisely what it said: Congress could make *no* law establishing religion or prohibiting its free exercise, or abridging freedom of speech or of the press or of the rights to assemble peaceably and to petition the government. But while he took a strong stand on the importance of protecting First Amendment freedoms, Black also defined these freedoms somewhat narrowly. For him, conduct such as picketing a store or marching in the streets— even if done in order to publicize an idea—was not "speech" protected by the First Amendment. Such conduct, he felt, could be regulated by appropriately drawn statutes (or injunctions), provided the regulations were applied to all groups alike. During the 1960s, as lawyers for civil rights demonstrators pressed on the court their argument that sit-in demonstrations and protest gatherings were forms of speech and assembly protected by the First Amendment, Black repeatedly demurred in strongly worded opinions.

Justice Byron White was at one time known to millions of Americans as "Whizzer" White, the all-American halfback who led the University of Colorado to an undefeated season in 1938 and went on to star in the National Football League. He was also a Rhodes scholar and an outstanding student at Yale Law School. During the 1946–47 term of the Supreme Court, he was the law clerk for Chief Justice Fred Vinson, author of the court's opinion in the *Mine Workers* case. A long-time friend of John Kennedy, White was active in Kennedy's 1960 presidential campaign. After the election he was appointed Deputy Attorney General (the number-two position

in the Justice Department), and was one of the chief archi-
tects of the Justice Department's strategy of using court
orders as a basis for compelling local officials in the South to
acknowledge the constitutional rights of Negroes. In 1961 he
had taken charge of the force of federal marshals organized to
protect the Freedom Riders in Alabama, pursuant to Judge
Johnson's order. In the spring of 1962, when Charles Whittaker resigned from the court and Kennedy had his first opportunity to appoint a new justice, he chose White.

Although many observers expected White's appointment to
"tip the balance" in the court toward the libertarian, activist
position, White proved them wrong. He did join with the
"activist" wing in some important and closely contested
reapportionment and criminal due process cases during this
period, but he was to be found voting about as often with the
more conservative members such as Harlan and Clark. In the
demonstration cases of the mid-1960s White frequently
joined Black and Harlan in dissenting from majority decisions that vacated convictions on narrow grounds, and he
made it clear that he did not approve of demonstration tactics. However, his separate concurring opinion favoring reversal of demonstrators' convictions in *Brown v. Louisiana,* a
1966 case arising out of a sit-in in a public library, indicated
that he would examine a record carefully to see whether a
regulatory law had been applied to protesters in a non-
discriminatory fashion.

The ninth justice, Potter Stewart, had been only forty-three
when President Eisenhower appointed him to the Supreme
Court in 1958, after having appointed him four years earlier
to the U.S. Court of Appeals for the Sixth Circuit. Early in
his tenure on the Supreme Court, Stewart came to be
regarded as a key "swing justice" in close cases involving
claims of governmental deprivation of individual rights. At
the time he joined the court in 1958, it was composed of four
liberal-activist justices (Warren, Black, Douglas, and Bren-

nan), and four appreciably more conservative justices (Frankfurter, Whittaker, Harlan, and Clark) who were more likely
to stress the importance of judicial self-restraint and the values of federalism. Stewart tended to take a middle position
on many of these cases, voting with the conservative wing
more than half the time but frequently basing his vote on narrow grounds which left room for further consideration of the
direction the law should take in a particular area.

Stewart's votes in the demonstration cases of the early
1960s followed this pattern. In 1963 he wrote the opinion for
the court in *Edwards v. South Carolina,* a case involving
breach-of-peace convictions of black demonstrators who had
marched peacefully on the grounds of the South Carolina
statehouse to protest racial discrimination in the state. In
holding that the conviction must be reversed, Stewart emphasized the vagueness of the statute upon which the demonstrators were convicted, the fact that their views were being
expressed peacefully, and the fact that the state capitol was
an appropriate place to assemble and petition for redress of
grievances. The circumstances of the case, he said, reflected
an exercise of First Amendment rights "in their most pristine
form." He also stated, however, that it would be a different
case if the petitioners had been in violation of a law regulating traffic or if they had disobeyed a law reasonably regulating the hours the state capitol grounds were open to the
public. In a number of sit-in cases involving breach-of-peace
or trespass laws, he voted to reverse convictions on grounds
of lack of evidence or—after passage of the Civil Rights Act
of 1964—to remand the cases for reconsideration by lower
courts in light of the supervening legislation. In 1965 he
voted with the majority to reverse the conviction in *Cox v.
Louisiana,* but the following year he voted to sustain both the
breach-of-peace convictions in *Brown v. Louisiana* and the
trespass convictions in *Adderley v. Florida.* In a very real
sense, the constitutional law of the United States on First

Amendment rights of demonstrators hinged on what Justice Potter Stewart would think of a given situation.

For the Inc. Fund lawyers, sizing up the court and selecting the arguments most likely to persuade swing justices was a prelude to the hard work of actually preparing their appellate brief. Next they had to organize it, formulate the questions to be treated, write a statement of facts so as to present the petitioners' case in as favorable a way as possible, and draft the central legal arguments.

13

Arguments Before the Bench

I<small>T</small> <small>WAS</small> A<small>NTHONY</small> A<small>MSTERDAM</small> and James Nabrit, more than anyone else, who shaped the Inc. Fund's brief in the *Walker* case. Tony Amsterdam was a young man, only thirty-two in 1966, but he had already become something of a legendary figure in the civil rights movement. A summa cum laude graduate of Haverford College and the University of Pennsylvania Law School, he had been a clerk to Justice Felix Frankfurter for a year, worked briefly as an Assistant U.S. Attorney in Washington, and then returned to teach law at Penn. But teaching occupied only a relatively small part of Amsterdam's time. From 1963 on he was involved in criminal defense cases and civil rights lawsuits all over the country, conferring with lawyers on strategy, writing memos and briefs, and presenting oral arguments. Jack Greenberg, impressed by Amsterdam's ability the first time he heard him speak, had asked him to become a consultant for the Inc. Fund in 1963, and Inc. Fund lawyers had come to rely heavily on his aid in some of their most important cases.

Amsterdam's theory about how to organize the brief in *Walker* was consistent with the views of Nabrit and Greenberg. Basically, it called for relegating discussion of the *Mine Workers* doctrine to a secondary position in the brief and placing major emphasis on arguments addressed to less fundamental issues. Amsterdam felt, and the others agreed, that given the temper of the times there was virtually no chance to persuade a majority of the court to overturn or even limit *Mine Workers*. The four liberals might well be willing to do this, but it was the fifth vote that was crucial. They decided to emphasize some of the more narrow arguments of the sort that had consistently garnered a majority for reversal in the sit-in cases.

Thus, the opening point in the "Argument" section of the brief attacked Judge Jenkins' rulings excluding the evidence which the Inc. Fund lawyers had tried to introduce at the trial to show that the parade-permit ordinance was administered in an arbitrary manner by city officials. This point had been covered in two paragraphs in the certiorari petition, but in the brief it was developed into a ten-page argument. Its main thrust was that the trial court's rulings had denied the defense an opportunity to show that the ministers could not have obtained the parade permits that the injunction ostensibly required them to have. The proffered evidence, they said, would have shown that the permit ordinance was administered in a racially discriminatory fashion, in violation of the petitioners' constitutional right to equal protection of the laws. The effect of excluding it, they argued, was to convict them without due process of law.

In an effort to meet the city of Birmingham's argument that the case was not reviewable because it had been decided on an "adequate state ground," the Inc. Fund lawyers researched Alabama law on contempt. They found and cited several cases indicating that in the past some Alabama courts reviewing contempt convictions had inquired into the validity of an underlying injunction. Since the rule of law followed by the Alabama supreme court in its affirmation of the contempt conviction had not been uniformly followed, they contended, it could not bar review of the petitioners' constitutional claims.

Although the Inc. Fund lawyers tried to emphasize the narrow arguments, they still devoted considerable attention to the *Mine Workers* doctrine. First, they contended that as a general proposition it did not apply in cases where injunctions restrained First Amendment rights. Second, they said, even if the court held otherwise, it was wrong to apply the *Mine Workers* doctrine in the particular circumstances of the *Walker* case. Here, they said, the injunction was "patently unconstitutional," had been issued *ex parte,* and was aimed at "effecting the wholesale repression of speech in a volatile political situation" at "precisely the moment when repression could be most crippling."

At the same time that the Inc. Fund lawyers were working on their brief, three of the top lawyers in the Department of Justice were busy preparing an *amicus curiae* (friend of the court) brief in support of the petitioners. Thurgood Marshall, the former Inc. Fund director who had served for four years as a federal appellate court judge, had replaced Archibald Cox in 1965 as Solicitor General, the Justice Department official primarily responsible for representing the government before the Supreme Court. Marshall was acutely aware of the abuses to which injunctive powers of courts had been put in the past, especially in civil rights contests. He decided that his office should enter the case on the side of the petitioners, even though he felt that King and his lawyers should have made some effort to dissolve Judge Jenkins' order in court before the Good Friday march.

Marshall, Assistant Solicitor General Louis Claiborne, and Civil Rights Division Chief John Doar collaborated on a twenty-five-page brief arguing that the *Mine Workers* doctrine should not be applied in a situation like the *Walker* case. After emphasizing that the government was "strongly committed to securing respect for judicial decrees" and disclaiming any disagreement with the decision in the *Mine Workers* case itself, they argued that the combination of factors in

Walker—"the unconstitutionality of the underlying ordinance, the plain invalidity of the *ex parte* injunction based on that ordinance, the practical unavailability of prompt relief, and the ultimate effect of a prior restraint upon rights guaranteed by the First Amendment"—should prevent the *Mine Workers* doctrine from being applied to bar the petitioners from challenging the constitutionality of the injunction.

Early in February the issues were joined when the city of Birmingham filed its brief. Again prepared by J. M. Breckenridge and Earl McBee, the brief continued the city's emphasis on *Howat v. Kansas* to support the Alabama supreme court's affirmance as resting upon an adequate state ground. They acknowledged that some Alabama appellate court opinions in contempt cases had considered the question of whether an injunction was "void on its face," but they argued that these and other such cases were dealing not with the terms of the injunction involved but whether the issuing court had "usurped jurisdiction."

In an attempt to capitalize on the growing public concern about riots and protest, Breckenridge and McBee included a new section emphasizing the disastrous consequences that might result if the *Howat* and *Mine Workers* precedents were abandoned and court orders were to be ignored. They cited President Johnson's remarks during the summer of 1966 condemning riots that had broken out in several cities and Mayor Daley's charges that King's staff had spurred on the summer riots in Chicago, thereby linking the protest marches of 1963 in Birmingham with the ghetto riots of 1965 and 1966. Past encouragement of civil disobedience and defiance of court orders, the brief suggested, was resulting in "street violence, disregard for law, rioting, bloodshed, arson and destruction of property."

The required forty copies of the city's brief were received at the Supreme Court on February 2, 1967. A few days later copies of the briefs of the Inc. Fund, the Solicitor General, and the city were distributed to the nine justices. At about the same time the court clerk's office notified the lawyers that the case of *Walker v. City of Birmingham* was scheduled for oral argument on Monday, March 13.

Presenting the case for the petitioners would be Jack Greenberg, a veteran of numerous Supreme Court arguments. Greenberg, knowing the high regard in which the justices held the Solicitor General's office, was quite willing to share his hour with Assistant Solicitor General Louis Claiborne. Greenberg would emphasize the defects in the parade-permit ordinance and the injunction, and would also discuss the Alabama law. Claiborne, who had argued before the court many times as a member of the Solicitor General's staff, would discuss the constitutionality of applying the *Mine Workers* rule in this kind of case.

The city's attorneys, Breckenridge and McBee, were no strangers to the Supreme Court either. Both of them had argued previously before the court, generally in losing causes wherever racial issues were involved. This time, however, they felt they had a good chance to win.

Perhaps even more than the briefs, oral argument provides an opportunity for the lawyer to apply persuasion to the justices. Justices who have publicly discussed the decisional process of the court have stressed the importance of oral argument. Justice Brennan, for example, once commented that "oral argument is the way we get answers to things that are bothering us about the case."

Knowing this importance of oral argument, the Inc. Fund staff had a standard practice of holding "dry runs." The lawyers would assume the roles of Supreme Court justices and pepper the attorney who would argue the case (most frequently, Greenberg) with the most difficult questions they could formulate. In early March, before going to Washington for the argument, they had a dry run in New York, and on the eve of the actual argument they had another one in a Washington hotel room. Norman Amaker later recalled that these sessions were not particularly encouraging. "We all knew that this was a tough case. We were fairly sure we could get four votes, but the trick would be to get the fifth."

At the Supreme Court Building on the morning of March 13 small knots of tourists and schoolchildren milled about in the long, marble-columned corridor that leads from the entrance of the building to the door that opens into the courtroom itself. Men with briefcases and preoccupied looks on their faces walked to and fro, talking with companions; these were the lawyers in the four cases to be argued that day. As ten o'clock drew near, the tourists formed into a single line outside the door to the courtroom; those who wanted to see the court in session could sit in the section of the courtroom set aside for spectators. Newspapers are not allowed to be taken inside the courtroom, but those who had bought a Washington *Post* earlier in the morning probably noticed a front-page story telling about a march which Martin Luther King had led the day before through one of Washington's ghetto neighborhoods. King was not in the Supreme Court on the morning of March 13, though, because of speaking engagements in the Midwest. Of the eight ministers, only Wyatt Walker—whose name the case now bore—was present at the oral argument.

Inside the courtroom, at precisely ten o'clock the court crier banged his gavel sharply. Everyone stood up, and the nine justices entered through the dark-red velour draperies behind the raised platform where the court sits. They remained standing at their places while the crier made the traditional announcement: "Oyez, Oyez, Oyez! All persons having business before the Honorable, the Supreme Court of the United States, are admonished to draw near and give their attention, for this Court is now sitting. God save the United States and this Honorable Court.''

There were three cases ahead of *Walker* on the court's calendar for that day, and it was not until 2:10 in the afternoon that the argument in the third one was concluded. Then, with about twenty minutes left in the day's session, Chief Justice Warren called the next case, "Number 249." The lawyers involved in *Walker v. City of Birmingham* moved to the two long counsel tables located directly in front of the bench. Jack Greenberg put his briefcase on one of the tables, then moved quickly to a lectern between the two tables and began his presentation of the petitioners' case.

Greenberg had just started to develop his argument about the constitutional infirmities of the injunction and the parade-permit ordinance which it embodied when Justice Harlan interrupted him: "There is a threshold thing that you have got to get over, the question of adequate state grounds. . . . If there is an adequate state ground, everything else you say is irrelevant. Therefore, I would suppose you would address yourself to first things first.''

Greenberg used Harlan's statement as a basis for launching into a discussion of Birmingham in 1963. This context was important, he said, to an understanding of all the issues in the case. Greenberg was describing how Bull Connor had rudely rebuffed two efforts of the demonstrators to obtain a parade permit and had sent them a telegram stating that the request for a permit would have to be referred to the entire City Commission, when Justice Stewart remarked, "Of course, that is what the ordinance says, does it not?''

> GREENBERG: Yes, the ordinance says that. But at the trial there was evidence to the effect that the permits were issued by the City Clerk on the recommendation of the Traffic Division, which was under the Police Commissioner, and all those proffers were refused.

JUSTICE STEWART: Well, but the ordinance does say the license must be secured from the Commission.

GREENBERG: That is right.

JUSTICE STEWART: The telegram also informed you that the license had to be secured from the Commission.

GREENBERG: That is correct.

JUSTICE STEWART: So that whatever might be done in the case, you were told by words of the ordinance and specific language of the telegram that your application for license had to be made to the Commission?

GREENBERG: That is correct. But if the evidence had been allowed, it would have developed, as the record shows, that in fact this ordinance was enforced in quite a different way; that the City Commission in fact had never granted a parade permit; that the parade permits were granted by the City Clerk on the recommendation of a subordinate of Commissioner Connor. I think that would make quite another story, if that were established in the record.

JUSTICE STEWART: Except the telegram told you the entire Commission had to grant it, and that is what the ordinance says.

GREENBERG: We were trying to prove that . . . the Commissioner was sending these petitioners to a procedure which all other citizens of Birmingham did not have to follow . . .

Greenberg had made his point that the petitioners had never had an opportunity to show the discriminatory way the permit requirement had been administered, but Stewart did not seem much impressed. It was not a good omen, since Stewart was the swing justice whom the Inc. Fund lawyers were most hopeful of persuading. A few minutes later, when Greenberg noted that Judge Jenkins' injunction had been issued without a hearing or even notice to the petitioners, Stewart again broke in:

JUSTICE STEWART: There is nothing wrong about that, is there? Are you implying that that's shocking, that you have a temporary restraining order without a hearing?

GREENBERG: Yes—not in the abstract, but I think we are dealing here with the First Amendment context, assessing the validity of the injunction and assessing the validity of contempt convictions. I think that all adds up to a general oppressive atmosphere, the way this type of proceeding was being used in the City of Birmingham. Essentially this TRO was granted on the affidavit of Bull Connor requesting the court to remit the petitioners back to Bull Connor if they wanted to march.

At this point the clock in the courtroom showed 2:30 P.M., and Justice Warren announced that the court would take its usual recess until the next morning. Jack Greenberg welcomed the break; it gave him an opportunity to discuss the justices' questions with the other Inc. Fund lawyers and to plan how to make best use of his remaining few minutes of time.

Talking about the argument over dinner that evening, the Inc. Fund lawyers felt that their initial instincts about the case were right: individual justices might be interested in the broad questions about the soundness of the *Mine Workers* rule, but their best chance to win the case lay in convincing one or more of the swing justices that they could strike down the convictions without having to reach the *Mine Workers* issue. They were not optimistic, however. The first day's argument had not gone well, and Stewart, in particular, had seemed very skeptical about their arguments.

When the argument resumed on Tuesday morning, Greenberg began by stressing that the court could reverse the Alabama judgment without reaching the great constitutional issue. This was a point that might carry weight with some of the more conservative members of the court—it is a traditional canon of judicial decision-making (albeit one that is frequently honored in the breach) that a court should not rule on important questions of constitutional law unless a case cannot be decided without doing so.

Greenberg then turned to what Justice Harlan had termed the day before the "threshold question" of whether the *Mine Workers* doctrine was an adequate state ground. Whatever the validity of the *Mine Workers* doctrine as an abstract matter, Greenberg stressed, it had not been fairly applied in this case. Since previous Alabama opinions had never unambiguously embodied the *Mine Workers* rule, he argued, the petitioners were entitled to believe they could challenge the injunction in a contempt proceeding. In several contempt cases of a few years earlier, he noted, the Alabama supreme court had apparently looked at both the question of the jurisdiction of the court which issued the injunction and the question of whether the injunction was void. Finally, responding to an observation by Justice White that a state is "free to change its own law" and adopt the *Mine Workers* rule as firm policy, Greenberg maintained that the petitioners were entitled to rely on Alabama law as they found it at the time the injunction was issued. Since Alabama had not clearly followed the *Mine Workers* rule prior to the issuance of the injunction in 1963, invocation of the rule by the Alabama supreme court could not bar consideration of the petitioners' First and Fourteenth Amendment arguments.

At this point a small white light on the lectern went on, indicating that Greenberg had only five minutes of his argument time left. Wishing to save a little time for rebuttal to the arguments that the city's attorneys would make, he closed by returning briefly to his contention that the petitioners had not had a chance to show at the trial how discriminatorily the parade-permit ordinance was administered. Before the court decided a far-reaching question such as the extent to which First Amendment rights can be frustrated by an injunction, he observed, it should at least have a complete record.

As Greenberg sat down at the counsel table, Louis Claiborne stepped to the lectern, dressed in the formal frock coat worn by lawyers from the Solicitor General's office when they argue before the court. Claiborne, a Southerner with more than a trace of accent in his voice, went immediately to the gravest issue in the case. "Our argument begins," he said, "with the premise that the Court will reach the *Mine Workers* issue here."

The *Mine Workers* doctrine, he observed, is "a remarkably extraordinary rule," in that it allows "the imposition of criminal penalties for the violation of a court order which is contrary to the law or contrary to the Constitution." Why, he asked, should violation of court orders be treated differently from violations of statutes which are invalid or of a policeman's orders which are unconstitutional? One answer, he said, is that court decrees must be obeyed because in our system courts are the final authority with respect to controversies, and if we do not obey them we "altogether abandon the rule of law." And, he continued, since courts need time to decide cases, it can be argued that their temporary orders to preserve the status quo must be respected.

But, said Claiborne, "in applying those rationales to this case it seems to us that in important respects they don't fit.
. . . [Here], the issuance of the injunction, if it had to be obeyed, mooted the legal controversy—because for all practical purposes these parades or marches could not be postponed indefinitely. Their timing was important in the context of Birmingham in 1963. This protest could not serve its purpose several months or years later when this injunction was ultimately vacated on appeal . . . ."

Justice Stewart interrupted Claiborne here, pressing him to state precisely why the Supreme Court should not allow the Alabama courts to apply the *Mine Workers* doctrine:

> JUSTICE STEWART: The Constitution prohibits the state in this case from following the *Mine Workers* rule. Is that your argument?
> CLAIBORNE: Yes, especially in the light of First Amendment rights which are affected on the other side.

JUSTICE STEWART: Is not your argument simply that this is an inadequate state ground? Or is that another way of putting the same thing?

CLAIBORNE: I suppose the inadequacy of the state ground would have to turn on its unconstitutionality.

JUSTICE STEWART: Not necessarily. Often a state ground is inadequate even though it may be perfectly constitutional.

CLAIBORNE: It wouldn't be here. . . . We rest on the rationale of the Green case—*In re Green*—in which, as I read the opinion, this Court held that the Fourteenth Amendment prohibits a state from denying the defense of invalidity with respect to an injunction issued by a court in an area which was pre-empted by federal legislation. Here we say that the area was pre-empted by the First Amendment and that the state court here, in issuing the over-broad injunction stifling First Amendment rights, was acting unconstitutionally beyond its jurisdiction in an area pre-empted by the Constitution—by the First Amendment. . . .

JUSTICE STEWART: Is your argument then confined to the First Amendment? Or is your argument the same if any provision of the Constitution deprived a state court of jurisdiction to issue the injunction, and, if not, why not? In other words, how can it logically be confined to the First Amendment, if it is?

CLAIBORNE: I do accept those rulings of this Court which view the First Amendment as more absolutely pre-empting from state courts—for that matter from federal courts—power to interfere in the First Amendment area than is true with respect to other constitutional guarantees. I don't see the necessity for reaching the question whether the same principle would apply elsewhere.

JUSTICE STEWART: Well, perhaps not in this case, but when we think of an argument and decide a case, it's certainly the better part of valor to think how far it does reach, isn't it?

Stewart pressed on, asking Claiborne a hypothetical question about a federal court order enjoining a person from getting a divorce under state law. Such an injunction would clearly be a violation of the Ninth or Tenth Amendment, he observed (since divorce is a matter clearly within the jurisdiction of state courts); could a person disobey it in his own discretion? When Claiborne answered "yes," to Stewart's evident surprise, Fortas helpfully broke in, saying, "Really all you are talking about is not whether the injunction can be disobeyed with impunity but whether the person who disobeys the injunction has the right to have his claim that the injunction was void examined by the court. Is that not right?" "Exactly so," replied Claiborne.

As Claiborne neared the close of his argument, he stressed the vagueness and overbreadth of the injunction and the parade-permit ordinance. Both the injunction and the ordinance, he observed, allowed the City Commission to withhold a permit on what amounted to "absolute unconfined discretion." "But," remarked Justice Stewart, "the Commission has never withheld a permit from these people because they never applied to the Commission."

For Justices White and Black, the critical issue seemed to be not the breadth of the injunction or the ordinance, but rather the nature of the petitioners' actions. "Do you have on the tip of your tongue," asked White, "cases in this Court which hold that parades like these are protected by the First Amendment?" Claiborne cited the line of cases which held that overly broad licensing statutes could be disregarded, but was immediately challenged by Justice Black. "Are you right now saying," asked Black, "that the right to parade on the streets of a city may be beyond the constitutional power of a city to control? . . . That seems to me to be the whole basis of this case, and I haven't yet heard a single case pointed to where this Court has held that to be the constitutional rule." Claiborne had to agree that no case had so held.

It was exactly 11 A.M. when Claiborne finished answering questions from the justices and Earl McBee rose to begin his presentation of the city's case. McBee started by reviewing some earlier Alabama supreme court decisions in contempt cases. These cases made it clear, he maintained, that the Alabama courts had for many years been applying the rule that a person charged with contempt could not challenge the validity of an injunction in the contempt proceedings. The application of the *Mine Workers* rule by the Alabama supreme court in affirming the petitioners' conviction was, he said, no change from prior Alabama law.

McBee then turned to the petitioners' contention that the injunction itself was unconstitutionally broad and vague. Shrewdly, he made the point that the injunction referred to specific acts designated in the bill of complaint, such as "mass picketing" and "mass demonstrations," thus turning the discussion to the demonstrations:

> McBee: In the Easter March there were approximately 1,500 to 2,000 . . . The entire street and sidewalks and everything was covered from side to side. On the march which occurred on the 12th of April most of the time they were on the sidewalks, using each sidewalk, but sometimes the street. But in the main on the sidewalks on Good Friday.
>
> Justice Black: Did they claim to have a constitutional right to march with that many people blocking the streets?
>
> McBee: The only constitutional right they claimed was when they came into court and said you are violating our constitutional rights—when they filed the motion to dissolve the injunction after the act had been committed. They committed the Good Friday marches and also the march on the 14th, Easter Sunday, before ever making any effort at all to obtain any sort of relief or permit. . . .
>
> Justice Black: How many marched [on Good Friday]?
>
> McBee: Well, on one side of the street the evidence is over 50 because over 50 were arrested, but they did not arrest all of them because they couldn't get to all of them. They were on the two sides of the street. Altogether the evidence is that there was some thousand involved in the entire proceedings.

Warren, who up until this point had been listening silently, now broke in with a series of questions which left little doubt that his sympathies lay with the petitioners. Three decades earlier, the silver-haired Chief Justice had been a vigorous prosecutor in California, and he now hunched forward and began cross-examining McBee:

CHIEF JUSTICE WARREN: Now those were the people who gathered—those weren't the people who marched on the 12th, were they? I find in the statement there were about 50 persons who marched on the sidewalks headed by Reverend Martin Luther King, Ralph Abernathy, and Fred L. Shuttlesworth. Is that wrong?

McBEE: That is only a part. That group, it is true, did march. But on the other side of the street the evidence is—Mr. Painter, a witness for the city, testified—that on the other side of the street the group outside the church also engaged in a march along with the other marchers. In other words, this technique of having the crowd and the marchers intermingled apparently had been followed in the other cases in movements in other situations.

CHIEF JUSTICE WARREN: I suppose if they had a crowd they would have to go home, wouldn't they? Is that a march when a crowd went home?

McBEE: Mr. Chief Justice, they joined in and went with the group. They were engaged in heading, so they said, to the City Hall. That is where their objective was and they were going in that direction at the time the arrests took place.

CHIEF JUSTICE WARREN: Where is it in the record, the number of people who were in the march? Not the people who had been assembled, who were going home, but how many people were in that march?

McBEE: I believe the testimony of Inspector Haley was that there were approximately 50. . . .

CHIEF JUSTICE WARREN: Where were those 50 walking? Were they in the street blocking traffic or were they walking along the sidewalk?

McBEE: The 50 basically were on the sidewalk and I believe the others were on the sidewalk too. They were on the other side of the street.

CHIEF JUSTICE WARREN: Now has your Supreme Court ever determined whether it is a violation of this ordinance to walk along the sidewalk?

McBEE: No, sir. The *Shuttlesworth* case, which the Court of Appeals has ruled upon, is now before the Supreme Court.

Warren's questions were clearly aimed at differentiating the actions of the marchers from those of the assembled crowds, but McBee was not ready to concede the distinction. Referring the justices to the trial testimony of state police lieutenant Willie Painter, McBee emphasized that on both Good Friday and Easter Sunday the onlookers had joined in a procession following the marchers, and that one of the defendants—Walker—had stated to Painter that he could "control" the crowds. He then went on to stress the same aspects of the Easter Sunday march that he had focused on at the trial:

> The crowd became unruly, became violent. At least one person was injured. A police officer was narrowly missed by a large brick. Damage to some city property occurred in that a three-wheeler was damaged, the radio antenna, I believe, and the windshield and some other things possibly, and there were a number of persons arrested for resisting arrest. There were a number arrested for assault and battery in connection with throwing of rocks and so on. . . . We simply say, may it please the Court, that we have more than a First Amendment freedom case.

When Breckenridge replaced McBee at the lectern at 11:30, the tone of the city's argument became more strident. The petitioners, Breckenridge said, came into Birmingham as "outsiders," at a time when the voters had just voted to change the city's form of government. They started demonstrations "at a time when it seemed to me reasonable to wait." Then, he went on, they chose to disobey the injunction, when "All they had to do under Alabama law was to dissolve the injunction or modify it, and have a hearing in a few days. There was nothing urgent about these demonstrations, about the timing, because they should have waited until the new government took place."

Stewart interrupted sharply, with a question which suggested that he might not yet have made up his mind about the case:

> JUSTICE STEWART: That was open to them—it was not up to you to decide how urgent it was, was it?
>
> BRECKENRIDGE: Well, they have raised the question. The appellants have raised the question of the urgency of the situation and the timing of the demonstrations.
>
> JUSTICE STEWART: They wanted to have the parade on Good Friday and Easter Sunday and those days come only once a year.

Outwardly unruffled by Stewart's comment, Breckenridge moved on to the heart of his argument—a portrayal of King and the other petitioners as militants who would not hesitate to flout the law:

> BRECKENRIDGE: Before this Court for the first time is a clear-cut statement of a theory that "we do not obey a law which we believe unnecessary."
>
> JUSTICE BLACK: What statement is that? Where is that statement?
>
> BRECKENRIDGE: Complainants' Exhibit 2.
>
> JUSTICE CLARK: Where is it in the record?
>
> BRECKENRIDGE: Page 410 of the record says: "Just as in all good conscience we cannot obey unjust laws, neither can we respect the unjust use of the courts."

JUSTICE BLACK: Who testified to that?

BRECKENRIDGE: This is a statement in a news release. It is a written statement by M. L. King, Jr., F. L. Shuttlesworth, Ralph Abernathy, *et al.*, for engaging in peaceful desegregation demonstrations.

Before Breckenridge could go further with his characterization of King as a lawbreaker, Earl Warren interrupted to ask him about official Birmingham's faithfulness to its own laws:

CHIEF JUSTICE WARREN: What was the practice in the city of Birmingham prior to this time for granting permits? You are the City Attorney.

BRECKENRIDGE: Mr. Chief Justice: I don't believe there was any established practice. I would not deny that there were times when probably a permit was issued by the city clerk, but if it was issued it was issued without authority of law or ordinance. Had our office been referred to, we would require it to be considered by the government as we required later that it be by the city council. . . .

CHIEF JUSTICE WARREN: Do the records of your city show that as a practice permits were granted by vote of the city commissioners or was it done *ex parte* through the clerk and the police officers?

BRECKENRIDGE: I am going to have to say I have not personally examined those records. I will say I believe they will show they were granted by the city clerk on approval of at least two commissioners rather than after formal action in the city commission meeting. Now that would be my thought. I have not reviewed the records. But I do think that would be the result. Of course I still say that is not relevant to this case. . . .

CHIEF JUSTICE WARREN: You mean that the city granted permits through the clerk without any reference to the city commission at all over a long period of time and when these people came in they said we don't have authority to do that—you have to go to the city commission and have it determine it at some future date?

BRECKENRIDGE: Mr. Chief Justice, I would say that you are correct if this was a prosecution for a violation of an ordinance. But not if it goes to the higher prosecution for contempt for violating a court order. A court order commands greater respect and must under our system of government command greater respect than an ordinance. If this order is wrong, come in and tell the judge. That is what these cases say all through the country—you come to the judge and get it modified. . . .

Breckenridge's argument ended just at noon, and the court took its usual luncheon recess. In 1967 the lunch break lasted only half an hour (it has since been extended to an hour), and Greenberg used the time to consult with the Inc. Fund lawyers on what points to try to make in the five minutes he had saved for rebuttal. He decided to try to respond to Justice Black's concerns about the nature of the demonstrations and the power of a municipality to control the use of its streets.

When the afternoon session began, he moved quickly to a discussion of these issues. Certainly, he said, he would concede that a municipality could regulate use of the streets "and perhaps under some circumstances prohibit use of the streets." But, he added, "we think the law is clear that it must be done under precise standards and it must be done on the basis of equality." As for the demonstrations involved in the *Walker* case, he observed, none of the marchers had been involved in any disorders and the city police had not found it necessary to seek assistance from the sheriff's office or the state police.

The argument closed with Justice Black inquiring whether there had been any effort to obtain a parade permit. Greenberg responded by telling of Lola Hendricks' attempt to obtain a permit on April 3 and Bull Connor's response: "No, you will not get a permit . . . to picket. I will picket you over to the City Jail."

14

The Court Chooses Order

WITH THE CONCLUSION of oral argument on Tuesday, March 14, the lawyers had finished their input to the court. Now it was up to the justices. During the years of the Warren court, most of the justices would meet with their two law clerks on Thursdays to go over the cases that would be discussed and voted on at the court's Friday conference. Typically, there would be a review of the facts and legal issues in each case, especially as these had been illuminated (or obscured) by the oral argument. A justice might tell his clerks that he had a firm idea how he would vote the next day, and solicit ideas about the best supports for his position. Or he might ask the clerks how they saw the case, and listen to them rehearse or debate the issues. It was also common for the group to speculate about how the other justices would be likely to line up on the case.

Such speculations about the Friday conference vote in *Walker* must have gone on in quite a few of the nine oak-paneled suites that Thursday, since the outcome of the case was far from clear at that point. Questioning by the justices at the oral argument had not revealed how each of the court's members would vote. And, on its merits, the case was a difficult one. Like so many of the "hard cases" in American constitutional jurisprudence, *Walker* presented a difficult choice between two fundamental values of the American constitutional system; in this instance, between the First Amendment right to protest and the principle that court orders should be respected and reviewed through orderly judicial processes.

However, it was not absolutely necessary that the court reach this fundamental question. The justices could find a technical procedural ground on which to send the case back to the lower courts for further proceedings or they could void the conviction on a narrow basis, as the court did in the demonstration cases between 1962 and 1964.

These were the kinds of choices that the justices brought into the conference room of the Supreme Court at 11 A.M. on Friday, March 17. By long tradition, the justices shook hands with each other on entering the room, moved to their respective name-plated chairs around the long rectangular conference table, and settled down to a full day's work. To safeguard the secrecy of the proceedings, only the justices are permitted in the room—no clerks, no secretaries, not even a messenger. Again by custom, the junior justice (Abe Fortas that day) goes to the door to receive or pass out messages. The room is both warm and stately, lined with ceiling-to-floor bookcases filled with the volumes containing federal court decisions. A portrait of the great nineteenth-century Chief Justice, John Marshall, is the only wall decoration.

Chief Justice Earl Warren took his assigned place at the head of the table, at the south end of the room, facing Justice Hugo Black, the senior associate, at the opposite end. In front of ''the Chief,'' as he was usually called by his colleagues, was a large docket book in which their votes would be recorded. Justice Clark has described the protocol by which conference deliberations proceed:

> We first take out our assignment sheets or list of cases for the day. . . . The Chief Justice starts the conference by calling

the first case and discussing it. He then yields to the senior Associate Justice and on down the line seniority-wise until each Justice who wishes to be heard has spoken. There is no time limitation. The order is never interrupted nor is the speaker. . . . After discussion of a case, a vote is taken. . . . Ever since John Marshall's day the formal vote begins with the junior Justice and moves up through the ranks of seniority, the Chief Justice voting last.

Even though we have no information about what actually took place when the *Walker* case was considered that day, by knowing the order in which the case was discussed and voted upon, we can venture some speculation. The discussion would have begun with the Chief Justice and continued in this order: Hugo Black, William O. Douglas, Tom C. Clark, John M. Harlan, William J. Brennan, Jr., Potter Stewart, Byron R. White, and Abe Fortas. On the basis of their prior positions in the relevant cases and the way they eventually cast their votes in *Walker,* and assuming that each justice expressed his viewpoint, we can visualize a scene such as this: The Chief Justice would have stated the facts of the case, framed the issues, and declared the reasons of law and policy why he believed the *Walker* convictions had to be overturned. Justice Hugo Black would have spoken next, making it clear that he would uphold the convictions. Douglas would have added a second voice for reversal, and Clark a second for affirmance, and expressions by Harlan (affirmance) and Brennan (reversal) would have brought the situation to a 3–3 tie when it came to Justice Stewart. Since he could fairly expect the two remaining justices to adopt opposite positions (White for affirmance and Fortas for reversal), Stewart was obviously the pivotal man. His resolution of the conflicting constitutional values, his selection between the alternative lines of precedent, and his notion of the sociopolitical message that the court should be sending out at that moment would be critical. Judging from the intensity of the opinions that were ultimately filed in the case, there was probably animated discussion among the justices after their initial statements, and then the vote would have been taken: from Fortas up the ladder to the Chief. Since it is rare for the justices to change their vote between the time they cast it at the conference and the final vote after circulation of draft opinions, we can assume that the vote on March 17 was probably 5–4 to uphold the convictions, with Justice Stewart providing the decisive vote.

By custom, if the Chief Justice is not among the majority justices, the senior associate justice—in this case, Hugo Black—assigns the writing of the majority opinion, usually a few days after the conference has ended. The senior justice can take this function for himself, but it is common in closely divided cases for the senior associate to choose one of the "centrist" members of the majority to do this. The idea is that such a justice will usually seek a careful and limited way of formulating the ruling and explaining it to the public, and his working out of the competing interests is most likely to keep the majority's five or more votes intact. In this tradition, Black assigned the opinion to Stewart.

The drafting of a majority opinion, its circulation to the other justices for their comments and suggestions, any revisions undertaken, and the writing and circulation of dissenting opinions may take anywhere from a few weeks to several months. When that process is completed and the final drafts of the opinions are ready, the case is presented at a Friday conference and a final vote is taken. Then it will be scheduled for public announcement, and the printed opinions will be made up, under tight security procedures, in the court's own basement printing plant.

While these procedures were being followed between March and June 1967, racial conflicts and the activities of Dr. Martin Luther King, Jr., continued to be front-page news in the nation. After the urban riots in Chicago, Cleveland, and San Francisco during the summer of 1966 and the spread of "black power" rhetoric among several formerly integrationist and nonviolent organizations like SNCC and CORE, white public opinion in the nation swung into what came to be called "backlash" against further major Negro demands. The Johnson Administration's latest civil rights bill, which would have desegregated juries, protected civil rights workers, extended fair employment practices, and instituted fair housing guarantees, could not overcome Senate filibuster opposition and was pronounced dead for 1967.

On March 24 King announced that he had decided to make an attack on the Administration's war policy in Vietnam a major priority, since it had become "the major obstacle to the civil rights movement in America." Not only was it shifting governmental and public attention away from civil rights but it was also draining off the funds needed to make antipoverty programs more than Band-Aid measures. In an interview published on April 2, he said he would have to "weigh" leading a civil disobedience campaign if the government continued to step up the war, and this was soon followed by a major speech at New York City's Riverside Church in which he pledged such massive antiwar protests. On April 15 he marched in New York City with 125,000 people in the Spring Mobilization Against the War in Vietnam. Throughout April and May, King came under sharp criticism for getting into the "war issue" and not "sticking to civil rights." His critics included Vice-President Humphrey, Solicitor General Thurgood Marshall, FBI Director J. Edgar Hoover, Roy Wilkins, Senator Jacob Javits, Ralph Bunche, and many others. A Louis Harris poll reported that 60 percent of the total population (though only 30 percent among Negroes alone) believed King's stand would damage the civil rights movement.

King not only persisted in linking the war and civil rights, but he also declared that the civil rights movement was now moving into a new, second stage. In an article in *The New York Times Magazine* on June 11, he said the rights movement would seek to spur a radical restructuring of the nation's economic and political institutions. Negroes must organize politically and use their power to force the government to reorder its priorities. Unless this was done, he warned, the "language of the unheard"—urban riots—would be the tragic result.

On Sunday, June 11, Martin Luther King had spoken. The next day it was the turn of the U.S. Supreme Court.

June 12 was the last day of the court's 1966–67 term. Since a large number of important cases argued in earlier months would be "coming down" this last Monday, the courtroom was packed with reporters and members of the Washington bar, along with the usual tourists.

The court had over a dozen major rulings to announce. The practice is for the Chief Justice to nod to the justice who wrote the majority opinion in the case ready for announcement, then that justice states the case number (and sometimes its title) and the judgment reached. How fully a justice wishes to make his oral announcement of the decision is up to him. Some justices, especially in litigation of high legal or public interest, make full-dress presentations of the facts and read large parts (or even all) of the majority opinion. In the most highly charged cases, they may add some pointed extemporaneous comments that do not appear in the written opinion. Other justices announcing opinions content themselves with a straightforward indication of the result and mention of who joined the majority and who dissented. Whether a dissenting justice wishes to make extemporaneous remarks about his opinion or read it all is also a matter of his choice, and dissenters too sometimes enliven opinion day with pertinent asides.

On the morning of June 12 Justice Fortas first summarized the decision in three business-regulation cases. Then the Chief Justice nodded to Justice Potter Stewart. "I have the opinion for the Court in Number 249, *Walker v. City of Birmingham*," he began. His presentation was very full and firm, but not emotionally declaimed. Stewart believes that since decisions of the court are announced publicly, this ought to be an educational occasion, with a cogent outlining of the facts, issues, judgment, and reasons, and that was the way he treated *Walker*. When he finished, he noted that the Chief Justice and Justices Douglas, Brennan, and Fortas dissented. Because of the large number of cases to announce, none of these justices gave oral presentations of their reasons for dissenting.

As soon as Stewart started announcing the decision, the court clerk's office gave the full printed opinions in *Walker* to the waiting newsmen. With so many important decisions on this last day, *Walker* had to vie for space in newspaper and television coverage. But one item was featured in all the media: the United States Supreme Court had upheld Alabama's contempt conviction of Martin Luther King.

Stewart's opinion began with a dry recital of the history of the case, starting with the allegations of potential disorder on which the city of Birmingham had based its successful request for an injunction. The opinion then related the statements of the movement's leaders at their April 11 press conference and at the church meeting that evening declaring that they intended to violate the injunction; the actual participation of three of the petitioners in the Good Friday march and of four of them in the Easter Sunday march; and the size and behavior of the crowds that had congregated to see the demonstrations, particularly on Easter Sunday, when rocks had been thrown by members of the crowd. There was nothing said in the majority opinion about why the demonstrations were held or about the patterns of segregation which had existed in Birmingham in 1963. Martin Luther King, Jr., was not mentioned anywhere by name, nor any of the other Negro leaders; the opinion referred to them only as "the petitioners."

Stewart concluded his review of the proceedings in Alabama by quoting from the Alabama supreme court's reliance on *Howat v. Kansas* for the proposition that an injunction's validity could not be challenged in a contempt proceeding. In the *Howat* case, he said, the U.S. Supreme Court had "not only unanimously accepted but fully approved the validity of the rule of state law upon which the judgment of the Kansas court was grounded." Such a rule, he noted, citing the *Mine Workers* case and several lower federal court decisions, was consistent with the rule followed by the federal courts.

For Stewart, the question was whether the rule approved in *Howat* should now be held "constitutionally impermissible." "We are asked," he said, "to say that the Constitution compelled Alabama to allow the petitioners to violate this injunction, to organize and engage in these mass street parades and demonstrations, without any previous effort on their part to have the injunction dissolved or modified, or any attempt to secure a parade permit in accordance with its terms." Stewart had little difficulty in rejecting that suggestion.

He acknowledged that the language of both the parade-permit ordinance and the injunction itself were "subject to substantial constitutional question." But, he added, citing cases which recognized "the strong interest of state and local governments in regulating the use of their streets and their public places," this was "not a case where the injunction was transparently invalid or had only a frivolous pretense to validity." Since this was so, the way to raise constitutional questions about the ordinance, the injunction, and the allegedly arbitrary manner in which the permit requirement was administered would be by presenting these issues to the Alabama courts, not by violating the court order. In Stewart's words:

This case would arise in quite a different constitutional posture if the petitioners, before disobeying the injunction, had challenged it in the Alabama courts, and had been met with delay or frustration of their constitutional claims. But there is no showing that such would have been the fate of a timely motion to modify or dissolve the injunction. There was an interim of two days between the issuance of the injunction and the Good Friday march. The petitioners give absolutely no explanation of why they did not make some application to the state court during that period. The injunction had issued *ex parte;* if the court had been presented with the petitioners' contentions, it might well have dissolved or at least modified its order in some respects. If it had not done so, Alabama procedure would have provided for an expedited process of appellate review. It cannot be presumed that the Alabama courts would have ignored the petitioners' constitutional claims. Indeed, these contentions were accepted in another case by an Alabama appellate court that struck down on direct review the conviction under this very ordinance of one of these same petitioners.

Nor was this a case, said Stewart, in which the Alabama courts had departed from prior precedents and applied a newly enunciated rule of law against a litigant. Citing several earlier Alabama supreme court decisions in contempt cases, he observed that the Alabama court had "apparently never in any criminal contempt case entertained a claim of nonjurisdictional error." These precedents, he said, "clearly put the petitioners on notice that they could not bypass orderly judicial review of the injunction before disobeying it. Any claim that they were entrapped or misled is wholly unfounded, a conclusion confirmed by evidence in the record showing that when the petitioners deliberately violated the injunction they expected to go to jail."

Stewart ended his relatively short opinion with a strong rhetorical flourish:

The rule of law that Alabama followed in this case reflects a belief that in the fair administration of justice no man can be judge in his own case, however exalted his station, however righteous his motives, and irrespective of his race, color, politics, or religion. This Court cannot hold that the petitioners were constitutionally free to ignore all the procedures of the law and carry their battle to the streets. One may sympathize with the petitioners' impatient commitment to their cause. But respect for judicial process is a small price to pay for the civilizing hand of the law, which alone can give abiding meaning to constitutional freedom.

Despite the rhetoric in the closing paragraph, the majority opinion was not a sweeping one in terms of the constitutional issues involved. Stewart carefully avoided an explicit endorsement of the *Mine Workers* and *Howat* cases. Although he noted that the majority holding was consistent with those cases, he emphasized that the *Walker* decision was limited to the facts of this particular case: where the state's rule of law was long established; where no effort had been made to challenge the validity of the injunction in court before violating it; and where no explanation had been advanced for that failure. To lawyers and groups concerned with the long-range development of First Amendment law, the opinion could be seen as relatively narrow.

The dissenting justices expressed themselves in three separate, sharply worded opinions which attacked both the presentation of facts and legal reasoning in the majority opinion. These were written by Chief Justice Warren, Justice Douglas, and Justice Brennan.

For Earl Warren, writing one of his rare dissenting opinions, the crucial facts were not the actions of the petitioners and the crowds of onlookers, as Stewart had stressed. Rather, Warren emphasized the well-known opposition of Bull Con-

nor and other Birmingham officials to any attempts at desegregation, the indications in the record (particularly the testimony of Mrs. Lola Hendricks) that the petitioners had made
good-faith attempts to obtain a permit but had been frustrated
because the parade-permit ordinance was administered in a
discriminatory fashion, the symbolic importance to the protesters of marching on Good Friday and Easter Sunday, and
the fact that the petitioners had willingly submitted to arrest
and prosecution for violating the injunction. Where Stewart
had pointedly noted the rock throwing by onlookers that had
taken place on Easter Sunday, Warren characterized the two
marches simply as "peaceful demonstrations."

The facts of the case, said Warren, "lend no support to the
Court's charges that petitioners were presuming to act as
judges in their own case, or that they had a disregard for the
judicial process." Noting that the petitioners had readily submitted to the jurisdiction of the Jefferson County circuit court
the Monday following the marches, he brought in an analogy
that Stewart had ignored:

> They [the petitioners] were in essentially the same position as
> persons who challenge the constitutionality of a statute by
> violating it, and then defend the ensuing criminal prosecution
> on constitutional grounds. It has never been thought that viola-
> tion of a statute indicated such a disrespect for the legislature
> that the violator always must be punished even if the statute
> was unconstitutional. On the contrary, some cases have
> required that persons seeking to challenge the constitutionality
> of a statute first violate it to establish their standing to sue. In-
> deed, it shows no disrespect for law to violate a statute on the
> ground that it is unconstitutional and then to submit one's case
> to the courts with the willingness to accept the penalty if the
> statute is held to be valid.

The heart of the case, to Warren, lay in the failure of the
majority to acknowledge that the injunction simply incorpo-

rated a parade-permit ordinance whose vesting of "totally un-fettered discretion" in city officials made it "patently uncon-stitutional." The injunction, he commented sarcastically, was treated by the majority as "such potent magic that it trans-formed the command of an unconstitutional statute into an impregnable barrier, challengeable only in what likely would have been protracted legal proceedings and entirely superior in the meantime even to the United States Constitution." Warren minced no words in attacking the majority's conten-tion that obedience to a court injunction is always necessary to preserve respect for courts and law:

> I do not believe that giving this Court's seal of approval to such a gross misuse of the judicial process is likely to lead to greater respect for the law any more than it is likely to lead to greater protection for First Amendment freedoms. The *ex parte* temporary injunction has a long and odious history in this country, and its susceptibility to misuse is all too apparent from the facts of the case.

Even if the *Howat* decision was considered a precedent for upholding a state rule such as Alabama's, Warren read the court's later *In re Green* decision as a major modification of *Howat*. Stewart had attempted to distinguish the *Green* deci-sion by noting that the petitioner there sought to have the in-junction vacated before violating it, and that the court which had issued the injunction had agreed to its violation as an ap-propriate means of testing its validity. Warren maintained that those facts were irrelevant to the *Green* holding—that "a state court is without power to hold one in contempt for violating an injunction that the state court had no power to enter by reason of federal pre-emption." Therefore, he argued, a state court injunction can be challenged on First Amendment grounds in a contempt proceeding.

Finally, Warren insisted, neither *Howat* nor *Mine Workers* supported the majority's holding. In both those cases, the injunctions had been issued in order to preserve the status quo while the issuing court inquired into the merits of underlying labor/management disputes. In the *Walker* case, there was no underlying dispute before the court that issued the injunction: "The court in practical effect merely added a judicial signature to a pre-existing criminal ordinance." Whatever the scope of the *Mine Workers* doctrine may be, the Chief Justice concluded, "it plainly was not intended to give a State the power to nullify the United States Constitution by the simple process of incorporating its unconstitutional criminal statutes into judicial decrees."

Justice Douglas wrote a short dissent which focused on the circuit court's "jurisdiction" to issue its broad injunction. The *Howat–Mine Workers* rule has an exception, he noted, "where the 'question of jurisdiction' is 'frivolous and not substantial.' " For Douglas, it was clear from the record that the petitioners' First Amendment rights "peaceably to assemble, and to petition the Government for a redress of grievances" were abridged by the Jenkins injunction. Using a broader definition of the concept of "jurisdiction" than either Judge Jenkins or Justice Stewart had employed, he maintained that the state court, like any other instrumentality of the state, had no jurisdiction—no legitimate power—to abridge these rights:

> A court does not have *jurisdiction* to do what a city or other agency of a State lacks *jurisdiction* to do. The command of the Fourteenth Amendment, through which the First Amendment is made applicable to the States, is that no "State" shall deprive any person of "liberty" without due process of law. The decree of a state court is "state" action in the constitutional sense (*Shelley v. Kraemer,* 334 U.S. [1948]), as much as the action of the state police, the state prosecutor, the state legislature, or the Governor himself. An ordinance—unconstitutional on its face or patently unconstitutional as applied—is not made

sacred by an unconstitutional injunction that enforces it. It can and should be flouted in the manner of the ordinance itself. Courts as well as citizens are not free "to ignore all the procedures of the law," to use the Court's language. The "constitutional freedom" of which the Court speaks can be won only if judges honor the Constitution.

Justice Brennan began his dissent with an opening paragraph that was the most blistering in tone of all the minority opinions:

> Under cover of exhortation that the Negro exercise "respect for judicial process," the Court empties the Supremacy Clause of its primacy by elevating a state rule of judicial administration above the right of free expression guaranteed by the Federal Constitution. And the Court does so by letting loose a devastatingly destructive weapon for suppression of cherished freedoms heretofore believed indispensable to maintenance of our free society. I cannot believe that this distortion in the hierarchy of values upon which our society has been and must be ordered can have any significance beyond its function as a vehicle to affirm these contempt convictions.

Like Warren, Brennan reviewed the facts of the case in some detail, emphasizing points which Stewart had played down or ignored. Thus, for example, he commented that in April 1963 "Birmingham was a world symbol of implacable official hostility to Negro efforts to gain civil rights, however peacefully sought," and he directed considerable attention to the trial testimony about the petitioners' unsuccessful attempts to obtain a parade permit. In describing the Good Friday and Easter Sunday marches, he emphasized that the participants in both parades had been in every way orderly. According to a police inspector, he noted, the only episode of violence had been rock throwing on Easter Sunday, after the marchers had been arrested, by three onlookers who were immediately taken into custody by the police.

Turning to the legal considerations, Brennan acknowledged that a state had a valid interest in the enforcement of decrees of its courts and was free to adopt rules of judicial administration designed to ensure respect for those decrees. But, he went on, "a valid state interest must give way when it infringes on rights guaranteed by the Federal Constitution." In order to ensure that First Amendment freedoms have the necessary "breathing space" to survive, the Supreme Court had formulated legal rules to enable individuals to express themselves in the face of such restraints and to challenge subsequently the constitutionality of the restraints. One example he discussed was the long-established rule that an individual accused of violating a statute requiring a license to undertake certain activities could contest the constitutionality of the statute at his trial. "Yet," said Brennan acidly, "by some inscrutable legerdemain, these constitutionally secured rights to challenge prior restraints invalid on their face are lost if the State takes the precaution to have some judge append his signature to an *ex parte* order which recites the words of the invalid statute."

Brennan contrasted what he called the court's "religious deference" to Alabama's application of the *Mine Workers* rule here with the court's rejection of the asserted state interest in the *Green* case. It was "an odd inversion of values," he suggested, to overturn a state court contempt conviction because of an "arguable" collision with federal labor policy but to affirm the conviction in a case where the *ex parte* order, as well as the permit ordinance which it incorporated, were more than arguably repugnant on their face to the First Amendment of the Constitution.

Brennan also discussed the practical effect of the majority's insistence that the petitioners should have tried to have the injunction dissolved before holding their demonstrations. A cessation of the protest activities, he noted, might have dealt a crippling blow to their efforts to arouse community support for their assault on segregation in Birmingham. The timing of the marches—deliberately scheduled for Good Friday and Easter Sunday—was critically important to them, and there was no way of knowing how long dissolution proceedings might take. To preach "respect for judicial process" in this context, said Brennan, "is to deny the right to speak at all."

15

Back to Birmingham Jail— and to Memphis

SOME OF THE SCLC leaders were surprised by the *Walker* decision; others were not. But all were dismayed. "Martin was terribly saddened by the ruling," Bayard Rustin recalled. "He saw it as the courts saying, 'Go slow, let things catch up.' But it threatened the whole future of the movement, giving a sharp weapon to the forces of the status quo." To Wyatt Walker, King remarked that the injunction procedure "will be a license to thwart our demonstrations. We used to have the Supreme Court as an ally; now even they have turned against us." Walker himself called the decision "the biggest disappointment I ever had in the civil rights movement. . . . I couldn't believe we had lost."

Charles Hamilton, who had been in Birmingham in 1963 as part of the SNCC group, remembered his reactions to the *Walker* ruling vividly. "Black people weren't looking at the *Walker* case before it was handed down, since Birmingham was a thing of the past by then. The action was in the North, with a whole new language, ideology, and issues. But when the ruling was announced, black people got the message loud and clear: this is it, the turning point of the 1960s. The honeymoon is over. The day of looking to the high court is finished. We knew that if the justices ruled against King, then no other black leader could expect much when he ran afoul of racist justice." Hamilton added, "The white media didn't play up the decision much, but it had a deep psychological effect within the black community."

The prospect of spending five days in jail was not very frightening to King and the other ministers, of course. They had been in jail before, and expected to be there again in the pursuit of racial justice. Ralph Abernathy even joked about the decision with one of SCLC's legal advisers, Harry Wachtel. Abernathy had a long-standing "agreement" with Wachtel. "If you keep me out of jail, Harry," he would say, "I'll keep you out of hell." On the day the *Walker* case was announced, Wachtel received a call from Abernathy. "Well, Harry," the minister said, "I guess this lets me off the hook."

The *Walker* ruling was praised editorially in *The New York Times,* Washington *Post,* and other newspapers, though the *Times* added that having "one of the nation's foremost religious leaders and a Nobel Prize laureate in jail is profoundly embarrassing to the good name of the United States."

Many black and white leaders active in civil rights felt that the court's ruling was predestined by the flow of events on the racial front during 1965–67. Ramsey Clark, then Attorney General, recalled recently that while he regretted the opinion when it was announced, "I didn't think it was absolutely horrible. It was technical, and rather limited. In the broader sweep, I didn't think it was all that significant. It really wouldn't have made any difference in the national civil rights picture if it had gone the other way." The real change in the civil rights situation, he felt, came with the change in public attitudes after the riots. *"Walker* just capped the mood. It followed the country." As Clark saw it, the movement in 1967 "desperately needed to reestablish its moral focus, to persuade the nation of the continued importance of the equality struggle." It was time, he felt, for "persevering through the storm, not going slow. New goals had to be developed, and better organization."

In Birmingham, Mayor Albert Boutwell hailed the *Walker* decision, stating that "the dignity of the courts and the orderly process of law that required trial before courts and not on the streets have been widely and properly sustained by this ruling." An adverse ruling, he said, "would have opened the door to chaos instead of the rule of law."

The Inc. Fund lawyers naturally were disappointed with the decision. They were also highly critical of the reasoning of the majority opinion, and vented this criticism in a petition for rehearing, which was filed in early July. In the petition the lawyers acknowledged that "rehearing is granted rarely, and never lightly." But, they concluded, after reviewing what they regarded as some of the more glaring defects in the majority opinion, "the implications of this decision are so dangerous to First Amendment freedoms that it deserves reconsideration."

> For those concerned with law and order, as well as equal justice and social progress, this is the worst of all possible decisions. The peaceful protest movement—no matter how dissonant it may have become—has channeled dissatisfaction with deeply ingrained injustices into constructive social change. In the face of boiling resentment against long-standing injustices and ugly traditions of oppression, the peaceful protest movement has achieved not only some measure of equal justice and social progress, but has contributed to stability. By this decision the Court devastates the peaceful protest movement and leaves the field to capture by those violent elements who do not stop to read injunctions.

In submitting the petition for rehearing, the petitioners were supported by two interest groups. Both the American Jewish Congress and the AFL-CIO filed *amicus curiae* briefs urging the court to grant a rehearing. The AFL-CIO brief emphasized the significance of the *Walker* ruling for union organizing activity:

> In a labor relations context this doctrine means that unions and workers must forego their right to picket or strike, in deference to an unconstitutional ordinance or an illegal injunction, at the height of a strike or organizing campaign. It means that an unscrupulous city council or judge can break any strike or organizing campaign, even if the organizers or strikers are so sure that the ordinance or injunction is illegal that they are ready to risk jail if they are wrong. We submit that any state procedural rule which requires forfeiture of federal rights in deference to an illegal ordinance or court order is itself an invalid restraint.

Early in the fall of 1967 the Supreme Court convened for the start of the 1967–68 term. The petition for rehearing in *Walker v. City of Birmingham* was one of several hundred matters the justices considered during their initial week of conferences. On Monday, October 10, in a brief unsigned order, the court denied the petition.

Three weeks later King and his associates flew from Atlanta to Birmingham to begin serving their sentences. While in jail King was cheered by the delegation of fifty SCLC supporters who gathered each afternoon and evening outside the jail to sing freedom songs and spirituals for the ministers and "keep a vigil" with them. Inside the jail, Wyatt Walker recalled, "we spent a good bit of time talking about the future of the movement. . . . It was a good week, a chance to be all together and talk seriously. We'd sing too—we had a fine jailhouse quartet." Between the planning and the singing, they spoke of the *Walker* ruling's meaning for the movement. "Martin's thoughts were that we would do what we had to do," Walker said. "We could not count on the Supreme Court any more. We might be coming to the point of having to spend real time in jail, maybe a year or two. Martin didn't like jail—no one did, really—but he said that maybe that was where we'd have to be.'' They also began to evolve plans for a black and white Poor People's Campaign to be initiated in local communities and then converge on Washington in the spring of 1968.

Later in November, at an SCLC staff retreat held in Frogmore, South Carolina, King analyzed the harsh realities confronting the SCLC and the civil rights forces two years after the Selma victory. ''The decade of 1955 to 1965, with its elementary constructive periods, has misled us,'' King said. ''Everyone underestimated the amount of rage Negroes were suppressing, and the amount of bigotry the white majority was disguising.'' The civil rights movement had failed so far in the Northern ghettos, he felt, because the forces of racial discrimination were more complex and intractable there than in the South. After discussing and rejecting the idea that riots and ''rebellion'' offered any hope for the American Negro, either in practical terms or as a morally proper course of action, King turned to the growing white attacks on ''black lawlessness.'' It is true, he noted, that residents of the black slums had rioted and that the crimes committed in the ghetto were destructive to person and property. ''But these are essentially derivative crimes,'' King declared, ''they are born of the greater crimes of white society.'' It was the dominant white society which created the frustrating slums that brought unemployment, poverty, and oppression, and it was in this context that obedience to law had to be discussed.

As the reexaminations and strategy meetings took place in late 1967, both friends and critics of Dr. King agreed that it was a lean and troubled time for the movement. More than two years had elapsed since King had led a victorious civil rights campaign. The direct-action movement rested on the engineering of such victories: the mounting of moral and political spectacles, the sharp dramatization of racism, national media attention, the unification of liberal and civil rights

forces behind King, federal executive intervention, new federal civil rights laws, and badly needed donations to the
SCLC bank account.

But the last such victory had been Selma. Now King was
under a barrage of sharp criticism. Black militants branded
his nonviolent strategy foolish and defeatist; Adam Clayton
Powell called him "Martin Loser King." Liberals, labor
leaders, and moderate Negroes allied with the Johnson Administration decried his increasingly vocal stand against the
Vietnam War and his growing alliance with New Left figures. After King's antiwar speech at Riverside Church in
New York in April 1967, for example, Carl Rowan, a Negro
journalist with close ties to the Johnson Administration,
wrote a slashing attack on King which appeared in the September *Reader's Digest*. At the same time, white radicals
condemned his campaigns in the Northern ghettos as ineffec-
tual, diversionary efforts.

King felt these attacks sharply, as he always did. But they
had been made before, in the interims between Montgomery
and Birmingham and between Birmingham and Selma. Those
experiences led him to believe that a proper confrontation
with racial injustice could bring the forces of equality
together again despite the disunity of 1967–68. The chosen
vehicle was the Poor People's Campaign.

This was to be King's first "class"- rather than "race"-based
effort, a national campaign to bring the poverty and discrimination faced by poor blacks and whites alike to the unwilling
attention of the nation's lawmakers. Announced in December
1967, King's plan called for an interracial delegation of three
thousand poor people—blacks, whites, Chicanos, and Indians—from ten cities and five rural communities throughout
the country to be organized by the SCLC staff and local
movement people. In April the delegations would make their
slow but well-publicized ways to the nation's capital, where
they would build an encampment, to be known as Resurrec-

tion City, along the Potomac. The assembled groups would then present their demands for a new economic agenda to the President and Congress, engage in direct-lobbying meetings with legislators, and undertake "creative dislocation" of national business-as-usual. If such an attempt at rearranging the congressional agenda meant going to jail, King advised, "we will accept that."

From the White House, most of the Negro leadership (the NAACP, Urban League, etc.), and most of the white liberal community came the reaction that this was an ill-timed and unwise move. There was doubt whether such a demonstration could be kept nonviolent in the post-Newark, post-Detroit era. Even within King's own circle, people like Bayard Rustin felt the Washington encampment offered no real leverage as a direct-action campaign; you could not deal with the Congress in the same way that you did with a local segregated community in the South. Furthermore, the Poor People's Campaign evoked memories of the Bonus Marchers who descended on Washington in 1932, also camping out in the open, to pressure Congress for legislation to aid jobless veterans of World War I. Congress refused to pass the bill, and President Herbert Hoover had ordered the veterans driven forcibly from Washington by federal troops, under General Douglas MacArthur. It was a nasty precedent to ponder, but the fact that driving the poor out of Washington this time would have to be done in full view of television cameras offered some hope for a different outcome.

In late February, while King was engaged in planning for the April march on Washington, several black ministers from Memphis, Tennessee, asked him to come to their city to help build support for a strike by thirteen hundred black garbagemen. As King's good friend, Rev. James Lawson of the Centenary Methodist Church, outlined the situation, it sounded like a promising update of the Montgomery struggle of 1956.

In 1966, newly chartered as Local 1733 of the American Federation of State, County, and Municipal Employees, the garbage workers of Memphis had sought recognition of their union from the city and had asked for a contract providing better wages and working conditions. The city refused to recognize the union and obtained a court injunction against a strike. The situation simmered for over a year. Then, in early February 1968, two members of a work crew who had taken refuge from a heavy rain in the barrel of their truck were crushed to death when the mechanism started accidentally. A few days later a number of men had their pay docked for refusing to go out in another heavy downpour. On February 12 the garbage workers walked off the job, demanding recognition of their union as the bargaining agent for garbagemen, higher pay, improved working conditions, a grievance procedure, and similar basic union-contract provisions.

For a time it looked as though the dispute would be resolved by negotiation with the City Council. These hopes were dashed on February 23 when the council voted to leave the matter to Mayor Henry Loeb, who flatly rejected all negotiations. Outraged by the council's action, the strikers marched in protest down Main Street. Some incidents broke out between marchers and the police, who rushed into the crowds using cans of Mace. Local black ministers who were with the marchers were deliberately Maced. Overnight the strike became the central issue of the Memphis black community, uniting the churches, the NAACP, the union, and the militants in what was now seen as a struggle of blacks for basic dignity. A campaign was developed that called for boycotts of downtown stores, nightly church rallies, a fund-raising campaign in the churches, and daily protest marches from Mason Street Temple to City Hall.

In many ways the garbagemen's strike in Memphis seemed to be a prototype of the class-based protest movement that King was trying to develop on a national scale through the Poor People's Campaign. In Memphis blacks were asking for decent wages and a place in the union movement that had helped lift millions of white workers into economic prosperity and dignity. Here was a chance to support black workers who were backed by a white national union confronting a white-supremacist local government; King agreed to go to Memphis. On March 18 he addressed a cheering throng packed into the huge Mason Street Temple, and after the speech he promised to return soon to join one of the daily protest marches. It was the kind of commitment he had made and kept many times in the past in order to aid local civil rights campaigns.

Memphis in 1967 was a city of over 600,000 persons, about 40 percent of them black. Much of the town's white population consisted of immigrants from rural areas of Arkansas, Mississippi, and Missouri, and there was a distinctly fundamentalist and rural-conservative cast to the town's culture. The mayor, Henry Loeb III, was an antilabor, antiblack hard-liner who had won election in 1967 despite losing 98 percent of the black vote. He clearly intended to pay his debts to the whites in the town who wanted no appeasement of blacks or unions in their city. The black community in Memphis included a few well-to-do businessmen and professionals, but there was not much of a middle class. Blacks in this city were mostly poor; they worked as unskilled laborers in the laundries and car washes, as domestic help, and as garbage collectors.

The SCLC's own element in Memphis was small and weakly organized. Authority over the protest marches rested with the sanitation workers' union and the local black ministers' association; these were the groups who were organizing the demonstrations. There was also a local black youth gang, the Invaders, who rejected the "moderate" black ministers' leadership and intended to use the big protest march which King would lead as a means of delivering a stronger message to the city's white establishment. At a meeting with the ministers, one of the gang's leaders reportedly told them that marching wasn't going to help anyone: "If you want honkies to get the message, you got to break some windows." King and his aides had done no staff work in Memphis, so they had no idea of the ferment within the black community when they returned to the city on March 28 to honor King's commitment.

The march on that day quickly turned into a debacle. The marchers had gone only a few blocks when teenage blacks began to jostle the leaders. On the sidewalks, signs appeared: "Damn Loeb—Black Power is here." Suddenly the sound of shattering glass was heard as store windows were broken and looting began. What followed was the familiar pattern: The police struck out in all directions with their clubs, hitting marchers, gang members, and bystanders without discrimination, the main target seeming to be black heads. Tear gas was lobbed into the fleeing crowd, the sounds of gunfire rang out, and the police swept the streets like a blue wash.

When it was over, windows in 155 stores had been smashed and a third of them looted. Sixty persons were injured, many of them beaten and gassed; one sixteen-year-old black youth, pursued by a policeman into an alley, was reportedly shot to death as he stood with his hands raised. Two hundred and eighty persons were arrested, forty-one charged with looting. Mayor Loeb imposed an immediate curfew and called on Governor Buford Ellington to send the National Guard to Memphis. The governor responded immediately, dispatching four thousand Guardsmen to patrol the city. From Washington, President Johnson announced that federal forces would also be available if needed. "We will not let violence and lawlessness take over the country," he declared.

There were sad and bitter discussions later in King's room. "We should have had some intelligence work done before we came here," Bernard Lee complained. "We walked right into this thing." They all agreed it had been a disaster, a stunning defeat for the cause of nonviolent direct action. Roy Wilkins of the NAACP was reported as saying that King should call off the march on Washington; that mass street marches now could only lead to violence, however peaceful the intentions of their leaders.

After the postmortems were over, King and his advisers agreed that he had to come back to Memphis, to show that he could still lead a peaceful march. "Yes, we must come back," King said. "Nonviolence as a concept is now on trial." Before, Memphis had been but a brief and minor detour, the kind of itinerant aid to local civil rights campaigns that King supplied perhaps a hundred times each year. Now, he and the movement were trapped in Memphis, Tennessee. He would never get to Washington in April unless he could first lead a peaceful march through Memphis. The waiting press was given a message: Dr. King would lead another march in Memphis in about a week, and this one would be entirely peaceful. Back in Atlanta later that week, King and his aides went into detailed planning for the next march: meetings in Memphis with all the local groups; development of march plans; bringing in outside "celebrities" to force Mayor Loeb and the police to restrain their conduct. Rooms were booked for King and his aides at a black motel, the Lorraine.

Jesse Jackson, Bayard Rustin, and others were busy recruiting public officials, labor leaders, churchmen, and entertainment figures to come to Memphis. On Monday, April 1, in his study in Atlanta, King went over all the details with his staff. Among the matters they discussed was the probability that the city would go to court to enjoin the march as a threat to public safety, and probably to a federal rather than a state judge. They were right. Mayor Loeb instructed city attorney Frank Gianotti to file in the U.S. district court for a temporary restraining order prohibiting "non-residents of the city acting in concert" from organizing or participating in a street demonstration.

On Wednesday, April 3, King and his staff took a 7 A.M. flight from Atlanta to Memphis. By midmorning King was settled in Room 306 of the Lorraine Motel, a large, plainly furnished bedroom on the second floor, facing the inner courtyard's parking lot and covered swimming pool. Andrew Young was sent to the federal courthouse to attend the injunction hearing before Judge Bailey Brown. King's lawyers agreed that the federal court would probably grant the injunction. "Whether it is granted or not," King told Ralph Abernathy, "I am going to lead that march."

Shortly after noon King was at James Lawson's church attending a ministers' meeting. He went over the march plans with them carefully, demanding assurances that this would be an orderly, nonviolent demonstration. Word came that a temporary restraining order had been granted, and federal marshals served him with it about 2 P.M.

King then went to his room to meet with a group of local lawyers led by Lucius Burch, an outstanding white lawyer in Memphis and a cooperating attorney for the American Civil Liberties Union. Burch had been sent a telegram by Charles Morgan, director of the ACLU's Southern Regional Office, asking him to represent King in the injunction proceedings, and Burch had agreed to do so, without fee, to protect King's constitutional rights. Burch and the other lawyers went to see the city attorneys to try to negotiate some conditions under which the march could be held. These were completely rejected. At that point the lawyers settled down for the night to work on their presentation to the federal court the next day, a motion to have the injunction dissolved or modified.

Later that afternoon there were more meetings with local

ministers and King's inner circle. A statement was drafted to the press in which King termed Judge Brown's order an "illegal and unconstitutional" violation of the First Amendment. His lawyers would be in federal court seeking to have it dissolved or limited, but "beyond that, it is a matter of conscience." Some of the reporters, remembering Selma, were skeptical that he would defy a federal court order. King reminded them that he had been in jail just the past fall for violating an "unjust" court order in Birmingham in 1963, and said that there was "a real possibility" that he would not obey even a federal court order in Memphis. "We are not going to be stopped by Mace or injunctions," he declared, but added that "we'll cross that bridge when we come to it."

As the issue of obeying the court order sharpened, there were no high-level contacts with Justice Department aides or White House staff in the Albany–Birmingham–Selma pattern. King's relations with the White House were now "very cool," as one SCLC aide recalls them. King's antiwar speeches and criticism of the cutbacks in domestic programs had angered President Johnson, and White House concerns over urban riots and black-violence advocates were a major influence on Administration thinking about protest marches. At the Justice Department, Ramsey Clark, a generally liberal Attorney General, had approved the prosecution of Dr. Benjamin Spock, Rev. William Sloan Coffin, and others for conspiring to impede the draft. King had met shortly before with leaders of the Concerned Clergy Against the War to map out strategy to fight this Justice Department prosecution.

The attention of the Justice Department was not focused on Memphis in early April 1968. The Civil Rights Division, not much larger than it had been in the mid-1960s, now had the 1964 and 1965 Civil Rights Acts to administer, a national task of formidable proportions, and the campaign to enact a Civil Rights Bill of 1968 was also under way. After Newark and Detroit, the Justice Department was organized into the nation's prime riot-watch command post, monitoring pressure points and preparing "response capacities." President Johnson had laid it down that he wanted the federal government better prepared to deal with urban disorders than it had been in the Detroit episode. "We were spread thin," Ramsey Clark recalls, "scanning the country. A wildness was in the land, and groups a lot different than Dr. King's were out there."

The "riot watch" ensured that some Justice Department people were watching Memphis. "It was about twenty-fifth on our crisis charts," according to one Justice Department aide. But there were no grounds the first week in April for the Justice Department to intervene there. The garbage dispute was labor relations, and was not viewed as presenting a violation of citizens' federal rights by local officials acting under color of law, as with Birmingham and Selma. Nor was it a major campaign by Dr. King in which the department felt it should be involved. Ramsey Clark and several of his assistants had been negotiating during the winter directly with King, Andy Young, and SCLC aide Walter Fauntroy over arrangements for the Poor People's Campaign, which was scheduled to arrive in Washington later in April, and they knew that this was King's principal effort for 1968. Memphis was only a detour on the route to Resurrection City.

As a result of these factors, only a low-level representative of the U.S. Community Relations Service was on the scene in Memphis. As the injunction dispute deepened, there were no calls to King from Attorney General Clark or top Civil Rights Division staff asking him to obey the court order or trying to press Mayor Loeb into negotiating. The Justice Department's general legal position was well known: federal injunctions must be obeyed, and the U.S. Attorney in Memphis, Thomas Robinson, told the press that the injunction would be enforced against any violators.

None of this came as a surprise. King and his colleagues

were not counting on the Justice Department to aid them in Memphis, nor were they trying to draw the Johnson Administration into the labor dispute as a force for supporting civil rights legislation. According to Bernard Lee, violating a court order, even from a federal court, and jeopardizing the goodwill of the federal executive branch just didn't mean what it had to the SCLC in Birmingham or Selma. "We were on our own," Lee said.

By now, it was early evening of Wednesday, April 3. A heavy rain had swept the area in the afternoon and was still coming down steadily. King had asked Abernathy to go in his place to the evening rally scheduled for the Mason Street Temple. He was tired, he had a lingering cold and sore throat, the crowd would probably be small, and he wanted to be alone, to think through his course of action.

At about 8:30 P.M. the phone rang. It was Abernathy at the Mason Street Temple. Though there were only two thousand people in the huge hall, they were waiting enthusiastically to hear King, not Abernathy. The TV people were also there. Wouldn't he change his mind and come to the rally? King went, and soon he was reviewing the events in Memphis for his listeners. He spoke of the injunction obtained in federal court, branding it a "violation of First Amendment privileges," and he declared that he *would* lead the march on Monday. The hall shook with cheers. But the march would be entirely peaceful and lawful, he continued, with nothing said or done to precipitate a conflict with the police. Then he moved into the now famous conclusion, reviewing the times he had been close to death, warning that "we've got some difficult days ahead," saying that he didn't know what was going to happen, but that he wasn't afraid, he had "been to the mountaintop," his eyes had "seen the glory." On this moving but troubled note, he ended abruptly, hurrying off with Andy Young to a meeting with Judge Ben

Hooks, one of the local black leaders. Later, back at the Lorraine Motel, he worked late into the night on the Sunday sermon he was due to preach at his church in Atlanta.

On Thursday, April 4, King met during the morning with Abernathy, Lee, Jesse Jackson, and other staff members, going over plans to bring in the notables, to keep the march peaceful, and to be sure that all of the staff were themselves committed to nonviolence. Andrew Young was sent to the federal courthouse again, where the city's injunction was being defended against the motion by King's lawyers to dissolve it. Memphis police director Frank Holloman testified that anger in the black community was so high that another mass march could lead to something "worse than Watts or Detroit." He said reports had been received that Memphis Negroes were buying guns in nearby Arkansas and that instructions for making Molotov cocktails had been circulating among local black youths. The city attorney, Frank Gianotti, told the court that the city was "fearful that in the turmoil of the moment someone may even harm Dr. King's life, and with all the force of language we can use we want to emphasize that we don't want that to happen." In the back of the courtroom, to emphasize his official interest, sat Mayor Henry Loeb.

Unlike the *ex parte* proceeding Judge Jenkins had held in Birmingham before the Good Friday march or the one Judge Brown had conducted the day before, this hearing was an adversary one. In addition to Burch, Chauncey Eskridge, a black lawyer from Chicago and the SCLC's general counsel, had flown in that morning to join in the legal defense. King's counsel cross-examined the police witnesses closely, stressing that it was the duty of the police to provide adequate protection to peaceful demonstrators and to apprehend anyone, black or white, who sought to engage in violent acts; that to allow threats of violence to justify a ban on marches was to jeopardize basic First Amendment rights. Burch called two main witnesses of his own, Rev. James Lawson and Rev. Andrew Young. "Their testimony was memorable," Burch remembers, "a lucid presentation of the role that peaceful demonstrations play in the black community—as a means of communicating information to people who don't read the newspapers, as a way of getting people together for civic action, and to be a community. It was a magnificent philosophical presentation."

At this point Judge Brown called the lawyers to a hearing in his chambers, giving no indication in the courtroom of what action he was going to take. "About three thirty," Chauncey Eskridge recalls, "we were seated in Judge Brown's chambers. After some give and take among the lawyers, the judge said he wanted to work out with us the terms of an order we could all agree on. There *would* be a march on Monday, he said. A reasonable route was specified, marchers could be only six abreast, one parade marshal would have to be stationed every four ranks, etc. The order was not actually drafted then, but its terms were outlined. We knew that it would satisfy Dr. King, and we could have the march on Monday as we planned." King had followed the route called for by the majority's ruling in the *Walker* case, and in this instance his invocation of First Amendment rights had been promptly respected by a court.

Eskridge and Andy Young hurried back to the Lorraine to inform King. Eskridge poured out the day's developments, concluding with the comment, "We're home free!" King was joyous. He grabbed Young and wrestled him to the bed in a burst of horseplay. For about ten minutes everyone in the room was laughing and joking at the welcome news. "It was a great lift for our spirits," Eskridge recalls, "and then we all went to get dressed for dinner."

Two hours earlier Attorney General Ramsey Clark had

received a call from Tennessee governor Buford Ellington informing him that the KKK intended to march in counter-demonstration if there was a civil rights march on April 8. They did not know that Judge Brown was about to lift the injunction and set forth conditions for an orderly march, and so their conversation assumed the violation of the court order and the necessity for federal intervention. Both feared that there would not be enough federal marshals available to cope with the situation. Governor Ellington was worried that the National Guard troops in Tennessee were overtired from their duty since the violence on March 28; he expressed the hope that it would not be necessary for them to be federalized. The conversation ended with Clark facing a decision as to what he would do if Dr. King were to head a march in defiance of a federal court order.

A few minutes before six o'clock that evening, King and his associates stepped onto the open balcony outside Room 306, on their way to a "soul food" supper that Rev. Billy Kyles's wife had made for them. King, in his shirt sleeves, went back to his room to get his jacket. He came out at 5:59 and stood on the balcony talking to Kyles and several other persons in the courtyard below. At 6:01 a single shot rang out. King fell, mortally wounded. He was pronounced dead at St. Joseph's Hospital at 7:05 P.M., Memphis time.

The next day Judge Brown issued a modification of his temporary restraining order, setting forth conditions for a peaceful march on April 8. A somber memorial march was held, with Coretta King filling in for her husband. The marching days of Dr. Martin Luther King, Jr., were ended.

On April 16 the garbage strike was settled. Local 1733 was accepted as the bargaining agent for the black garbagemen, and a wage increase, grievance procedures, and other benefits were provided. It was the first time that the city of Memphis had entered into a contract with a labor union.*

* For weeks after King's murder, riots erupted in cities all over the country as blacks raged through the streets in fury over what had happened to the most admired black man of this era. In one Eastern state the governor called a meeting of a hundred "responsible" local Negroes, urging them to uphold law and order and denounce the "disciples of violence." No militants had been invited to the meeting, the governor explained, none of what he called the "caterwauling, riot-inciting"–type Negroes. And this "was no accident, ladies and gentlemen," said Maryland governor Spiro T. Agnew. "I do not communicate with lawbreakers."

16

King, Courts, and Protest

THREE OF THE MAIN protagonists of the Birmingham protests are dead now. Martin Luther King and Robert Kennedy were killed by assassins' bullets in 1968, and Bull Connor died of a heart attack in 1973. King's major aides are widely scattered. Ralph Abernathy, Bernard Lee, and several others are striving to keep the SCLC alive. Fred Shuttlesworth and Wyatt Walker are serving as full-time pastors, Shuttlesworth in Cincinnati and Walker in Harlem. Andrew Young is in Washington as Georgia's first black congressman since Reconstruction days.

Many of the lawyers who argued the *Walker* case have remained in the roles they occupied between 1963 and 1967: Jack Greenberg directing the Inc. Fund, Breckenridge and McBee handling legal affairs for the city of Birmingham, and Arthur Shores and Orzell Billingsley running their own law offices. Norman Amaker and Leroy Clark are now law professors; Constance Motley is a federal district judge. Judge Walter Jenkins resigned from the bench in 1964 to resume the private practice of law; now a pillar of the local bar, he served for a time as president of the Jefferson County Board of Education. The lawyers who led the Justice Department under Presidents Kennedy and Johnson went into political exile with the arrival of the Nixon Administration. Most of them are in private or corporate law practice, or teaching in law schools.

In Birmingham there have been some marked changes. Politically, as a result of vigorous voting registration efforts in the late 1960s, following the federal Voting Rights Act of 1965, blacks now constitute 35 percent of the voters in the Magic City, a percentage about equal to their proportion in the total population. Arthur Shores is now one of two Negroes on the City Council, and there are other blacks on the city's various boards and agencies. Blacks and white "moderates" in the city make up a coalition that has kept power out of the hands of the right-wing white elements that formerly supported Bull Connor. The present mayor of the city, Republican George Seibels, was elected with black support.

There has been progress in other aspects of the city's life as well. The lunch counters in the downtown department stores have been fully integrated since the mid-1960s. There are black clerks in the department stores, black policemen and black firemen, and black children in all the city's high schools and most of the elementary schools. Black spectators sit next to whites at sports events at Birmingham's Legion Field, and during the football season they can see an integrated University of Alabama football team in action. A *New York Times* story in 1971 reported that Birmingham had become part of "Mainstream, U.S.A."

It is a phrase that accurately depicts contemporary Birmingham, for the problems of Birmingham's blacks today mirror the problems of black people throughout the United States. For example, although city agencies now hire Negroes, they generally do so only in token numbers. Early in 1974 there were only two black firemen in the city and only thirty black policemen on a force of 650. Few black civil service workers are in supervisory positions, few black craftsmen are in any of the construction trades unions, and the plumbers and carpenters unions are still all white. Although the school system is integrated, more than half the schools are over 90 percent black or white. Delivery of municipal services in black neighborhoods still leaves much to be desired. Black insurance executive John Drew, a key figure in the negotiations that took place in May 1963, summed up the situation: "Before 1963 Birmingham was the hell-hole of the world. It's not the greatest place in the world today, but at least it's livable and there are people of both races who are trying to make it a better place to live."

Birmingham is also in the American mainstream now in another sense. Most of the basic problems of its black poor can be dealt with effectively only when new economic and political measures are developed to alleviate the problems of employment, housing, education, and medical care for the poor in America generally—white, red, brown, and black. These are no longer "civil rights" questions, but fundamental social-reform issues.

Though King is dead, and so is the era of civil rights activity typified by the Birmingham campaign of 1963, the *Walker* decision lives on as one of the Supreme Court's important rulings—both legally and politically—on how social protest must be conducted under the American Constitution. Its impact has, to be sure, been moderated in some respects. In November 1968 a unanimous decision of the Supreme Court in a case called *Carroll v. President and Commissioners of Princess Anne* established the rule that injunctions restraining the exercise of First Amendment rights cannot be issued *ex parte* where it is possible to notify the opposing parties and give them an opportunity to be heard. Under the *Carroll* holding, the kind of *ex parte* procedure employed by Judge Jenkins in issuing the injunction in the *Walker* case would be unconstitutional, since notice was not given to the other side. Martin Edelman, a commentator highly critical of the *Walker* decision, felt that in *Carroll* the court "had begun the process of applying its cool, sober, second judgment." Significantly, however, the court in *Carroll* did not deal with the question of whether such an unconstitutional injunction could be ignored without penalty or still had to be contested first in judicial proceedings.

A few months after handing down their decision in *Carroll*, the justices decided *Shuttlesworth v. City of Birmingham*, an appeal by Fred Shuttlesworth to reverse a misdemeanor conviction for marching on Good Friday in 1963 without a parade permit. This time, disobedience of an injunction was not involved; Shuttlesworth had been convicted for not having a permit before he marched, and his defense was that the permit ordinance was unconstitutional. Apart from that difference, the case was identical with the facts in *Walker*, and the justices heard arguments from the same lawyers as in 1967—Jack Greenberg for Shuttlesworth and Earl McBee for the city. This time, however, the city lost. Eight justices agreed in March 1969 that Shuttlesworth's conviction had to be overturned. (The ninth, Thurgood Marshall, who had replaced Tom Clark in June 1967, did not participate.)

Ironically, it was Justice Potter Stewart who again wrote the court's opinion about the 1963 events in Birmingham. Reviewing the language of the ordinance, he noted that it gave the City Commission "virtually unbridled power to prohibit any 'parade,' 'procession,' or 'demonstration' on the city's streets or public ways." Therefore, he said, it fell "squarely within the ambit of the many decisions of this Court over the last 30 years holding that a law subjecting the exercise of First Amendment freedoms to the prior restraint of a license, without narrow, objective, and definite standards, is unconstitutional." Citing a long line of cases, he observed that these decisions "have made it clear that a person faced with such an unconstitutional licensing law may ignore it and engage with impunity in the exercise of full expression for which the law purports to require a license."

With the *Shuttlesworth* decision, the Supreme Court issued a warning to local police officials and city governments: vaguely worded licensing laws could not be used to thwart legitimate demonstrations, and protesters would be legally free to march without first securing such permits, so long as there were no court injunctions forbidding it.

But, even as tempered by *Carroll* and *Shuttlesworth,* the majority opinion in *Walker* has played an important role in controlling social protest. The approach approved by the justices in *Walker* has been used by local governments and private institutions as the basic technique for dealing with protest movements of all kinds—minority rights demonstrators, student protest groups, antiwar movements, labor and civil service unions, and groups pressing for welfare rights, women's liberation, and homosexual rights. Whenever demonstrations reach a point that the authorities consider too "disruptive," an injunction has been sought in state or federal court.

For example, the *Walker* case had been on the books only a few months when the University of Wisconsin obtained a temporary injunction in November 1967 barring students from interfering with job-recruitment interviews on its Madison campus. During the year that followed, at least fifty-three more injunctions against various forms of allegedly disruptive behavior, especially building seizures, were obtained by colleges and universities. The advantage of the injunction to university administrators was that it could be obtained quickly (particularly when *ex parte* procedures were followed) and that it placed student activists in the position of confronting not only the university but the courts. Facing injunctions directed specifically at themselves, rather than generalized statutory commands such as trespass laws and university regulations, most student dissidents between 1967 and the present have abandoned their enjoined activities without waiting for police action. As one university administrator commented, the use of injunctions has had "a great tranquil-izing effect." And, where injunctions obtained by colleges and universities have not been complied with by protesting students, courts have not hesitated to hold them in contempt, invoking the *Walker* precedent.

The *Walker* ruling has been put to similar use in those sec-tors of labor relations that are not covered by federal collec-tive bargaining and anti-injunction laws. These include groups such as farm workers and state or local government employees (teachers, sanitationmen, police, etc.). When union leaders have mounted organizational campaigns in these sectors or have resorted to strikes or demonstrations, government agencies have frequently obtained injunctions or-dering such activities to be halted. Failures to comply with the injunction and test it in court have been met with *Walker*-supported contempt convictions. One New Jersey court, for example, recently upheld the contempt conviction of a group of Newark teachers by telling them that the only lawful re-sponse to what they believed was an overly restrictive injunc-tion was to "seek the court's assistance" in requiring the school board to negotiate in good faith. Citing the *Walker* decision, the court emphasized that the teachers could not defy the court order and "take the law into their own hands."

Despite the complaints of various protest groups, many ob-servers—and not simply those who have a vested interest in perpetuation of the status quo—believe that the *Walker* ruling is an eminently sound one. Their approval is measured in terms of four criteria: sound interpretation of the concept of "jurisdiction"; considerations of federalism; the proper limits on protest; and the ideal of the "rule of law."

The first criterion has to do with a somewhat technical but highly significant problem in American law: the determina-tion of when a court has the power to decide issues that involve special remedies such as injunctions. (Lawyers refer to these as issues of equitable jurisdiction.) One of the Inc. Fund's arguments was that because Judge Jenkins' injunction had been unconstitutionally broad, he had no "jurisdiction" to issue it; that the order was therefore "void" and could be disobeyed at will. By the 1960s only a few state courts had accepted the concept that an overly broad order was void on its face and could be ignored, not merely challenged as void by a motion to dissolve it. One reason why the *Walker* decision won acclaim in legal circles was that it did not accept the "constitutional voidness" approach. Many legal scholars felt that this approach would have introduced undesirable uncertainties as to when persons named in injunctions were bound to obey them, and would have rendered the definition of "jurisdiction" even more vague and metaphysical than it had been before. Moreover, such scholars argue, allowing defiance of court orders to be justified in later contempt proceedings would deprive the courts themselves of the opportunity to bring hurriedly issued *ex parte* injunctions into line with the Constitution. In Memphis, for example, when King sent his lawyers into federal court to contest the *ex parte* injunction, Judge Brown was given a chance to reexamine his order. The result was the drawing up of reasonable conditions, satisfactory to King and his aides.

Second, many of those who agree with the Stewart opinion believe that it set the proper balance between uniform federal law and the divergent systems desirable at the state level in American government. The rule barring collateral attack on injunctions was not an "Alabama special"; it was and is the rule followed by all but a few states in the nation. While any state should be free to place vindication of constitutional claims ahead of the interest in orderly equity procedure if it wishes to, it is quite another use of judicial power by the U.S. Supreme Court to force all states to adopt that doctrine. To do this, it is argued, would be to carry the Supreme Court dangerously deep into the writing of state procedural codes and upset the principle of local option that has been regarded as highly desirable in federal/state relationships.

Third, the *Walker* decision has been praised for its timely definition of the proper limits on protest activities, a declaration that many commentators regarded as badly needed from the high court in 1967, even somewhat overdue. *Walker* told all black protest movements, from King's group to far more militant forces, that they could no longer count on the Supreme Court to immunize many of their direct-action activities from the control of local police. While the justices had never ruled that civil rights groups had a clear First Amendment right to sit-in and conduct mass demonstrations in the 1960–66 cases, they had found sufficient faults in the prosecutions to free demonstrators who had challenged the flouting of equality decisions by Southern officials. These rulings had the effect of overturning convictions obtained by Southern officials under the general law of American municipalities—breach of the peace, disorderly conduct, licensing, trespass laws, etc.—when these laws were being used to repress the expression of black demands for an end to unlawful racial segregation.

By 1967, though, the dislocation of local business and social life and the rioting by onlookers that were increasingly accompanying such confrontations had alienated national public opinion. When the Supreme Court in *Walker* quoted sympathetically from Birmingham's petition for an injunction, with its stress on keeping the public peace, and placed First Amendment rights behind the procedural rules of equity enforcement, it was telling local government authorities across the nation that their peacekeeping powers were now being recognized in a way that had not been the case in the high court for many years. Together, the *Adderley* decision of 1966 and *Walker* were praised by many observers as restoring the proper balance between protest rights and public interest, and helping "cool off" the fevered political situation.

Though the *Walker* case helped restore more "orderly" conduct to public protests, larger political and social forces were obviously at work. These included the spread of "white backlash" sentiments in 1967–69; the electoral choice of Richard Nixon in 1968 and 1972 on a conservative, law-and-order platform; the ending of the Vietnam War; the use of strong police and prosecutive measures; the shift of black movements to electoral politics and the rise of black separatist sentiment; and the sheer exhaustion of many of the social movements active in the 1960s. But the *Walker* ruling and the state and federal decisions after 1967 that followed its principle, also played a role in winding down social protest.

Finally, the *Walker* case has been seen by its admirers as a valuable reaffirmation of the rule-of-law principle in American political life. We noted in Chapter 1 the direct relevance of Justice Stewart's language about no man judging his own case to the claims of executive privilege that President Nixon invoked against Judge Sirica's order on the Watergate tapes. But the relationship between *Walker* and Watergate has another dimension also. When several of the President's aides involved in illegal surveillance or burglary activities testified before the Senate Watergate Committee they explained their willingness to break the law on the ground that they had watched antiwar leaders and other protest figures of the 1960s engage in unlawful conduct and felt that people who were defending the country had to take some similarly dedicated actions. They never acknowledged a distinction between actions taken by private citizens and those by public officials sworn to uphold the law. And though they never quite said that the nation's laws had been suspended by executive order, they did attempt to portray a sort of "higher law" justification for their actions, based on national security interests. It was *Walker*'s clear message that not even the highest-minded appeals of this kind should lead judges to set aside the regular application of the nation's criminal and civil law. The public support given to the prosecutive actions in the Watergate case can be seen as resting on a fundamental belief in the rule-of-law principle, an outlook that many believed the *Walker* decision helped to nurture during one of its recurring moments under attack.

For all these reasons, the *Walker* decision has developed a strong following among judges, editors, lawyers, and "constitutionalists" of both liberal and conservative persuasion. If a national opinion survey were conducted today, there is little doubt that the *Walker* principle would draw overwhelming approval from the general public. Even among civil libertarians who adopt the most generous definition of First Amendment rights, there are many who would argue that the proper way to assert such rights in the face of restrictive *ex parte* injunctions is through immediate challenge in the courts rather than by open defiance of a specific order. In short, the weight of national opinion is that the *Walker* rule arises out of the logic of the American constitutional blueprint and that its enunciation by the Supreme Court in 1967 was proper and timely.

Despite the attractiveness of these arguments, we believe that the *Walker* case was mishandled by the Supreme Court in 1967. Furthermore, *Walker*'s continued vitality as a precedent is exerting a harmful effect on our social and political processes. In our view, the Supreme Court should have ruled in favor of Martin Luther King in 1967, and could have done so in a fashion that recognized the importance of both the rule-of-law concept and First Amendment principles. To understand why this should have been done and how it could have been accomplished requires some examination of the historical relationships between social change and the judicial process.

Americans have a tendency to repress memories of the harsh conflicts that spurred much of the nation's progress toward more democratic institutions, from the colonists' dumping of tea in Boston harbor to the civil rights sit-ins of the 1960s. But the cold historical fact is that democratization has come only through a series of confrontations between various disadvantaged and disenfranchised groups and the dominant interests of the day. Though this is only one part of the large and varied tapestry of American history, we associate such confrontations with vital periods of domestic reform: the efforts of small farmers and workingmen in the Jacksonian age; blacks and white abolitionists before the Civil War; trade unionists in the early twentieth century; and groups such as Negroes, Mexican-Americans, Puerto Ricans, women, and cultural nonconformists in the contemporary period. In each era groups denied legal and political equality have had to demand first-class citizenship by waging continuous and determined struggles. This required not only proving that their claims were morally justified in terms of democratic ideals but also demonstrating that their group was so unified and determined to persist that its call for change could no longer be denied.

Since those upholding the status quo make the laws, and police and judges who are part of that system enforce them, disadvantaged groups have usually had to violate laws in the course of pressing their campaigns for major social change. The legal constraints have dealt with rights to organize, to hold meetings, to disseminate ideas, to engage in public demonstrations, and to use weapons such as boycotts and strikes. None of the major disenfranchised groups of the nineteenth and twentieth centuries would have altered their status if their leaders had not been willing to violate openly discriminatory laws or generally valid laws that were being applied against them in unfair ways. Such confrontations were the essential force that led to changes in the rules, as the famous Negro publicist Frederick Douglass wrote in 1857:

> Those who profess to favor freedom and yet deprecate agitation, are men who want crops without ploughing up the ground. They want the rain without thunder and lightning. They want the ocean without the awful roar of its many waters. The struggle may be a moral one; or it may be both moral and physical; but it must be a struggle. Power concedes nothing without a demand. It never did and never will. . . . Men may not get all they pay for in this world; but they must certainly pay for all they get.

In all these historical conflicts, the courts have been one of the central battlegrounds. Most judges, consciously or unconsciously, tend to reflect the values of the political interests that installed them in office, and American constitutional law has rarely moved very far ahead (or lagged very far behind) the dominant national opinion of the day. But the Supreme Court justices have played a very important role in defining what Robert G. McCloskey has called the important margins of power and public policy. The way the Supreme Court defines what is legitimate and illegitimate protest activity by social movements is just such an area.

When they rule on this issue, judges can help to keep the moment of social debate and institutional change open in the society, enabling the protesting groups to keep their cause on the national political agenda and resisting the onset of political reaction and retrenchment. Or they can rule the other way, helping to bring on closure by holding that certain protest tactics or political justifications are not legally valid, and thereby bringing powerful legal pressures to bear on those social movements and their leaders. This latter course was the one the Supreme Court adopted in the *Debs* case of 1895. When the federal courts enjoined Debs and the American

Railway Union officials from leading the Pullman strike and they were arrested for continuing in defiance of the court order, this action broke the back of a strike that otherwise seemed destined to win an expansion of workers' rights. One union leader described what happened in testimony before the United States Strike Commission: "As soon as the employees found that we were arrested and taken from the field of action, they became demoralized, and that ended the strike. It was not the soldiers that ended the strike. It was not the old brotherhoods . . . It was simply the United States courts."

In the *Walker* case the key issue was whether the court in 1967 would side with the white majority to effect closure. How important to the achievement of basic racial justice it was for the courts to keep the way open to further reform is clear in terms of where King, the nonviolent movement, and the nation stood in 1967–68. Birmingham had led to the Civil Rights Act of 1964, providing blacks with rights to equal treatment in public accommodation facilities; the stigma of inferiority created by "whites only" facilities was now barred by law. Selma had led to the Civil Rights Act of 1965, guaranteeing voting rights for Negroes in the South; this accelerated a process of political participation that has seen black officials elected to local offices in many areas of the South and has led most Southern white candidates and office-holders to treat black interests with newfound respect.

King and the nonviolent civil rights movement had then turned in 1966–68 from challenging discrimination based on the color of a person's skin, whatever his class status, to a broader attack on social and economic inequalities that cut across racial lines but that particularly affected blacks because of their position at the bottom of the economic ladder. In Memphis, King was trying to help blacks enter the American labor-union mainstream of economic opportunity. The Poor People's Campaign was directed at mobilizing the black and white poor to demand jobs, job training, income maintenance, ghetto reconstruction, and a variety of other social programs. The assumption was that the black masses in America could only achieve the next step toward freedom and equality when employment, education, housing, and social services were fundamentally improved for all the poor.

In 1966–68, therefore, King was developing a campaign against class-based social and economic discrimination, from which blacks, though they were not the sole sufferers, were the most consistently victimized. This was what President Lyndon Johnson had said he would do with his Great Society programs. But by 1967 those programs were being sapped by Vietnam War demands, and the energies of both Administration officials and social-reform groups were being shifted to the pro- and antiwar confrontations. What was sad in 1967 was that the Supreme Court majority chose to apply legal sanctions against King and the nonviolent movement at just that moment.

This is not to argue that, had the *Walker* case gone the other way, King would have overcome the fragmentation of black forces, the divisiveness over the war, and the growing white demands for law and order that marked those years. We will never know how King might have ridden out those events had he lived, and whether he would have moved in the 1970s to lead a new social-reform movement. What we do know is that the moral authority of the Supreme Court was withdrawn from the nonviolent civil rights movement at its moment of greatest need.

This did not have to be done. The justices could have reversed King's conviction with a narrowly based ruling that did not attempt to determine the exact circumstances under which groups could defy court orders but took into account the very special circumstances of the *Walker* case. This would have been in keeping with the well-accepted principle of constitutional adjudication that the court ought not to decide disputes on broader constitutional grounds than are absolutely necessary; i.e., it should avoid choosing between major competing principles when this is not essential to the wise decision of a particular problem. While such cautious restraint is often praised by lawyers and judges, it also tends to run counter to the expectations of most Americans that the justices will face up to the great legal issues of the day. Thus the question is why the Supreme Court in 1967 should have considered developing a narrow rule and reversing King's conviction.

One basic answer is that *Walker* was a relic of a bygone era. It arose at the moment in 1963 when direct-action protest was directed against Southern public officials who were in open defiance of the law of the land. Only a four-year delay in the progress of the appeal—a delay in no way attributable to King or his lawyers—explains the appearance of this historical artifact before the court in the entirely new context of racial disorders and violence in 1967. Justice, in its most elemental sense, could not be well served by sending King back to Birmingham jail with a lecture on obedience to law that bore no relation to the realities of law in Bull Connor's Birmingham.

Another reason for attempting a narrow ruling would be to recognize the distinction between King's basic respect for law and the courts and the actions of militant groups that openly counseled violence, disrespect for law, and revolutionary challenges to the legal order. There was no doubt that it was the special situation in Birmingham that forced King to exercise his federally protected rights of expression in defiance of an injunction embodying an ordinance which the Supreme Court itself was to declare patently unconstitutional. For the Supreme Court not to appreciate the difference between that conduct and the ghetto rioting and disruptive confrontations that marked 1966–67 was to ignore the critical social distinctions on which a sensitive constitutional jurisprudence ought to rest. Segregationists in the South and defenders of de facto racism in the North might lump all "demonstrators" into one condemned camp, but the nation had a right to expect finer sorting from its highest tribunal of justice.

On what narrow grounds could the court have reversed the *Walker* convictions? The simplest way would have been to anticipate by one year its decision in the *Carroll* case, and to apply its policy to the particular context of Birmingham. In its *Carroll* opinion the court declared there was a "basic infirmity" in the use of *ex parte* procedures for enjoining the exercise of First Amendment freedoms when it was feasible to notify the opposing parties. Unless there is a genuine emergency situation requiring immediate action, only an adversary proceeding provides the critical elements of notice and opportunity to be heard on which due process of law depends, even when injunctions are involved. Since the city's attorneys could easily have served notice to King at the time they applied for an injunction, and an adversary hearing been arranged, the justices could have found a "basic infirmity" in the initial proceedings before Judge Jenkins. Quite simply, the convictions in *Walker* grew out of proceedings that violated fundamental concepts of due process of law.

Had the court voided King's conviction on such grounds, the ruling would not have had to express any official approval of King's failure to initiate a legal protest against the injunction before he marched. If they wished, Justice Stewart and any other members of the court's center or conservative wing could have noted in concurring opinions their view that injunction orders—when they are issued under proper procedures—must ordinarily be complied with, even in First Amendment cases. That warning would have been well understood by the Inc. Fund lawyers and all others working in the civil rights movement, and there would have been later protest cases involving disrespectful and violent demonstrators in which the court majority could then have enunciated guidelines for protest on the post-1967 scene. Such a treatment of *Walker* would not have constituted "bending the law" for Martin Luther King, Jr., and his colleagues. Rather, it would have been a ruling in the spirit of Judge Frank Johnson's opinion on the Selma march, calling for courts to measure the enormity of the wrongs done to people denied their constitutional rights when considering the pleas of public officials to apply the "normal" processes of the law. It would have been the "civilizing hand of the law" at its best.

It is not hard to explain *why* the Supreme Court majority chose not to reverse the convictions along these lines. The court often responds in barometric fashion to major shifts in public mood, and there is no doubt that white America was anxious for some law-and-order guidelines in 1967. But it was still a tragic failure of judicial sensitivity. This was especially true of Justice Stewart, the swing man whose reckoning of the relative equities determined how the court decided.

In many other cases Justice Stewart has argued strongly in favor of narrow rather than sweeping dispositions of constitutional questions. This was his view, for example, in the famous death-penalty case of 1971, *Furman v. Georgia*. For him to reject First Amendment claims and uphold the use of the *ex parte* injunction here was a departure from his customary judicial style. If only a little of the social reality and constitutional outrage that Stewart put into his *Shuttlesworth* opinion two years later could have broken through the syllogistic reasoning he penned in *Walker*, the court could not have voted to wash its hands of Martin Luther King and turn him over to the authorities of Alabama.

Of course, the *Walker* case is now history. An even more important question than what might have been in 1967 is what should be the law for the 1970s. Even as modified by *Carroll*, the *Walker* doctrine warns all groups today that they must go to court to contest injunctions limiting the exercise of what they believe are their legally protected First Amendment rights. We think this is too rigid and restrictive a rule for a society that depends on the vigorous exercise of First Amendment rights to achieve significant progress toward social justice.

This is especially true in the era of rapid social change and urbanization through which our advanced technological society is now passing. The disenfranchised and deprived groups of our time have to depend on the politics of protest to bring their discontent to the attention of majority opinion and political leaders. Unless such peaceful but vigorous protest is allowed, people with deep grievances are likely to turn to revolutionary activity or withdraw from political life, either of which would weaken the vitality of democratic institutions. Of course, any protest movement must be judged on the merits of its claims, and its demands can be posed so broadly and aggressively that the majority ultimately turns it off as a noisy and illegitimate activity. But the right to initiate protest movements and carry them as far as their cause can persuade has become a vital aspect of contemporary mass society.

In this setting, the First Amendment has become even more central than it was during earlier periods of our history. For in a society that seeks to work through lawful methods and foster peaceful change, judicial protection of the rights to speak, publish, associate, assemble, and petition government for redress of grievances enables new social demands to be voiced, to be examined in terms of American values and ideals, and, where justified, to be ultimately incorporated into regular political and legal channels. The Supreme Court between the late 1950s and the *Walker* case in 1967 recognized that paramount function for First Amendment rights during the civil rights movement, striking down attempt after attempt by local officialdom in both North and South to use traditional police powers to outlaw black protest.

Any rule of constitutional law that threatens to stifle the exercise of First Amendment rights is extremely dangerous to the process of democratic social change. It puts a powerful and illegitimate weapon in the hands of local officials seeking to protect the status quo by denying the right of peaceful protest. It tells deprived groups in American society that the First Amendment isn't really for them, but only for those with the money and power to influence the establishment-dominated channels of politics.

While First Amendment rights are vital, it is also true that not every kind of protest demonstration falls within even the most generous definition of free speech or assembly. How far the borderline activities of protest groups should be given legal protection often depends on the specific context—the place they want to use, how long they wish to demonstrate, the emotional setting of the community, the availability of protection against disorders, and similar factors. Given these aspects of the protest issue, courts are the best instrument we have available in our political system not only to make judgments on the basis of constitutional principle but also to tailor these to the occasion. No general statute can be expected to set out all the rules in advance, nor is this a determination that can safely be left to administrative officials. It is preeminently a problem for the courts, operating under general constitutional guidelines from the U.S. Supreme Court as to the scope of First Amendment rights and drawing on adversary proceedings to get at the true facts and problems. Yet history also shows that many local judges have a tendency to undervalue protest and overvalue public peace. This is especially true where controversial social movements are involved.

The problem of legal statecraft is to fashion a constitutional rule that protects the conflict-resolving role of the American judiciary and supports popular respect for law but does *not* encourage arbitrary rejection of First Amendment rights by the courts. The *Walker* rule—because it calls for absolute compliance with court injunctions regardless of their breadth or the procedures by which they were issued—places no significant pressure on the local courts to keep their rulings in line with U.S. Supreme Court definitions of First Amendment rights. Local judges who enjoin unpopular protest movements will usually be applauded by community leaders; if their rulings are reversed years later by nine men in Washington, this does not generate the kind of creative tension that the adjustment of competing constitutional interests calls for in our legal system. In short, a rule forbidding any hearing of First Amendment claims in prosecutions for violation of court orders weakens constitutional responsibility in the judiciary while demanding the highest constitutional rectitude of those seeking to exercise First Amendment rights.

Furthermore, the *Walker* rule is nowhere near as benign as some of Justice Stewart's language would make it appear. When he suggested that if the petitioners had made some kind of "gesture" toward compliance with the injunction, the case might have been different, he implied that there might have been a way for King and his co-defendants to have paid minimal respect to the judiciary and still enjoyed their First Amendment rights. But filing a motion to dissolve would have trapped King on the flypaper of the Alabama judicial process. Having filed a motion, he would have had to postpone his marches while the motion was being heard. Then he would have had to wait while the predictable rejection of his motion by Judge Jenkins was appealed in the Alabama courts, since the inescapable logic of the *Walker* case is that no one can defy a final (permanent) injunction order with any more impunity than the temporary (preliminary) one. And so any group today in the same situation as King was in Birmingham is put to the choice between two extremely undesirable options: exercise First Amendment rights in defiance of court order and expect a contempt conviction, or give up timely protest in favor of lengthy litigation up the ladder of state and federal courts.

Because of the defects in the *Walker* rule, it has been urged that a group whose exercise of First Amendment rights has been enjoined, particularly in an *ex parte* hearing, should be legally free to engage in their protest as it was scheduled and then to raise the defense that the injunction was unconstitutional in any contempt proceedings that are initiated. This is the position presently adopted in California, whose streets do not seem to be in any greater turmoil than in the other states of the Union. But those supporting the position that violation of injunctions should be as subject to constitutional defense as are statutes go further than saying this should be a matter of local option. They believe that a proper respect for due process and First Amendment freedoms requires the U.S. Supreme Court to guarantee this by federal law, taking it out of the hands of any state to require automatic compliance with court orders as a matter of state procedure.

Though there is a good deal to recommend this policy, we think that it suffers from some of the same rigidities and unrealities as the *Walker* rule. Putting no pressure on protest groups to come into court to dissolve a temporary injunction, as King's lawyers did in Memphis, deprives the local court of the opportunity to hear conflicting argument on what the situation really is at that moment in the community and precisely what the group wishes to do. Judges ought not to have to depend on newspaper accounts and police testimony for their information on the intentions of those seeking to be heard in the public arenas. And, since there may not be authoritative guidelines from the U.S. Supreme Court on every type of protest activity, or every kind of setting in which the conflict between community interests and free expression is posed, there is a strong value in having the local court hear constitutional presentations from both sides before it rules on the request of authorities for injunctions. Finally, there is something that offends the spirit of justice in saying that a court order can simply be treated like a recommendation by a presidential commission or a civic group. Courts are not always right, to be sure; but the process of judicial inquiry and its search for ways to balance the interests of expression and public safety is so valuable (and superior to any other institutional alternative) that persons given directions by a court should be required to use the procedures of law to make their response—*if the available procedures of law are fair*.

That, of course, is the pivot of the issue. Before obedience to court orders should be sustained as a rule of conduct, society must be assured that the judges as well as the parties come into the court of equity with clean hands. This means that two basic conditions must be satisfied: the procedures available to parties whose First Amendment rights are being jeopardized must be timely and fair, and the proper weight must be assigned, in advance, to the exercise of freedom of expression as a value in democratic society.

We do not propose here to write a code detailing how a golden mean might be applied between the poles of the *Walker* rule and the rule permitting court orders to be treated the same way as statutes. That would take extensive, case-by-case adjudication by the U.S. Supreme Court, with the final doctrine built up by decisions placing situations on one or the other side of the line. But we can illustrate what we see as clear cases of what should and should not be done, and this would represent a step toward the development of a new position.

We can start by reformulating one part of the rule in a way that would have disposed of the *Walker* case in what we believe to be exactly the right fashion. Where a court issues an *ex parte* injunction even though there was time to bring the affected parties into court before the scheduled events took place, where the injunction places such broad limits on protest activities that it effectively defeats the timely exercise of First Amendment rights in the particular situation, and where the group believes that the court's order applies patently unconstitutional restrictions on its rights of expression, then there should be no application of the *Walker* rule of automatic contempt conviction. In any prosecution for violating an *ex parte* injunction affecting the exercise of First Amendment rights, the person or group enjoined should be able to raise constitutional objections to the terms of the injunction, and to have the merits of these objections considered by the court as a defense to the contempt charge.

This would mean that where a group has been correct in its assumption that the *ex parte* injunction contained unconstitutional terms, *and* where the group's activities were indeed protected by the First Amendment, its members would avoid conviction for contempt. Of course, if they adopted an inflated or nonsensical definition of what the First Amendment protects—for example, by claiming a "right" to stall cars on the George Washington Bridge to call attention to their cause after an injunction had forbidden such conduct—a court considering the contempt issue would have no difficulty under the rule we suggest in holding such conduct to be contempt. Such a rule would also increase the incentive for local officials and courts to hold adversary hearings and avoid ex parte procedures. This would increase the possibility that all sides of a dispute would be heard before any injunction might be issued.

In considering the usefulness of this approach, it should be noted that authorities always have the option of prosecuting a group for violation of the criminal law if it engages in conduct that incites to riot, destroys private or public property, or violates any of the other laws that punish use of one's own liberty in ways that harm others. Generally, because of American law's proper hostility to the placing of prior restraints on speech—forbidding it in advance—rather than prosecuting acts after they have taken place, we ought to use the criminal law as the rule and resort to the injunctive approach only rarely. Injunctive relief should be reserved for those truly exceptional cases for which equity powers were devised—where the threat of imminent harm is so serious that it cannot be dealt with by ordinary protective measures (rules of march, adequate police presence, etc.). Indeed, the courts have warned frequently that injunctions ought not to be used in place of the criminal law, or to administer the criminal law. A major problem with the *Walker* rule is that it encourages just such behavior by public officials.

We can specify, at the other pole, a situation in which the constitutional defense clearly should not be permitted in a contempt proceeding. Suppose public officials serve a group with an order to show cause why their planned demonstration should not be enjoined as a threat to public safety, and a reasonable time is set for a judicial hearing. Again, this would be the situation presented in Memphis, or even in Selma. Under these conditions there would be a duty on the group to come into court and contest the show-cause order. If they refused to do so, they would be barred from raising constitutional defenses in an ensuing contempt hearing.

Even here, however, there would still be one further avenue open to them. They should be able to allege—and prove, if they can—that the procedural rules of that jurisdiction (the state involved, or the federal government) did not provide an accelerated special procedure for passing on appeals from injunctions placing limits on First Amendment rights. What this means is that the U.S. Supreme Court, as a requirement of due process of law under the Fifth and Fourteenth Amendments, would insist that the federal and state courts create rapid appellate review procedures for such situations. In some situations, this could be a few hours; in others, a few days or as long as a week or two.

This has been the general approach followed by the U.S. Supreme Court in dealing with censorship of motion pictures.

In *Freedman v. Maryland,* decided in 1965, the court held that due process requires a speedy hearing and appeal for censorship rulings involving movies, with the burden on the state to prove the availability of such procedures before it can enforce a ban on the film. This is just the kind of position that would make good political and legal sense in the protest-and-injunctions context.

In suggesting development of a rule by the Supreme Court along these lines, we have in mind a practical distinction between those groups that are deliberately engaging in civil disobedience to make a political witness (and therefore both want and should be "permitted" to go to jail) and those groups that are seeking to use their constitutional rights of free expression to make their voice heard as forcefully and fully as possible in what are usually the establishment-dominated arenas of mass communication. It was just this distinction that the Supreme Court failed to consider and respond to in the *Walker* case, and our law will continue to be out of balance until that is corrected.

The fact that this is far from a hypothetical concern can be illustrated by a recent case that involved not protest groups but the press. In November 1971 reporters for two Baton Rouge, Louisiana, daily newspapers were sitting in the local U.S. district court covering a hearing. It involved a local VISTA worker who brought suit against state officials alleging they had trumped up murder charges against him solely because of his race and his civil rights activities. The presiding judge issued an order at the start of the hearings forbidding any newspaper, radio, or TV reporting of the proceedings, to "avoid undue publicity which could in any way interfere with the rights of the litigants" in future proceedings. Such an order was in direct contradiction to U.S. Supreme Court decisions holding that trials are public proceedings, that judges cannot forbid reporting by those present, and that the judiciary may not "suppress, edit or censor events which transpire before it.'' Knowing this to be the law, and facing the usual newspaper deadlines, the two reporters wrote factual accounts of the hearing, and these appeared the next day.

The presiding judge cited the two reporters for criminal contempt and fined them each three hundred dollars. When the case was appealed, the U.S. Court of Appeals for the Fifth Circuit ruled that the judge's ban on reporting was in flat violation of the First Amendment. But, following the *Walker* rule, the appellate court upheld the contempt convictions. Although it acknowledged that "the difference between 'news' and 'history' is merely a matter of hours,'' the court insisted that "newsmen are citizens too" and they "sometimes have to wait.'' Complying with court orders, and testing their validity in judicial proceedings, the court held, is "an experience-proved" requirement for "the system to work.'' When an appeal was taken to the U.S. Supreme Court in 1973, the justices declined to review the case. Although Justice Douglas dissented, the court allowed the Fifth Circuit decision to stand. Journalism groups, editors, and civil liberties groups have vigorously protested, but the decision remains in force. It is a pointed reminder that the *Walker* rule is a repressive doctrine that can be applied to many interests exercising First Amendment rights besides protest groups, and that its hold over American constitutional law cannot be reexamined too soon.

In a very real sense, we owe it to Martin Luther King, Jr., and what he did for American law, to reformulate the *Walker* doctrine. From his first direct-action campaign in Montgomery until his last in Memphis, King's efforts to secure rights of equality were met by local officials in the South who misused the law by obtaining sweeping local court injunctions that denied him First Amendment rights. He continually voiced his belief in the U.S. Constitution, the Supreme Court, and fidelity to the law, and only wished that Southern segregationists and their de facto colleagues in the North would display an equal commitment, in action. But King was too much of a political realist, and an opponent of corroding tokenism, to let the enemies of equality make him play their game of lengthy court appeals and administrative round robin. The cry of black Americans in this era was to begin the achievement of "Freedom—Now!"

Jack Greenberg summed it up eloquently in a commemorative speech for Martin Luther King in 1968:

> Dr. King made such a deep impact on his times, and all those who knew him, because he maintained, in inspired fashion, [the] tension between the legal and the moral. He knew that law without justice is tyranny, but he also knew that disorder tears the fabric of society. He was always willing to negotiate. But if negotiation was futile, or if others sought to use it as a cloak for inaction, he was prepared to march.

King knew that if he agreed in advance to submit his critically important civil rights campaigns to every restrictive *ex parte* order of a local judge, he might just as well have stayed in his pulpit preaching or gone out on the lecture circuit. He could not function as a man trying to channel the force of the Negro revolt into peaceful and effective social change. And when he walked this delicate line between respect for law and commitment to justice, he had good reason to expect the Supreme Court of the United States to make a fundamental distinction between his behavior and that of the black-power advocates and pro-violence groups, as well as to look behind the façade of white Birmingham's invocation of the rule of law. The answer to those who lamented that, in the end, King erred by breaking the law, is that five justices of the nation's highest court failed to define the law of the land in a way that made it possible for those seeking basic justice to stay within its boundaries.

Selected Bibliography
and Case List

WE HAVE LISTED HERE the sources used directly for the writing of this book; no effort has been made to include all the leading works on such large topics as race relations, civil disobedience, or the work of the United States Supreme Court. Books and articles are listed together under six main topics: race relations and civil rights; Martin Luther King, Jr., and Negro movements; Alabama history, law, and politics; national politics and political leaders; the U.S. Supreme Court and the judicial process; and protest, contempt, and civil disobedience. A seventh section lists the cases discussed in the text. The personal interviews we conducted are listed in the Preface.

Race Relations and Civil Rights

Amaker, Norman. "The 1950's: Racial Equality and the Law." *Current History,* November 1969.

Brink, William and Harris, Louis. *The Negro Revolution in America.* Simon and Schuster, New York, 1964.

Civil Rights: Excerpts from the 1961 United States Commission on Civil Rights Report. U.S. Government Printing Office, Washington, D.C., 1961.

Civil Rights in the United States. Congressional Quarterly Service, Washington, D.C., 1963.

Greenberg, Jack. *Race Relations and American Law*. Columbia University Press, New York, 1959.

Keesing's Research Report No. 4. *Race Relations in the U.S.A., 1954–1968*. Charles Scribner's Sons, New York, 1970.

Konvitz, Milton R. *Expanding Liberties: Freedom's Gains in Postwar America*. The Viking Press, New York, 1966.

Lewis, Anthony and *The New York Times*. *Portrait of a Decade: The Second American Revolution*. Bantam Books, New York, 1971.

Masotti, Louis H.; Hadden, Jeffrey K.; Seminatore, Kenneth F.; and Corsi, Jerome R. *A Time to Burn? An Evaluation of the Present Crisis in Race Relations*. Rand McNally and Company, Chicago, 1969.

O'Neill, William L. *Coming Apart*. Quadrangle, New York, 1971.

Revolution in Civil Rights. Congressional Quarterly Service, Washington, D.C., June 1968.

Silberman, Charles E. *Crisis in Black and White*. Random House, New York, 1964.

United States Commission on Civil Rights. *Freedom to the Free: Century of Emancipation*. U.S. Government Printing Office, Washington, D.C., 1963.

Westin, Alan F. (ed.). *Freedom Now: The Civil Rights Struggle in America*. Basic Books, Inc., New York, 1964.

Woodward, C. Vann. *Origins of the New South, 1877–1913*. Louisiana State University Press, Baton Rouge, 1951.

Martin Luther King, Jr., and Negro Movements

Ahmann, Matthew (ed.). *The New Negro*. Fides Publishers, Notre Dame, Indiana, 1961.

Alabama Christian Movement for Human Rights, "Birmingham: People in Motion," 1966.

Anderson, Jervis. *A. Philip Randolph: A Biographical Portrait.* Harcourt Brace Jovanovich, New York, 1972.

Bennett, Lerone, Jr. *Confrontation: Black and White.* Pelican Books, Baltimore, Maryland, 1965.

————. *What Manner of Man: A Biography of Martin Luther King, Jr.* Johnson Publishing Company, Chicago, 1964.

Carmichael, Stokely and Hamilton, Charles V. *Black Power: The Politics of Liberation in America.* Vintage Books, New York, 1967.

Clark, Kenneth B.; Farmer, James; King, Martin Luther, Jr.; Randolph, A. Philip; and Wilkins, Roy. "What Next? Five Negro Leaders Reply." *The New York Times Magazine,* September 29, 1963, p. 27.

Clark, Leroy D. "The Lawyer in the Civil Rights Movement—Catalytic Agent or Counter-Revolutionary?" *Kansas Law Review,* Vol. 19, 1971, pp. 459–473.

Cleghorn, Reese. "Martin Luther King, Jr.: Apostle of Crisis." *Saturday Evening Post,* June 15, 1963, pp. 15–19.

Connery, Robert H. (ed.). *Urban Riots: Violence and Social Change.* The Academy of Political Science, New York, 1968.

Dunbar, Ernest. "A Negro Leader Talks about the Struggle Ahead." *Look,* February 12, 1963, pp. 92–96.

Fager, Charles. *Uncertain Resurrection: The Poor People's Washington Campaign.* William B. Eerdmans Publishing Company, Grand Rapids, Michigan, 1969.

Forman, James. *The Making of Black Revolutionaries*. The Macmillan Company, New York, 1972.

Frank, Gerold. *An American Death*. Bantam Books, New York, 1973.

Goldman, Peter. *The Death and Life of Malcolm X*. Harper & Row, New York, 1973.

Grant, Joanne (ed.). *Black Protest: History, Documents, and Analyses, 1619 to the Present*. Fawcett Publication, Inc., Greenwich, Connecticut, 1968.

Greenberg, Jack. "Dr. Martin Luther King, Jr.: The Law and Nonviolence." Text of speech, May 17, 1968.

Hamilton, Charles V. *The Black Preacher in America*. William Morrow and Co., New York, 1972.

Holloway, Harry. *The Politics of the Southern Negro*. Random House, New York, 1969.

King, Coretta Scott. *My Life with Martin Luther King, Jr.* Holt, Rinehart and Winston, New York, 1969.

King, Martin Luther, Jr. "Behind the Selma March." *Saturday Review,* April 3, 1965, p. 16.

———. "The Civil Rights Struggle in the United States Today." *The Record of the Association of the Bar of the City of New York,* Vol. 20, No. 5, May 1965 (Supplement), pp. 3–24. (Address delivered April 21, 1965.)

———. "A New Sense of Direction." *Drum Major,* August 1971, pp. 1–13.

———. *Stride Toward Freedom: The Montgomery Story*. Perennial Library, Harper & Row, 1958.

————. *The Trumpet of Conscience*. Harper & Row, New York, 1967.

————. *Where Do We Go From Here: Chaos or Community?* Bantam Books, New York, 1968.

————. *Why We Can't Wait*. Signet Book, New American Library, New York, 1964.

Kunstler, William M. *Deep in My Heart*. William Morrow and Co., New York, 1966.

Lewis, David L. *King: A Critical Biography*. Praeger Publishers, New York, 1970.

Lincoln, C. Eric (ed.). *Martin Luther King, Jr.: A Profile*. Hill and Wang, New York, 1970.

Lokos, Lionel. *House Divided: The Life and Legacy of Martin Luther King*. Arlington House, New Rochelle, New York, 1968.

McKean, Andrew J. "Ministers Go to Jail; Birmingham People March." *The Southern Courier*, October 28–29, 1967, p. 1.

"Man of the Year: Never Again Where He Was." *Time*, January 3, 1964, pp. 9–19.

Meier, August. "On the Role of Martin Luther King." *New Politics*, Winter 1965, Vol. IV, pp. 52–59.

Meier, August and Rudwick, Elliott. *CORE: A Study in the Civil Rights Movement, 1942–1968*. Oxford University Press, New York, 1973.

Muse, Benjamin. *The American Negro Revolution: From Nonviolence to Black Power, 1963–1967*. Indiana University Press, Bloomington, 1968.

Peck, James. *Freedom Ride*. Simon and Schuster, New York, 1962.

Rowan, Carl T. "Martin Luther King's Tragic Decision." *The Reader's Digest*, September 1967, pp. 37–42.

Rowe, Jeanne A. *An Album of Martin Luther King, Jr.* Franklin Watts, Inc., New York, 1970.

Rustin, Bayard. *Down the Line*. Quadrangle Books, Chicago, 1971.

Sellers, Cleveland and Terrell, Robert. *The River of No Return: The Autobiography of a Black Militant and the Life and Death of SNCC*. William Morrow and Company, New York, 1973.

"The Talk of the Town: King." *The New Yorker*, May 1, 1965, p. 35.

Watters, Pat. "St. Augustine." *New South*, September 1964, p. 4.

Williams, John A. *The King God Didn't Save: Reflections on the Life and Death of Martin Luther King, Jr.* Coward-McCann, Inc., New York, 1970.

Zinn, Howard. *The Southern Mystique*. Alfred A. Knopf, New York, 1964.

Alabama History, Law, and Politics

Alabama Supreme Court Library, *Alabama Appellate Courts*. Ellis Litho. Co., Montgomery, Alabama, 1968.

Alabama Writers' Project. *Alabama: A Guide to the Deep South*. Hastings House, New York, 1941.

Bloodworth, James N. "Remodeling the Alabama Appellate Courts," *Alabama Law Review*, Vol. 23, 1971, pp. 353–367.

Brown, Joe David. "Birmingham: City in Fear." *Saturday Evening Post,* March 2, 1963, pp. 12–18.

"The Change in Birmingham." *Newsweek,* December 8, 1969, pp. 79–80.

"Civil Rights: Birmingham Revisited." *Time,* November 10, 1967, pp. 28–29.

Fite, Arthur, "In Alabama Supreme Court," *The Alabama Lawyer,* Vol. 33, 1972, pp. 156–162.

Harding, Vincent. "A Beginning in Birmingham." *The Reporter,* June 6, 1963, pp. 13–19.

Hawley, Langston T. "Negro Employment in the Birmingham Area," *Selected Studies of Negro Employment in the South,* National Planning Association Committee of the South, Washington, D.C., 1955, pp. 213–328.

Johnson, Haynes. "The Sixties: A Look Back; Article 1: Birmingham." *New York Post,* January 5, 1970, p. 45.

Leighton, George R. *Five Cities.* Harper and Brothers, New York, 1939.

Morgan, Charles, Jr. *A Time to Speak.* Harper & Row, New York, 1964.

Osborne, George R. "Boycott in Birmingham." *The Nation,* May 5, 1962, pp. 397–401.

Rowan, Carl T. *South of Freedom.* Alfred A. Knopf, New York, 1952.

Salisbury, Harrison. "Fear and Hatred Grip Birmingham." *The New York Times,* April 12, 1960, p. 1.

"The Sixties." *The Birmingham News,* December 31, 1969, special insert.

Spero, Sterling D. and Harris, Abram L. *The Black Worker: The Negro and the Labor Movement.* Columbia University Press, New York, 1931.

Vines, Kenneth, "Southern State Supreme Courts and Race Relations," Western *Political Quarterly,* Vol. 18, March 1965, pp. 5–18.

Warren, Robert L. "Birmingham: Brinkmanship in Race Relations," *Christian Century,* May 30, 1962, pp. 619–689.

National Politics and Political Leaders

Guthman, Edwin. *We Band of Brothers: A Memoir of Robert F. Kennedy.* Harper & Row, New York, 1971.

Harris, Richard. *Justice: The Crisis of Law, Order and Freedom in America.* Avon Books, New York, 1970.

Navasky, Victor S. *Kennedy Justice.* Atheneum, New York, 1971.

Sorensen, Theodore C. *Kennedy.* Bantam Books, New York, 1966.

The U.S. Supreme Court and the Judicial Process

Abraham, Henry, Jr. *Freedom and the Court: Civil Rights and Liberties in the United States,* Second Edition. Oxford University Press, New York, 1972.

Bickel, Alexander M. *The Least Dangerous Branch: The Supreme Court at the Bar of Politics.* The Bobbs-Merrill Company, Inc., Indianapolis, 1962.

Black, Charles L., Jr. *The People and the Court: Judicial Review in a Democracy.* Spectrum Book, Englewood Cliffs, New Jersey, 1960.

Friedman, Leon (ed.). *Southern Justice.* Meridian Books, The World Publishing Company, Cleveland, 1967.

Friedman, Stephen J. *An Affair with Freedom: Justice William J. Brennan, Jr.; A Collection of His Opinions and Speeches Drawn from His First Decade as a United States Supreme Court Justice.* Atheneum, New York, 1967.

Garraty, John A. (ed.). *Quarrels That Have Shaped the Constitution.* Harper Colophon Books, Harper & Row, New York, 1966.

Harlan, John M. "Mr. Justice Black—Remarks of a Colleague." *Harvard Law Review,* November 1967, Vol. 81, p. 1.

Kalven, Harry, Jr. *The Negro and the First Amendment.* University of Chicago Press, Chicago, 1966.

Lewis, Anthony. *Gideon's Trumpet.* Vintage Books, New York, 1966.

McCloskey, Robert G. *The American Supreme Court.* University of Chicago Press, Chicago, 1960, p. 229.

Meltsner, Michael. *Cruel and Unusual: The Supreme Court and Capital Punishment.* Random House, New York, 1973.

Mendelson, Wallace. *Justices Black and Frankfurter: Conflict in the Court.* University of Chicago Press, Chicago, 1961.

Mitau, G. Theodore. *Decade of Decision: The Supreme Court and the Constitutional Revolution, 1954–1964.* Charles Scribner's Sons, New York, 1967.

Murphy, Walter F. *Elements of Judicial Strategy.* University of Chicago Press, Chicago, 1964.

Murphy, Walter F., and Pritchett, C. Herman. *Courts, Judges, and Politics.* Random House, New York, 1961.

Peltason, Jack W. *Fifty-eight Lonely Men: Southern Judges and School Desegregation.* Harcourt, Brace and World, Inc., New York, 1961.

Pritchett, C. Herman and Westin, Alan F. (eds.). *The Third Branch of Government: 8 Cases in Constitutional Politics.* Harcourt, Brace and World, Inc., New York, 1963.

Rice, Charles E. "Justice Black, the Demonstrators, and a Constitutional Rule of Law." *UCLA Law Review,* January 1967, p. 454.

Schmidhauser, John R. *The Supreme Court as Final Arbiter in Federal-State Relations: 1789–1957.* University of North Carolina Press, Chapel Hill, N.C., 1958.

Steel, Lewis M. "Nine Men in Black Who Think White." *The New York Times Magazine,* October 13, 1968, p. 56.

Strickland, Stephen (ed.). *Hugo Black and the Supreme Court: A Symposium.* The Bobbs-Merrill Company, Indianapolis, 1967.

Weaver, John D. *Warren: The Man, The Court, The Era.* Little, Brown and Company, Boston, 1967.

Protest, Contempt, and Civil Disobedience

Blasi, Vince. "Prior Restraints on Demonstrations." *Michigan Law Review,* August 1970, pp. 1482–1574.

Bork, Robert H. "We Suddenly Feel that Law Is Vulnerable."

Congressional Record-Senate, December 11, 1971, pp. S 21411–S 21414.

"Can Law Survive?" (special issue). *Trial,* June/July 1970, Vol. 6, No. 4.

Cohen, Carl. *Civil Disobedience: Conscience, Tactics, and the Law.* Columbia University Press, New York, 1971.

Crockett, George W., Jr. "Reflections of a Jurist on Civil Disobedience." *The American Scholar,* Autumn 1971.

"Defiance of Unlawful Authority." Note, *Harvard Law Review,* Vol. 83, 1970, pp. 626–647.

Edelman, Martin. "The Absurd Remnant: *Walker v. Birmingham* Two Years Later." *Albany Law Review,* Vol. 34, 1970, pp. 523–538.

"Equity on the Campus: The Limits of Injunctive Regulation of University Protest." Note, *The Yale Law Journal,* Vol. 80, 1971, pp. 987–1034.

Fortas, Abe. *Concerning Dissent and Civil Disobedience.* Signet Book, New American Library, New York, 1968.

Goldfarb, Ronald L. *The Contempt Power.* Anchor Books, Doubleday and Company, Garden City, New York, 1971.

Graham, Hugh Davis and Gurr, Ted Robert. *Violence in America: Historical and Comparative Perspectives,* Vol. 1. Staff Report to the National Commission on the Causes and Prevention of Violence, Washington, D.C., 1969.

Greenberg, Jack. "The Supreme Court, Civil Rights and Civil Dissonance." *The Yale Law Journal,* Vol. 77, 1968, pp. 1520–1544.

Johnson, Frank M. "Civil Disobedience and the Law." *Tulane Law Review,* Vol. XLIV, No. 1, December 1969, p. 1.

Katzenbach, Nicholas deB. "Protest, Politics and the First Amendment." *Tulane Law Review,* April 1970, pp. 439–451.

Ledsky, Charles. "Parade Ordinances and Prior Restraints." *Ohio State Law Journal,* Vol. 30, 1969, pp. 857–865.

Leibman, Morris I. "Civil Disobedience: A Threat to Our Law Society." *Vital Speeches of the Day,* October 1, 1964, p. 768.

"The Limits of Protest: Are There Means No End Can Justify?" *City,* August–September 1970, p. 35.

Lipsky, Michael. "Protest as a Political Resource." *The American Political Science Review,* Vol. LXII, No. 4, December 1968, pp. 1144–1158.

Lusky, Louis. "The King Dream: Fantasy or Prophesy?" *Columbia Law Review,* Vol. 68:1011, 1968, p. 1029.

Marshall, Burke. "The Protest Movement and the Law." *Virginia Law Review,* Vol. 51, 1965, pp. 785–803.

Melton, Michael Ward. "Collateral Attack of Injunctions Restraining First Amendment Activity." Note, *Southern California Law Review,* Vol. 45, 1972, pp. 1083–1108.

"Memphis." *Soul Force,* February 1972, p. 3.

Neier, Aryeh. "Protest Movements Among the Disenfranchised." *The Civil Liberties Review,* Vol. 1, 1973, pp. 49–74.

Poswall, John M. "The First Amendment and the Right to Violate an Injunction." *California Law Review,* Vol. 56, 1968, pp. 517–524.

Power, Paul F. "Civil Disobedience as Functional Opposition." *The Journal of Politics,* Vol. 34, 1972, pp. 37–55.

Regan, Richard J., S.J. *Private Conscience and Public Law: The American Experience.* Fordham University Press, New York, 1972.

Rendleman, Doug. "More on Void Orders." *Georgia Law Review,* Vol. 7, Winter 1973, pp. 246–309.

Report of the National Advisory Commission on Civil Disorders, Special Introduction by Tom Wicker. Bantam Books Edition, 1968.

Rosen, Sanford Jay. "Civil Disobedience and Other Such Techniques: Law Making Through Law Breaking." *The George Washington Law Review,* Vol. 37, No. 3, March 1969, pp. 435–463.

Rosenthal, Robert R. "Injunctive Relief Against Campus Disorders." *University of Pennsylvania Law Report,* Vol. 118, 1970, pp. 746–765.

Rostow, Eugene V. "Of Civil Disobedience." *Freedom At Issue,* No. 6, 1971, pp. 3–20.

Rudman, Norman G. and Solomon, Richard C. "Who Loves a Parade? *Walker v. City of Birmingham.*" *Law in Transition Quarterly,* Vol. IV, No. 4, December 1967, pp. 185–219.

Schochet, Gordon J. "From Dissent to Disobedience: A Justification of Rational Protest." *Politics and Society,* February 1971, pp. 235–256.

Selig, Joel L. "Regulation of Street Demonstrations By Injunction: Constitutional Limitations on the Collateral Bar Rule in Prosecutions for Contempt." *Harvard Civil Rights-Civil Liberties Law Review,* Vol. 4, 1968, pp. 135–166.

Skolnick, Jerome. *The Politics of Protest: Violent Aspects of Protest and Confrontation;* a Staff Report to the National Commission on the Causes and Prevention of Violence. U.S. Government Printing Office, Washington, D.C., 1969.

Tefft, Sheldon. "Neither Above the Law Nor Below It." *The Supreme Court Review*, 1967, pp. 181–192.

Zinn, Howard. *Disobedience and Democracy: Nine Fallacies on Law and Order*. Vintage Books, New York, 1968.

Cases Discussed in the Text

Adderley v. Florida, 385 U.S. 39 (1966).
Brown v. Board of Education, 347 U.S. 483 (1954).
Brown v. Louisiana, 385 U.S. 863 (1966).
Carroll v. President and Commissioners of Princess Anne, 393 U.S. 175 (1968).
Cox v. Louisiana, 379 U.S. 536 (1965).
Gideon v. Wainwright, 372 U.S. 335 (1963).
Howat v. Kansas, 258 U.S. 181 (1922).
In re Debs, 158 U.S. 564 (1895).
In re Green, 369 U.S. 689 (1962).
Mapp v. Ohio, 367 U.S. 643 (1961).
NAACP v. Alabama, 377 U.S. 288 (1964).
Plessy v. Ferguson, 163 U.S. 537 (1896).
Shuttlesworth v. City of Birmingham, 394 U.S. 147 (1969).
United States v. United Mine Workers, 330 U.S. 258 (1946).
Walker v. City of Birmingham, 388 U.S. 307 (1967).

Notes

Chapter 1

Page 1. The description of King's arrival is from *The Southern Courier,* Montgomery, Alabama, Weekend Edition, November 4–5, 1967.

Pages 2–3. King's dress and reading material, and Judge Barber's remarks when King was released from jail, were reported in *Time* magazine, November 10, 1967, pp. 28–29. King's press conference on October 29 is described in *The Southern Courier, loc. cit.*

Page 4. The criticism of King is from Lionel Lokos, *House Divided: The Life and Legacy of Martin Luther King* (1968), Chap. 11. Justice Stewart's comment is at the close of the majority opinion in *Walker v. Birmingham,* 388 U.S. 307 (1967), 320–21.

Page 4. *The New York Times* editorial appeared on June 14, 1967, p. 46.

Chapter 2

Pages 8–9. William O'Neill's observations about life in America during the 1950s appear in his book *Coming Apart: An Informal History of America in the 1960s* (Quadrangle Books, 1971), p. 4.

Pages 10–12. The Salisbury article, headlined "Fear and Hatred Grip Birmingham," appeared in *The New York Times,* April 12, 1960, p. 1.

Page 12. Accounts of the founding of Birmingham can be found in George R. Leighton, *Five Cities* (Harper and Brothers, 1939), pp. 110–12, and in the Alabama Writers' Project book about the state, *Alabama: A Guide to the Deep South* (Hastings House, 1941), pp. 167–68.

Pages 12–13. The quotation on Northern absentee ownership is from C. Vann Woodward, *Origins of the New South, 1877–1913* (Louisiana State University Press, 1951), p. 292. The description of early violence in Birmingham is from the Alabama Writers' Project *Guide,* pp. 169–70. Birmingham's labor history is discussed in the *Guide* at p. 170; in Leighton, pp. 115–24; and in Sterling D. Spero and Abram L. Harris, *The Black Worker: The Negro and the Labor Movement* (Columbia University Press, 1961).

Pages 13–19. The discussion of Birmingham during the 1950s and early 1960s is drawn from a number of sources, including Carl T. Rowan, *South of Freedom* (Alfred A. Knopf, 1952), pp. 168–70; Langston T. Hawley, "Negro Employment in the Birmingham Area," in *Selected Studies of Negro Employment in the South* (National Planning Association Committee of the South, Washington, D.C., 1955), pp. 213–328; Charles Morgan, Jr., *A Time to Speak* (Harper and Row, 1964), pp. 25–122; and Joe David Brown, "Birmingham: City in Fear," *Saturday Evening Post,* March 2, 1963, pp. 12–18.

Page 13. The journalist quoted is Brown, p. 13.

Page 15. Bull Connor's remark is quoted by Morgan, p. 249.

Page 15–16. The NAACP litigation is treated in detail in George R. Osborne's case study, "Freedom of Association: The NAACP in Alabama," in C. Herman Pritchett and Alan F. Westin, eds., *The Third Branch of Government* (Harcourt, Brace and World, 1963), pp. 142–203.

Pages 16–18. The formation and early struggles of the ACMHR in Alabama are discussed in a pamphlet published by the ACMHR in 1966, entitled "Birmingham: People in Motion."

Pages 18–19. Connor's remarks about the arrest of the three ministers on vagrancy charges were reported in *The Afro-American,* November 22, 1958.

Pages 19–22. The discussion of events in the 1962–early 1963 period is drawn from Brown, *op. cit.;* George R. Osborne, "Boycott in Birmingham," *The Nation,* May 5, 1962, pp. 397–401; and Robert L. Warren, "Birmingham: Brinksmanship in Race Relations," *Christian Century,* May 30, 1962, pp. 619–89. Martin Luther King's perspective on Birmingham during this period appears in his book *Why We Can't Wait* (Harper & Row, 1963; Signet Books, 1964), pp. 52–53 (Signet ed.). Interviews with Fred Shuttlesworth and with Birmingham attorney David Vann also provided useful background information on this period.

Chapter 3

General. There are a number of books dealing with King and the campaigns he led. For the most part they mine essentially the same body of facts. In this chapter, and throughout the rest of the book, we have drawn particularly on five of them: Lerone Bennett, *What Manner of Man* (Johnson Publishing Co., 1964); William Robert Miller, *Martin Luther King, Jr.* (Avon, 1968); John A. Williams, *The King God Didn't Save* (Coward-McCann, 1970); David L. Lewis, *King: A Critical Biography* (Praeger, 1970); and Jim Bishop, *The Days of Martin Luther King* (G. P. Putnam's Sons, 1971). Two of King's own books, *Stride Toward Freedom* (Harper & Row, 1958, 1964) and *Why We Can't Wait,* are particularly valuable for gaining King's own perspective on the Montgomery, Albany, and Birmingham campaigns. Coretta King's story of these years, *My Life with Martin Luther King* (Holt, Rinehart & Winston, 1969), also provides some valuable material.

Pages 23–25. This account of King's childhood and student years is drawn from Lewis, pp. 3–45; Bishop, pp. 87–118; Bennett, pp. 3–51; Miller, pp. 13–40; Williams, pp. 25–26; and C. Eric Lincoln, *Martin Luther King, Jr.: A Profile* (Hill and Wang, 1970), p. xvii. King's comments are from *Stride Toward Freedom,* p. 72.

Pages 25–30. The discussion of Montgomery is drawn mainly from Bennett, pp. 55–78; Bishop, pp. 131–89; a *Time* cover story on King, February 18, 1957, p. 17; and King's own account in *Stride Toward Freedom,* pp. 53–165.

Pages 26–27. The quotations from King's speech are in Bishop, pp. 139–41.

Page 31. The founding of the SCLC is discussed in Bennett, pp. 82–83; Lewis, pp. 88–89; Bishop, pp. 189–90; and Miller, p. 85.

Pages 32–33. The account of the meeting with Eisenhower is from Bishop, pp. 205–07; and Bennett, pp. 91–93. For the sit-ins, see Miller, pp. 98–100; David Lewis, pp. 113–14; Anthony Lewis and *The New York Times, Portrait of a Decade: The Second American Revolution* (Bantam Books, 1965), pp. 72–73; and Bennett, pp. 112–13.

Page 34. The Shaw University conference and the formation of SNCC are discussed in Bennett, pp. 113–14, and Bishop, pp. 228–29.

Pages 34–38. The accounts of King's difficulties with the law in 1960 are from Bishop, pp. 231–41; Miller, pp. 111–12; Bennett, pp. 114–19; and Coretta King, pp. 185–87. The account of the libel case is from *The New York Times,* April 20, 1960, p. 25, and November 4, 1960, p. 67. The facts of the case are also discussed in the U.S. Supreme Court's opinion on the appeal from the Alabama judgment, *New York Times Co. v. Sullivan,* 376 U.S. 254 (1964).

Pages 38–44. The discussion of Kennedy Administration policy toward civil rights problems here and elsewhere in the book is drawn mainly from Edwin Guthman, *We Band of Brothers* (Harper & Row, 1971), pp. 154–78; Victor S. Navasky, *Kennedy Justice* (Atheneum, 1971), pp. 96–276; Theodore C. Sorensen, *Kennedy* (Harper & Row, 1965; Bantam Books, 1966), pp. 528–69 (Bantam ed.); and the authors' interviews with former Justice Department officials Nicholas Katzenbach, Ramsey Clark, Burke Marshall, Joseph Dolan, Louis Oberdorfer, and John Doar.

Pages 39–40. The attacks on the Freedom Riders, the newsmen, and Siegenthaler are described in Guthman, pp. 166–71; Lewis, pp. 132–33; and August Meier and Elliott Rudwick, *CORE: A Study in the Civil Rights Movement, 1942–1968 (Oxford University Press, 1973), pp. 135–75.* A personal account of the experience is contained in James Peck, *Freedom Ride* (Simon and Schuster, 1962).

Page 43. Robert Kennedy's speech is quoted in Guthman, pp. 161–62.

Pages 44–47. The account of the Albany campaign is drawn from Lewis, pp. 140–70; Bennett, pp. 129–31; Williams, pp. 52–55; Miller, pp. 124–41; Bishop, pp. 257–63; Coretta King, pp. 202–07; Howard Zinn, *The Southern Mystique* (Alfred A. Knopf, 1964), pp. 147–213; and William H. Kunstler, *Deep in My Heart* (William Morrow & Co., 1966), pp. 93–131.

Page 44. The quotation about Chief Pritchett appears in Lewis, p. 161.

Page 45. The terms of the injunction are quoted in Kunstler, p. 101.

Page 46. King's statement was reported in *The New York Times,* July 23, 1962, p. 13.

Chapter 4

General. The description of the preparations for the Birmingham campaign is based principally on King's own account in *Why We Can't Wait,* pp. 54–59 (Signet ed.), and David Lewis, pp. 173–76; supplemented by authors' interviews with former King aides Wyatt Tee Walker, Fred Shuttlesworth, and Andrew Young. Interviews with NAACP Legal Defense Fund director Jack Greenberg and with attorneys James Nabrit, Norman Amaker, and Harry Wachtel were very helpful in gaining an overview of the legal problems and strategies, as well as a sense of the role played by the lawyers in the SCLC campaigns. An excellent treatment of the law of contempt can be found in Robert L. Goldfarb, *The Contempt Power* (Columbia University Press, 1963; Doubleday Anchor, 1971).

Pages 56–57. The quotations from *In re Debs* are at 158 U.S. 564 (1895), 598–99.

Page 57. *Howat v. Kansas* is at 258 U.S. 181 (1922).

Page 58. Frankfurter's concurring views are in *United States v. United Mine Workers,* 330 U.S. 258 (1946), 309–10.

Pages 58–59. *In re Green* is at 369 U.S. 689. Harlan's dissent is at 693.

Pages 59–62. The quoted comments by Young, Katzenbach, Marshall, and Rustin were made in interviews with the authors.

Chapter 5

General. The description of events in Birmingham during the week of April 3–10 is taken chiefly from news stories in *The New York Times* and the Birmingham News: the books by Lewis, pp. 171–83, and Bennett, pp. 131–36; King's account in *Why We Can't Wait* (Signet ed.), pp. 59–71; and documents contained in the U.S. Supreme Court's "Transcript of Record" in the case of *Walker v. City of Birmingham.* No. 249, October Term, 1966. This official record, which includes all the trial testimony as well as other documents from the proceedings in the Alabama courts, is on file at the Supreme Court library and in other libraries which function as depositories for Supreme Court papers. In subsequent notes, it is referred to simply as *Record.*

Page 64. The "Manifesto" is quoted in Bennett, pp. 132–34. Boutwell's statement is from the Birmingham *News,* April 4, 1963, p. 7.

Page 65. The *Newsweek* story appears in the edition of April 15, 1963, p. 29.

Pages 65–66. The account of the ACMHR's attempt to get a parade permit is based on Mahoney's interview with Fred Shuttlesworth and on the trial testimony of Mrs. Lola Hendricks, *Record,* pp. 352–55. Connor's telegram is in the *Record,* p. 415.

Pages 66–67. Rev. Albert Foley's remarks were quoted in the Birmingham *News,* April 6, 1963, and in *Time,* April 19, 1963, p. 31. The attendance figure for the first meeting is from King, *Why We Can't Wait,* p. 58.

Pages 69–72. The court documents discussed in the text are all in the *Record.* The bill of complaint is at pp. 25–38; Capt. Evans' affidavit at pp. 39–41; and the injunction itself at pp. 42–45. Mahoney's interview with David Vann and Westin's interviews with Charles Morgan and George Peach Taylor were helpful in providing background information about court practices and procedures in Jefferson County.

Chapter 6

Pages 73–77. The discussion of the leaders' strategy session on

Wednesday evening, April 10, is based principally on the authors' interviews with Wyatt Walker, Fred Shuttlesworth, and Andrew Young, and on King's account in *Why We Can't Wait,* pp. 70–71.

Pages 74–75. The King quotation is from *Why We Can't Wait,* p. 70.

Page 77. The impromptu press conference held at the time the injunction was served at 1 A.M. on April 11 was described by Wyatt Walker and Fred Shuttlesworth in interviews with Mahoney and was the subject of trial testimony by Associated Press reporter J. Walter Johnson, Jr. The statements by Shuttlesworth and Abernathy were quoted by Johnson in his testimony, *Record,* p. 194. Wyatt Walker recalled King's comment.

Pages 77–81. The discussion of events on Thursday, April 10, is drawn from authors' interviews with Fred Shuttlesworth, Wyatt Walker, and Norman Amaker, trial testimony about those events, and a story about the press conference which appeared in the Atlanta *Daily World,* April 12, 1963. The full text of the press release is in the *Record,* pp. 409–10.

Page 81. King's comments at the Thursday night church meeting were quoted at the trial by newsman Elvin Stanton, *Record,* pp. 242, 244; and were the subject of a UPI news release, *Record,* p. 407.

Pages 81–83. The discussion of the bail-money problem and the Friday morning meeting at the Gaston Motel is based on authors' interviews with Wyatt Walker, Fred Shuttlesworth, Andrew Young, and Norman Amaker, and on King's account in *Why We Can't Wait,* pp. 72–73.

Page 84. Hailey's story about the march appeared in *The New York Times,* April 13, 1963, p. 1.

Pages 84–86. King described the jail conditions in *Why We Can't Wait,* pp. 73–74. Amaker's attempts to see King after the Good Friday arrests were related in an interview with Mahoney.

Pages 86–87. The Justice Department's views about the Birmingham campaign and the jailing of King were reported in *The New York Times,* April 14, 1963, p. 54. The *Time* article appeared in the edition of April 22, 1963, p. 28; the *Newsweek* piece in the edition of April 22, 1963, p. 28.

Chapter 7

General. The court papers and trial testimony discussed in this chapter are all to be found in the *Record,* which has a detailed table of references to documents and to the testimony of specific individuals. Much helpful background information about the court and the lawyers involved in the case was obtained in authors' interviews with Walter Jenkins, Charles Morgan, George Peach Taylor, David Vann, Jack Greenberg, and Norman Amaker, and via correspondence from J. M. Breckenridge and Earl McBee. The Martindale Hubbell directory of lawyers was also a useful source of biographical information.

Page 92. Judge Jenkins' statement that the contempt proceeding would be given precedence was reported in the Birmingham *News,* April 16, 1963.

Page 92. Kunstler's efforts are reported in Kunstler, pp. 179–80.

Page 93. A story about the witness list appeared in the Birmingham *News,* April 20, 1963.

Pages 92–93. King's release from jail and his comments to newsmen was reported in the Birmingham *News,* April 21, 1963.

Page 96. The exchange between Jenkins and Shores is in the *Record,* pp. 138–40.

Pages 99–101. Haley's testimony appears in the *Record,* pp. 145–85. Painter's testimony is at pp. 204–30; the quotations from his testimony are at pp. 211–12. Johnson's testimony appears at pp. 185–204. The Walker quotation is from p. 202. Ware's testimony is at pp. 230–38. Stanton's testimony appears at pp. 239–47, with the King quotation at pp. 243–44.

Page 101. House's testimony appears in the *Record,* pp. 247–53. The quotation is from p. 250. The testimony of the other officers appears at pp. 253–71.

Pages 101–102. The remarks of Shores and McBee are from the *Record,* p. 152. Haley's testimony discussed here appears at pp. 151, 153, 156–57. Shores's cross-examination is at pp. 159–71.

Pages 103–104. Cross-examination of Haley is from the *Record,* pp. 176–79.

Pages 104–105. Shores's motions and Jenkins' rulings are in the *Record*, pp. 271–75.

Pages 105–106. Hodges' testimony and the exchanges among the lawyers and the judge appear in the *Record*, pp. 281–87.

Page 121. Connor's testimony is at pp. 288–91 of the *Record*.

Pages 121–122. Moore's testimony appears at pp. 292–95. The attempt to portray segregation in Birmingham is at pp. 295–98. The testimony of the four ministers appears in the *Record*, pp. 298–339.

Page 122. Mrs. Hendricks' testimony is at pp. 352–55.

Pages 122–123. The text of the "Statement of Counsel" is in the *Record*, pp. 418–19.

Pages 123–125. Jenkins' ruling on the statement is in the *Record*, p. 357. Ware's testimony appears at pp. 358–60. Motley's argument appears at pp. 379–90. Greenberg's argument is in the *Record*, pp. 390–94.

Pages 125–126. McBee's argument appears in the *Record*, pp. 394–406. Jenkins' closing remarks are at p. 406.

Chapter 8

Page 127. Young's comments were made in an interview.

Pages 127–130. The ad placed by the Negro leaders and the clergymen's statement appeared in the Birmingham *News*, April 12, 1963.

Pages 130–140. King's *Letter from Birmingham Jail* has been widely reprinted. The portions of it quoted here are from the reprint made by the American Friends Service Committee in 1963. A slightly different version, "polished for publication," appears in *Why We Can't Wait*, pp. 76–95. King's description of the circumstances under which the *Letter* was written is from *Why We Can't Wait*, p. 76.

Page 140. Young's comment about the *Letter* was made in an interview with Westin.

Chapter 9

Pages 141–142. Judge Jenkins' opinion and order are in the *Record*, pp. 419–25.

Pages 142–150. There are a number of essentially similar accounts of the events in Birmingham during this period. We have drawn chiefly upon the following: Foster Hailey, "The Birmingham Story: Segregation Teetering Under Fire," in *The New York Times,* May 26, 1963, p. 58; Vincent Harding, "A Beginning in Birmingham, *The Reporter,* June 6, 1963, pp. 6–13; Miller, pp. 152–64; David Lewis, pp. 192–204; Bennett, pp. 151–56; and Harry Holloway, *The Politics of the Southern Negro* (Random House, 1969), Chap. 7. Interviews with Fred Shuttlesworth, Charles Hamilton, David Vann, John Drew (a black businessman who was a key figure in the negotiations), Burke Marshall, and Joseph Dolan were also helpful in providing details of the events and a sense of the differing perspectives of the parties involved in the conflict.

Page 145. The quotation is from the transcript of a tape recording of King's address, furnished to the authors by Professor Charles V. Hamilton.

Pages 146–147. Harding's account is quoted from his article in *The Reporter,* pp. 8–9.

Pages 147–148. The Reston column appeared in *The New York Times,* May 10, 1963, p. 32.

Page 149. The full statement of the movement leaders was quoted in *The New York Times,* May 11, 1963, p. 8. Malcolm X's remarks were quoted in *The New York Times,* May 11, 1963, p. 9.

Pages 151–153. This discussion of demonstrations and the use of injunctions draws on Bishop, p. 338; Keesing's Research Report No. 4, *Race Relations in the USA, 1954–1968* (Charles Scribner's Sons, 1970), pp. 156–57; and Meier and Rudwick, pp. 223–58. The quotation from Meier and Rudwick is at p. 258.

Pages 153–154. The text of Kennedy's speech is in *The New York Times,* June 12, 1963, p. 20.

Pages 154–155. The March on Washington is described in Miller, pp. 165–79, and Bennett, pp. 158–63.

Pages 155–156. Johnson's statement is from *The New York Times,* November 28, 1963, p. 20. The legislative history and contents of the 1964 act can be found in *Revolution in Civil Rights* (Congressional Quarterly Service, Washington, D.C., 1968), pp. 53–65.

Pages 157–158. Meltsner's essay is "Southern Appellate Courts: A Dead End," in Leon Friedman, ed., *Southern Justice* (Meridian Books, 1967), pp. 136–54. The quoted material is extracted from pp. 136–40.

Page 158. The study by Vines, entitled "Southern State Supreme Courts and Race Relations," is in *Western Political Quarterly*, Vol. 18 (March 1965), pp. 5–18.

Pages 158–159. The state court briefs for the ministers and for the city are in the *Walker v. City of Birmingham* case file at the offices of the NAACP Legal Defense and Education Fund Inc. in New York City, and were examined there on July 25, 1969.

Pages 159–160. For general background information on the Alabama supreme court we have drawn particularly on two Alabama law-review pieces: "Alabama Appellate Court Congestion: Observations and Suggestions from an Empirical Study," *Alabama Law Review*, Vol. 21 (1968), pp. 150–70; and "Editorial Comments," *Alabama Law Review*, Vol. 23 (Spring 1971). Useful information about the court's practices and procedures was also obtained in the authors' interviews with Charles Morgan, Jr., Janie Shores, George Peach Taylor, and Norman Amaker.

Chapter 10

Pages 161–164. This account of the St. Augustine campaign is drawn primarily from Miller, pp. 193–206; Bishop, pp. 339–48; David Lewis, pp. 240–44; and an article by Pat Watters, "St. Augustine," *New South* September 1964, pp. 3–20.

Pages 165–177. The discussion of Selma is based on the books by Bishop, pp. 339–48; and Lewis, pp. 240–44; an article by Martin Luther King entitled "Behind the Selma March," *Saturday Review*, April 3, 1965; and authors' interviews with Nicholas Katzenbach, John Doar, Andrew Young, and Harry Wachtel. The perspective of many of the SNCC activists is outlined in Cleveland Sellers, *The River of No Return* (William Morrow and Co., 1973), pp. 116–29. Judge Johnson's opinion in the injunction case, which also reviews many of the relevant facts, is reported as *Williams v. Wallace*, 240 F. Supp. 100 (1965).

Pages 170–171. The quoted remarks of Andrew Young were made in an interview with Westin.

Page 171. The King quote is from his article "Behind the Selma March," p. 17.

Pages 172–173. Doar and Katzenbach recalled their conversation with King in interviews with Westin. The King quote is from Bishop, p. 385.

Page 174. Burke Marshall's comment was made in an interview with Mahoney.

Page 178. The text of President Johnson's statement concerning the Watts riots is in *The New York Times,* August 15, 1965, p. 77. Clark's comments were made in a telephone interview.

Pages 179–180. The remarks of Judge Livingston were quoted by George Osborne in his essay on the *NAACP v. Alabama* litigation pp. 167–68. The 2-1 Alabama court of appeals decision is *Shuttlesworth v. Alabama,* 43 Ala. App. Ct. 68, 180 So. 2nd 114 (1965).

Pages 180–182. Justice Coleman's opinion for the Alabama supreme court in *Walker v. City of Birmingham* is at 279 Ala. 53, 181 So. 2nd 493 (1965).

Pages 183–184. The quote from the McCone Commission report is in *The New York Times,* December 7, 1965, p. 26. Rustin recalled his tour of Watts with King in an interview.

Chapter 11

General. The material in this chapter relating to the proceedings in the Supreme Court—and to the tactical and strategic problems of the lawyers for the two sides—is drawn from examination of the Inc. Fund's petition for a writ of certiorari and the city's brief in opposition to the petition, supplemented by the authors' interviews with attorneys Jack Greenberg, James Nabrit, Norman Amaker, and Harry Wachtel, and Washington *Post* reporter John P. Mackenzie.

Pages 191–195. This account of the Chicago campaign is based chiefly from David Lewis, pp. 331–53; Keesing's Research Report No. 4, pp. 216–17; and Mike Royko, *Boss: Mayor Richard J. Daley of Chicago* (E. P. Dutton, 1971), pp. 146–54.

Pages 191–192. Bayard Rustin's conversation with King was recalled by Rustin in an interview with Westin.

Pages 195–196. Shuttlesworth's view of the situation in Birmingham in 1966 appears in the ACMHR pamphlet "Birmingham: People in Motion."

Chapter 12

Pages 199–200. The discussion of the Reconstruction period draws on Woodward, *passim,* and on a report by the United States Civil Rights Commission discussing the civil rights progress of the nation during the century following the Emancipation Proclamation entitled *Freedom to the Free,* 1963, pp. 30–71. On Harlan, see Alan F. Westin, "The Case of the Prejudiced Doorkeeper," in John A. Garraty (ed.), *Quarrels That Have Shaped the Constitution* (Harper and Row, 1966).

Page 201. Walker's thoughts were expressed in an interview with Mahoney.

Pages 201–218. This discussion of the Supreme Court and the nine individual justices draws on a large body of literature, a portion of which is included in the bibliography. The cases discussed in the text are all included in the Table of Cases at p. 314.

Pages 204–205. The quote from Goldberg's opinion is in *Cox v. Louisiana,* 379 U.S. 536 at pp. 554–55. The quote from Black's dissent in this case is at pp. 483–84.

Pages 206–207. The quote from Black's opinion is in *Adderley v. Florida,* 385 U.S. 39, at pp. 47–48. The quote from the dissent is at pp. 50–51, 56.

Chapter 13

General. This treatment of the briefs and oral argument in *Walker v. City of Birmingham* is based mainly on the briefs themselves and on transcripts of the oral argument. The briefs are on file at the Supreme Court library and other depository libraries. A stenographic transcript of the argument was obtained from the Hoover Reporting Company of Washington, D.C. In addition, Mahoney listened to tapes of the argument, which are filed at the National

Archives in Washington. Helpful background material about the lawyers' handling of the case and their interaction with the justices at the oral argument was gained in interviews with Louis Claiborne, Jack Greenberg, James Nabrit, and Norman Amaker.

Chapter 14

Pages 238–241. The court's conference procedures and the practices of the justices in voting on cases and writing opinions are discussed in many places. See, for example, Alan F. Westin, *An Autobiography of the Supreme Court* (Macmillan, 1963).

Pages 241–242. This discussion of King's activities and other events on the civil rights front is drawn from Bishop, pp. 452–55, and Lewis, pp. 360–67, and from *New York Times* stories from January to June, 1967.

Pages 244–253. *Walker v. City of Birmingham* is reported at 388 U.S. 307. Stewart's opinion for the majority is at pp. 308–24. Warren's dissent is at pp. 324–34, Douglas' at 334–38, and Brennan's at 338–49.

Chapter 15

Pages 254–256. The comments by Rustin, Walker, Hamilton, Wachtel, and Clark were made in interviews with the authors.

Page 255. The *Times* editorial appeared June 14, 1967, p. 46.

Page 256. The Boutwell quote is from The Birmingham *News,* June 14, 1967.

Pages 256–257. The quotation from the Inc. Fund's petition for rehearing is at pp. 12–13 of that document. The quote from the AFL-CIO's *amicus* brief is from p. 16 of that brief.

Pages 257–258. Walker recalled the time in jail in an interview with Mahoney.

Page 258. King's address to the staff was published in *Drum Major* (an SCLC publication), November 1967, pp. 1–13.

Page 259. Powell is quoted in Miller, p. 286. Rowan's article is "Martin Luther King's Tragic Decision," *Reader's Digest,* September 1967, p. 37.

Pages 259–260. The discussion of plans for the Poor People's

Campaign is drawn chiefly from Bishop, pp. 368–85; Lewis, pp. 373–75; and Westin's interviews with Bayard Rustin, Andrew Young, Bernard Lee, James Orange, and Stoney Cooks. See also Charles Fager, *Uncertain Resurrection: The Poor People's Washington Campaign* (Eerdmans Publishing Co., 1969).

Pages 260–272. The section on Memphis is based chiefly on Bishop, pp. 3–72; Miller, pp. 264–90; Gerold Frank, *An American Death* (Bantam Books, 1973), pp. 11–138; and Westin's interviews with Young, Lee, Orange, Cooks, Lucius Burch, Chauncey Eskridge, and Ramsey Clark.

Page 272. The description of and quote from Agnew is from Lokos, pp. 61–62.

Chapter 16

Pages 274–275. The description of contemporary Birmingham is based on "The Change in Birmingham," *Newsweek,* December 8, 1969, p. 79; Roy Reed, "Proud Birmingham Steers into Mainstream, USA," *The New York Times,* March 28, 1972, p. 45; Fred Shuttlesworth, "Birmingham Revisited," *Ebony,* August 1971, pp. 114–18; Mahoney's interviews with Shuttlesworth, David Vann, John Drew, and Norman Amaker; and research assistant Helene Toiv's interviews with Birmingham attorneys Bill Pugh and Walter Jackson, city councilman Richard Arrington, George Quiggle, Massey Gentry, Jack Drake, Frank Parker, and Barney Weeks.

Pages 275–277. The *Carroll* case is at 393 U.S. 175 (1968). *Shuttlesworth* is at 394 U.S. 147 (1969). Edelman is quoted from his article, "The Absurd Remnant: *Walker v. Birmingham Two Years Later,*" *Albany Law Review,* Vol. 34 (1970), p. 530.

Pages 277–278. Examples of state and federal cases applying the *Walker* rule are: *Board of Education v. Federation of Teachers,* 46 Ill. 2d 439 (1970); *UMW Hospital v. United Mine Workers,* 52 Ill. 2d 496 (1972); *Dade County Classroom Teacher's Association v. Rubin,* 238 So. 2d 284 (Florida, 1970); *Board of Junior College v. Cook County Teachers Union,* 126 Ill. App. 2d 418 (1970); *State v. Cohen,* 489 P. 2d 283 (Arizona, 1971); *Kirstel v. State,* 284 A. 2d 12 (Maryland, 1971); *Mechanic v. Gruensfelder,* 461 S.W. 2d 298 (Missouri, 1970); *Apple Storage Co., Inc. v. Consumer's Edu-*

cation and Protective Association, 441 Pa. 309 (1971); *King v. Jones,* 450 F. 2d 478 (1971); and *United States v. Puerto Rico Independence Party,* 324 F. Supp. 1333 (1971). The statistics on campus injunctions are from "Equity on the Campus: The Limits of Injunctive Regulation of University Protest," Note, *The Yale Law Journal,* April 1971, p. 987. The university administrator quoted is John Cantini, in "Equity on the Campus," p. 1030. The New Jersey teacher's case is *In re Newark Teachers Union, Local 481,* 287 A. 2d 183 (New Jersey, 1972), p. 186.

Pages 278–282. For examples of legal commentary approving the *Walker* decision, see Sheldon Tefft, "Neither Above the Law Nor Below It," *The Supreme Court Review,* 1967, pp. 181–192 and Charles K. Ledsky, "Parade Ordinances and Prior Restraints," Note, *Ohio State Law Journal,* Vol. 30, 1969, 856–865. For an excellent summary of the general legal literature defending rules against collateral attack on injunctions, see Doug Rendleman, "More on Void Orders," *Georgia Law Review,* Vol. 7, Winter, 1973, pp. 246–309.

Pages 282–284. The protest movements of the 1960s prompted some excellent reports analyzing the role of protest in American history, and its function for democratization of our society. Among the most useful documents are: Jerome Skolnick, *The Politics of Protest: Violent Aspects of Protest and Confrontation,* Staff Report to the National Commission on the Causes and Prevention of Violence, U.S. Government Printing Office, 1969; Hugh Davis Graham and Ted Robert Gurr, *Violence in America: Historical and Comparative Perspectives, Vol. I,* Staff Report to the National Commission on the Causes and Prevention of Violence, U.S. Government Printing Office, 1969; *Report of the National Advisory Commission on Civil Disorders* Bantam Books edition, with special introduction by Tom Wicker, 1968; Michael Lipsky, "Protest as A Political Resource," *The American Political Science Review,* Vol. LXII, No. 4, December 1968, pp. 1144–1158; Paul F. Power, "Civil Disobedience as Functional Opposition," *The Journal of Politics,* Vol. 34, 1972, pp. 37–55. The Douglass quotation is from Frederick Douglass, "West India Emancipation Speech," August 1857, quoted in Stokely Carmichael and Charles V. Hamilton, *Black Power* (Random House 1967), p. x.

Pages 284–285. The reference to McCloskey is from Robert G. McCloskey, *The American Supreme Court* (University of Chicago 1960), p. 229. The union leader's testimony is quoted from *In re Debs,* 158 U.S. 564 (1895), at pp. 597–598.

Page 289. The *Furman v. Georgia* case is at 408 U.S. 238 (1972).

Pages 289–298. Our discussion here builds on a number of thoughtful law review articles criticizing the *Walker* rule and recommending various modifications of it. These include: Martin Edelman, "The Absurd Remnant: *Walker v. Birmingham* Two Years Later," *Albany Law Review,* Vol. 34, 1970, pp. 523–538; Norman G. Rudman and Richard C. Solomon, "Who Loves a Parade," *Law in Transition Quarterly,* Vol. 4, 1967, pp. 185–219; Vince Blasi, "Prior Restraints on Demonstrations," *Michigan Law Review,* Vol. 68, 1970, pp. 1481–1574; Doug Rendleman, "More on Void Orders," *Georgia Law Review,* Vol. 7, 1973, pp. 246–309; Joel L. Selig, "Regulation of Street Demonstrations By Injunction: Constitutional Limitations on the Collateral Bar Rule in Prosecutions for Contempt," *Harvard Civil Rights–Civil Liberties Law Review,* Vol. 4, 1968, pp. 135–166; Michael Ward Melton, "Collateral Attack on Injunctions Restraining First Amendment Activity," Note, *Southern California Law Review,* Vol. 45, 1972, pp. 1083–1108; and "Defiance of Unlawful Authority," Note, *Harvard Law Review,* Vol. 83, 1970, pp. 626–647.

Page 293. For the California rule, see *In re Berry,* 68 Cal. 2d 137 (1968), and discussion in Selig, "Regulation of Street Demonstrations . . ."

Page 297. *Freedman v. Maryland* is reported at 380 U.S. 51 (1965). The case involving the Baton Rouge newspapermen is *United States v. Dickenson,* 465 F. 2d 496 (5th Cir. 1972), cert denied U.S. (1973).

Page 299. The quote is from Jack Greenberg, "Dr. Martin Luther King, Jr.: The Law and Nonviolence," NAACP Legal Defense and Education Fund, Inc., 1968.

Index